POISONED LOVE

POISONED LOVE

A TRUE STORY

By

MELANIE CANE, M.D.

Bascom Hill Publishing Group
Minneapolis, MN

Bascom Hill Publishing Group

212 3ʳᵈ Avenue North, Suite 570

Minneapolis, MN 55401

612.455.2293

www.bascomhillpublishing.com

ISBN - 1-935098-11-x

ISBN - 978-1-935098-11-9

LCCN - 2008939761

Book sales for North America and international:

Itasca Books, 3501 Highway 100 South, Suite 220

Minneapolis, MN 55416

Phone: 952.345.4488 (toll free 1.800.901.3480)

Fax: 952.920.0541; email to orders@itascabooks.com

Cover Design by Brent Meyers

Typeset by Sophie Chi

Printed in the United States of America

BASCOM HILL
PUBLISHING GROUP

Isn't life mysterious? It hands us tragedies beyond comprehension and then gives us the strength to transform them into something of value to ourselves and others.

Edward Zalaznick
(1961-2004)

DEDICATION

This book is dedicated to the memory of my beloved cousin, Edward Zalaznick, shelter dogs everywhere, and to the millions of people who struggle to overcome the ravages of mental illness, from either side of the glass.

AUTHOR'S NOTE

This story is drawn from real events. I changed my name because I feel I am a different person now than I was when the events described in this book occurred. Most names have been changed.

In telling the story, I have verified my recollections against those of others. All of the major events are documented in hospital records, school transcripts, therapy videotapes, newspaper articles, court records, and/or petitions for re-licensure.

Recounting of court hearings and license petition hearings are verbatim from hearing transcripts that are available to the public. The events surrounding the licensing hearing are documented in a paper trail between my lawyer, the New York State Board of Regents and the Committee of the Professions.

The major characters in my story really exist. Most of the dialogue is reconstructed from memory, but communicates the gist of real conversations.

ACKNOWLEDGMENTS

In the years I took to get this book right, my mother, sister, and aunt stood by me with unwavering love and support even though my earlier actions brought them disappointment, shame, and hurt. Their fortitude, loyalty, and beauty of spirit allowed me to recover. Without them, I would be lost. They have my deepest love and gratitude.

My thanks also go to: Joe Scianameo, who kept me grounded; Tom and Meg Drago, who trusted and believed in me and kept me employed while working on the book; my editors, Sammie Justesen and Naomi Wax, who helped me with the early versions, taught me about the narrative voice and assisted me in figuring out how to tell my story; Vickie Frankmano and Lori Henry, who made me laugh and were always there when I needed them. They kept me focused on my goals and introduced me to new possibilities. My thanks also to: Sloan Harris, at ICM, whose enthusiasm propelled me forward; Mark Lawless, who taught me more about copyright law than I cared to know; my cousin Dana Zalaznick and friends, Chuck Bracken, Anna Quattrochi and Steven Polatnick, for reading the manuscript and providing the shot in the arm I needed when I became doubtful; my therapists, Dr. Samuel J. Langer and Tim Woehr, CSW who saved my life, believed in me and made me feel life was worth living; my lawyer, William L. Wood, Jr., for guiding me through the underground world of medical misconduct and helping me in my quest for redemption; to Bob Anello, whose sense of humor and legal expertise made my journey a little less scary; and my last editor, Marly Cornell, who read it, got it and helped me apply the finishing touches to this book.

Finally, I am grateful to my dogs, Jake, Scutch, and Baby Bop, whose unconditional love, constant company, and funny antics, kept me anchored, structured and smiling.

PROLOGUE

My knees buckled in horror when I saw Luke lying in the hospital bed. He looked so much worse than I anticipated. *This can't be happening. Why couldn't anyone else see what was so obvious? Luke didn't need anything or anyone but me.*

Luke was on his back with his head propped on two pillows. His face looked gaunt and his pasty skin blended with the white cotton blanket that covered him. His left arm was tied to the railing of the bed so he wouldn't disturb the IV line taped in the crook of his elbow. I reached for him tentatively, sliding around the IV pole to be next to him. Close up, I noticed a rivulet of drool sliding down his chin. He half-opened his eyes in response to my touch. "I have to pee," he mouthed.

I felt terrified as his brother, Jack, knelt beside the bed, untied Luke's rigid arm from the railing and hoisted him to his feet. Leaning his full weight on his brother, Luke's shoulders stooped and his head sagged. Jack practically dragged him across the room. I watched in horror, fighting the urge to scream, "It's all a big mistake!"

CHAPTER 1

The last time I saw my parents together was in my father's hospital room, a few days before he died. It was February 1990. They had divorced ten years earlier. My sister, Dani, had been estranged from my father for nearly two years and I was a fourth-year medical student.

My father had been diagnosed with advanced-stage cancer five weeks earlier. His doctor said he had three to six months to live. When my father was admitted to the hospital, I didn't even think to inquire after him. He had been a perpetual patient and hypochondriac. A week or so earlier, he began complaining of severe abdominal pain. I assumed it was another of his "crying wolf" episodes and was shocked when his doctor told me about the cancer.

I had called his doctor from the hospital where I was doing an elective in endocrinology. I was the only medical student on this rotation, so I had nobody to talk to. I had no idea what to do. My relationship with my dad was so conflicted; I wasn't even sure how I felt. I loved him and identified with him, yet he had hurt me again and again.

I called my boyfriend, Johnny, a psychiatric resident working in the same hospital as I was, but he was not at work. He was home, drunk, again.

I called my therapist, who was treating me for depression and ADD. He told me to go see my father immediately.

Next I called Mom. She had been furious at Dad for as long as I could remember, but she knew how I felt about him. I was close to my father; I had gone to medical school to appease him. Once I assured her I was okay, she told me to wash my face, have a drink of water and make the forty-minute drive "very carefully" to Dad's hospital.

Almost as an afterthought, I called Dani, who is six years younger than I am. She was working on her senior project in photography and was due to graduate from college at the end of the semester. We were very close. Dad had hurt her, too, so often and so badly that she refused to have anything to do with him. I was astonished that she was upset.

"Will you meet me at the hospital?" she asked.

"Of course," I told her. "And by the way, it's his birthday. He's fifty-five."

As I drove to the hospital, I imagined what I would do when I got there. I'd go to his bedside and talk to him about his diagnosis, comfort him and try to help him deal with it. The prospect of seeing my father so sick filled me with trepidation, but I wanted to be there for him.

When I walked into Dad's room, Pam, his wife, was there.

Her shoulder-length red hair was perfectly coiffed, her make-up impeccable. Her nail polish matched her silk blouse. She looked like a million bucks. Dad looked awful. Lying on his bed, tubes emanated from his arms like tentacles. His skin was ashen. She wiped crumbs from around his mouth and arranged his birthday cards on the windowsill. As I looked at him, my heart sank.

I wanted Pam to get out of the fucking room. When she finally left, I spoke to Dad in a sympathetic voice. Tears caught in my throat. "How are you doing?"

"Don't let her know," he demanded.

I hated his making believe everything was okay when *nothing* was okay. This was his approach to life. I couldn't stand it.

Dani arrived shortly after I did. Dad was ecstatic to see her.

Dad's health deteriorated quickly and dramatically over the next few days. Mom, as always, was the "Rock of Gibraltar" for Dani and me. Dani pleaded with her to come to the hospital, but Mom waited until my father asked for her. I couldn't blame her. He had treated her horribly since the divorce *and* while they were married. He was in and out of hospitals so often that she had grown inured to his many real and imagined illnesses.

Dani and I met her in the lobby. I was nervous because there'd been so much animosity between them for so long. The last time I'd seen them together was at my college graduation seven years earlier. Their interactions were strained. Dad's wife was with him and my mother loathed her.

The stench of death, mixed with antiseptic and urine, assailed us when we walked into his room. The curtain around his bed slid quietly back. Pam emerged carrying a full urinal. She mouthed hello as she exited the room. I was relieved there was not a scene between Mom and Pam.

Dad lay back with his sweat-soaked head on pillows. A white cotton blanket dangled from the side of the bed. His hospital gown hung off his shoulder, exposing his concave chest. Baby powder swirled like finger paint over his ribs. His dentures, a green plastic bedpan, and the remnants of his lunch were on a table next to his head. A bag of clear liquid hung on an IV pole.

I held my breath as Mom moved the table aside and leaned over his face. That she moved so close to him surprised me. She whispered to him and gently brushed his cheek with her hand. A smile gradually crossing his face accentuated his hollow cheeks. Tears slid from the corners of his eyes as he looked at her. Lines on Mom's face belied a lifetime of regrets. She didn't wear make-up, which made these lines all the more pronounced.

I was anxious about what she would do next. I felt embarrassed witnessing their intimacy and sad at the sudden realization that they still loved one another. Despite my training in psychiatry, and natural insight into people, I would not have guessed that they still cared for each other. I had only heard them berate one another for the last twenty years.

Dani passed my mother a chair. She and I sat across from each other near Dad's knees. We stared back and forth maintaining a reverent silence as Mom stroked Dad's head and cheek and softly cooed to him that he'd be okay. Mom dabbed at Dad's tears and shed a few of her own.

My heart was ripping from my chest. I had no memory of seeing my mother treat Dad so tenderly. It suddenly occurred to me how much I had longed for parents who were kind to one another. How painful this lack of love and constant acrimony had been for me. I wondered if Dani was thinking the same thing.

Soon their interaction became more upbeat, and the four of us started reminiscing about "the old days." We talked warmly about our summers in Cape Cod, the time our two Old English Sheepdogs were sprayed by a skunk, and funny things about Dad's mother.

If my father had not been gaunt, ashen, and intermittently gasping for air, this could have been mistaken for a family reunion. A family I barely recognized. But Dad was dying and this was Mom's way of forgiving him and saying goodbye. The sadness I felt was physically painful. It was as though I was finally mourning the tragic loss of my family that had happened two decades earlier. I realized what I'd missed, what I had needed and longed for with all my being--a unified family.

Shortly after my mother left, Dad pulled out his IV and fell on the floor while trying to climb out of bed. Half-naked and bleeding from the IV site, he clutched the leg of a chair and started screaming about the doctors and nurses. "It's a conspiracy," he bellowed. "They're trying to kill me. I need to go to a different hospital."

Despite having grown weary of my father's "conspiracy theories," which I'd been hearing for much of my life, I was moved by this pathetic display. I was also angry that he was likely to make the final days of his life as difficult as possible for me. He had been making things hard for me for as long as I could remember. Now that I was so close to graduating from medical school, *his dream* for me, he was once again threatening to sabotage my success. I was furious at him for making this difficult situation even more untenable. I felt guilty for being angry with a dying man and for thinking about how his transfer to a hospital further away would inconvenience me. I was mostly angry at the unpropitious timing of his illness. I was supposed to be celebrating my acceptance to a residency program, finishing my fourth-year electives and studying for the Medical Boards. His illness interfered with all these things.

I was devastated that Dad was not going to be around to see me graduate. It was *he* who had pleaded with me to go to medical school. It was *he* who promised to pay for it and then reneged on his promise. It was *he* who sued my mother and me a year earlier, devastating me emotionally and disrupting my studies for months.

A few months earlier, I had given him an ultimatum: "Either stop hurting me and sabotaging me, or I will no longer have a relationship with you. I love you more than anyone, but I cannot go on like this." He denied awareness of having done any of this to me. He apologized and promised not to hurt me again. Now he was playing his trump card.

Dad was transferred to another hospital. The following day, he became delirious. Over the next few days, Dani and I stayed there together. I sat by his bedside trying to study, held his head when he vomited and put his penis in the urinal, which he could no longer do by himself. Occasionally, I lay down next to him and cried. When Dani saw me holding him and crying, she reprimanded me, saying not to upset him. From then on, I detached emotionally from the situation.

A few days later, Dad's heart gave out. He was transferred, in a coma, to the intensive care unit. It was February 28, 1990, Pam's fortieth birthday. Pam, Dani, and I sat together in the waiting room of the ICU. We were only allowed to go into his room one at a time for fifteen minutes every hour. After twelve hours, his doctor came over to us. "It's time," he said.

We all went into his room. Pam stroked his face; Dani held his hand, and I stared at the monitors. When they flatlined, I felt Dad's soul leave his body.

Dani started crying. I did not. I asked her what she was feeling. "You can't borrow my emotions. You have to have your own," she replied.

But I felt nothing. It wasn't until my break up with Luke nearly two years later that I got in touch with the pain of my father's death.

CHAPTER 2

The day after Dad's funeral, I was scheduled to start a cardiology elective, but I felt so adrift, drained, and generally out of it that I dropped it. For the past six years I had been pursuing Dad's dream for me. Now I had no reason to continue medical school, or even living, I thought.

Toying with the idea of dropping out of medical school, I realized that would be a huge mistake. I only had to do one more month-long elective to graduate. Also, I knew my mother would be furious if I quit. It was very important to her that I "function" and see this through to the end.

I was scheduled to start a psychiatric residency program in New York in July, four months hence. Knowing I could not endure a rigorous program like cardiology, I decided to take time off to study for the Boards, and then do an easier elective in radiology.

By June, I still wasn't emotionally prepared to start a residency program. I considered taking a year off and going to California where I'd always wanted to live. But I feared that if I took time off, I would never pursue a medical career. Besides, accepting a residency position is like taking a sacred oath. I had to honor it. I was torn between doing what I knew was right and doing what felt easier in the instant.

Mom was irate that I was thinking about taking a year off. "That's irresponsible and reprehensible," she'd scolded. I knew her rage was more about fear than anger. She was terrified I'd turn into my father, take on his identity so to speak.

This phenomenon of "over identification" often happens when you lose someone you love. It's a way of trying to keep that person in your life. Everyone does it to some extent, but there's a fine line between a healthy amount of identification and a pathological amount. It's the difference between being *like* someone and trying to *be* someone.

I was like my father in many ways, both good and bad. My mother worried that the bad would end up dominating. That scared me, too. I'd spent the better part of my adult life trying to prevent that from happening.

Dad rarely completed anything he started. He went to law school but never practiced law. He'd been fired from every "real" job he'd had due to his refusal to obey authority. The only job he kept for more than a year was his own tutoring business, where he could work when he wanted to and make his own rules. He shirked responsibility and did not provide financially for our family. At the same time, he was generous to a fault. He'd give away the shirt off his back or his last piece of bread. He had a childlike curiosity and, when he wasn't too depressed to get out of bed, he loved to learn. He was extremely outgoing, to the point of embarrassing me. He talked to total strangers everywhere we went and picked up stray dogs, kids, and anyone else that needed help. He had a great sense of humor and nothing embarrassed him. His grandiosity and rebellion against authority made him unreliable, unpredictable, and generally unable to live in the real world. His underlying rage, which manifested as passive-aggressiveness, nearly destroyed the people he claimed to love most, his family.

I, too, had trouble dealing with authority and following rules, but I was not as rebellious as my father. I also had a history of depression, but it had not sidelined me as it did him. In many ways, I was a toned-down version of my dad, but my mom and I both knew that I had the potential to be just like him.

I did not attend my medical school graduation. "There's no point," I told my mom. "Daddy's not around to see it." Mom was disappointed and angry, but relieved that I started my residency program on time.

First year of a residency program, called the internship, is hell on wheels. The transition from being an independent and relatively carefree student, with tons of supervision and people to fall back on, to being a "real" doctor, working twelve-hour days with frequent overnight calls, is agonizing.

Besides the pressure and sleep deprivation, the worst part for me was treating dying patients, especially the ones that reminded me of Dad. Johnny was not supportive of me as his drinking problem continued to escalate. In September, he tried to kill himself by driving drunk in my car at top speed. The following day, he entered rehab. I was brokenhearted at this turn of events, but I knew it was best for both of us to end our relationship. Trying to save him would destroy me. Having already completed three months of my internship, I was determined to finish it, no matter what.

A month or so later, my friend Martin, also a psychiatric resident, had someone he wanted me to meet. I did not want to meet anybody. I barely had enough energy for work, never mind a date. Martin insisted. "His name is Luke. He's a psychiatrist I work with," he told me. "He'll be good for you."

Reluctantly, I agreed to meet Luke. "But don't expect anything to come of it," I said.

I had practically forgotten about it, when, in early November, Luke called me.

I was at my mother's house, lying on the bed in my old room. Immediately after a grueling thirty-six-hour shift, I made the half-hour drive to Mom's house. Going there was a form of therapy. I could see my dog, Brin, get some TLC, and be away from the dirty crowded city.

Talking to Luke on the phone was extremely stimulating. He was funny, a great audience for my humor, interesting, and bright. Not only that, he was professionally established, goal-oriented, open, and sensitive. He made me think, laugh and feel alive. Our conversation lasted more than two hours. We could have talked forever.

I started out lying on my back. As our chat continued, I became so excited and energized that I danced around the room, jumped on and off the bed, stared out the window and looked in the mirror.

Luke called me several times after that. Our conversations were titillating and I always hung up feeling exuberant. When he asked what I wanted to do on our first date, I replied, "Why don't we go to a movie? That way, if we discover we can't stand one another or you think I'm really ugly or something, we don't have to interact at all and it won't be too awkward. If we do like each other, we can go for a drink afterwards. Otherwise, I can take a cab home, you can go your merry way, and no hard feelings."

He found my diatribe entertaining and funny, but also considered it a bad idea. "Of course we'll like each other. Besides, how will we ever get to know each other if we don't interact?" He suggested going out to dinner instead. We met a few days later.

Coming off a thirty-six-hour shift and running on just a couple hours of interrupted sleep, I hurried home, cranked up my "get psyched" music on the stereo, showered and slipped into my size two slacks. I blew dry my long, brown, unruly hair and danced around playing air drums.

Luke arrived at my apartment at exactly seven. I liked that he was prompt and dependable. When the intercom rang, I turned off the stereo and ran down the hall to the elevator. I didn't know what he'd looked like, but when I saw him on the elevator, he looked kind of lost, so I assumed it was he. I said, "Hey handsome, are you going my way?" He looked at me as if I had two heads, then he laughed. I'd heard his deep warm laugh on the telephone many times. In person, his laugh came in quick bursts, as though he was holding it in for fear of letting go. His prominent Adam's apple moved up and out like a cobra emerging ready to pounce and then retreating. His lips parted into a wide warm smile that lit up his face, lining it with long dimples and laugh lines around his eyes.

Discreetly I sized him up. He was one of the nicest looking men I had ever seen. I knew I could look at his face for eternity. He was nearly a foot taller than I, slim, with straight blond hair combed back from his face. His light green eyes belied a life of sorrow. His skin was pale, his long straight nose fit his face perfectly, and he had a cleft chin to die for. He wore faded jeans, a button-down white shirt, gray sports jacket, and casual black shoes. He reminded me of a cross between James Woods and William Hurt, my favorite actor. While I loved the way he looked, I was surprised I wasn't exactly physically attracted to him. As my track record attested, my usual M.O. when meeting men with whom I fell in love was "lust at first sight." But this felt different. I couldn't even imagine kissing him.

We crossed the street to his silver Ford Bronco. I was very impressed when he held the door open for me, waited for me to get situated and closed the door behind me. *He's a real gentleman. Right out of the old school.*

As we drove down to Greenwich Village, we talked the entire way. He opened the conversation by asking for my advice on one of his female patients. "As a bright, insightful woman, I thought you might offer a fresh perspective on her situation," he said. I was thrilled that he divulged such intimate information to me, that he already trusted me and valued my opinion. Not wanting to let him down, I considered his questions and comments before answering thoughtfully and intelligently, as though I were taking an essay exam. More important to me than the conversation, or the impression I was making on him, was discerning his attitude toward his patient. In my mind, this translated to his attitude toward women in general. I was searching for something that would scare me off, but I didn't find anything. He clearly respected, admired and cared deeply about her. I hoped he would feel the same way towards me.

I stared at his hands, imagining what it would be like to hold one in mine. His fingers were long and not too thin, not too thick. They were masculine, but his perfectly manicured nails added a feminine touch. This yin-yang blend of strength and femininity intrigued me. These hands could just as easily karate-chop a board or hold a baby. He held the steering wheel precisely the way they teach in driver's ed. This was telling, too. He followed rules exactly, internalized his education and was a perfectionist.

I stared at his face and studied his mannerisms. I was mesmerized by his deep mellifluous voice and his words, which flowed fluently. He spoke with perfect pronunciation. I scrutinized him for any indication that he would eventually hurt me, if we were to become involved. I wanted to believe that he cared about his patient and was as enthusiastic about my feedback as he professed to be. At this point, I trusted him, guardedly, because I knew that eventually any man I really cared for would end up hurting me.

Walking around the village, I felt as though I'd known Luke for a long time. It was so comfortable and casual. We talked, laughed and wandered in and out of stores admiring the clothes, joking about some items and generally having a good time.

Throughout dinner, we meandered from lighthearted, mundane topics to heavier more personal ones. When I told him the story of how I got my therapist, a wannabe Freudian, to hug me, he said I was a handful and that he thanked his lucky stars I wasn't his patient, but that he was so glad he met me.

I was surprised that he appreciated stories about my manipulative antics. He seemed so straight-laced; I would have thought my behavior was antithetical to his code of conduct. I knew I intrigued him and as I stared into his doleful green eyes, I felt closer and closer to him. He quickly revealed the source of sadness in his eyes. His mother had committed suicide. "It was her fifth attempt," he told me. "She overdosed on antidepressant medication. I found her in the living room." Knowing his pain and having him confide in me sealed the deal for me. I was hooked, partly by my rescue fantasies and partly because of his candor. Not to mention his intelligence and deep, heartfelt laugh.

What I liked most about Luke was the way he listened. His soft, sympathetic drawn-out utterances of "um hmm" conveyed such empathy, as though he felt my pain and understood every word I uttered. He listened so attentively, offering such intelligent, perfectly timed responses; I was sure I'd never feel alone as long as he was in my life.

We didn't want our date to end, but we had to be at work early the next day. We finally decided it was time to go home. On the way back to my apartment, I grew anxious wondering if I had misread his interest in me. My insecurities kicked in as it suddenly occurred to me that he might not want to see me again. After all, he was handsome, accomplished, and I couldn't figure out what he could possibly see in me.

Outside my apartment, we sat talking in his truck. He gently stroked my hair, took my hand tentatively and asked if he could see me again. I laughed to myself realizing he was probably experiencing similar self-doubt. It struck me as funny that every person on the planet, no matter how good-looking, rich, or accomplished, probably experiences this apprehension, as well as the awkward moments, as a first date winds down.

His tender, gentlemanly approach melted my heart. As much as I liked him, I still wasn't sure I was attracted to him. But I was sure I wanted to see him again. We planned our next date for a few days later. He walked me to my door, kissed me gently on the top of my head, and thanked me for a lovely evening.

Back in my apartment, I reflected on the evening. That I had no desire to jump into bed with Luke confused me. He was by far the most sensitive, bright, and handsome man I'd ever dated, so why wasn't I physically attracted to him? Was my body holding back to give my mind a chance to connect with him? Was I so physically exhausted from my strenuous schedule that my body had temporarily shut down? Did he lack a sexual aura? Or was it something deeper? Whatever it was, I sensed that meeting Luke would change my life.

CHAPTER 3

My second date with Luke led to a third. The more time I spent with him, the more I liked him. In addition to the things that first attracted me, I discovered he was very deep and profoundly honest. Though somewhat stiff, he loosened up after a glass of wine, which he indulged in nightly. We had a lot in common, including our interest in psychiatry and love of tennis. We also liked the same kinds of books, music, food, and movies.

By the third date we were holding hands. By the fourth, we were discussing our hopes, dreams, and future aspirations. We wanted the same things: marriage, kids, and a rustic lifestyle. We were sizing each other up and liked what we saw. As far as I could tell, he was everything I wanted in a husband and a father for my children.

We had our fifth date a few weeks after we met. This night out, which turned into an entire weekend, closed the deal for both of us. It was the first time I went to his house in the suburbs. He cooked me dinner. We watched a movie and, before I knew it, he was lying on the couch with his head on my lap, crying. I could not resist a man who cries. After an hour or so of my caressing his head and listening to his sad tales, he took my hand and led me upstairs to the bedroom.

A wood-framed king-size bed was flanked by two dressers in the same dark wood. The dresser surfaces were empty. A clock radio and a book were on the nightstand next to his bed.

Still holding my hand, he asked shyly if I wanted to lie down with him. I nodded yes.

He turned out the light before unbuttoning his shirt and slipping out of his pants. Then he put them on a hanger in the closet. I followed his lead. Pulling back the green and gold paisley comforter, he guided me under the covers.

I found his diffidence endearing. I was used to more aggressive, passionate men. Pulling the covers over us, he held me and gently stroked me, as though I were fragile as a piece of glass. It felt so good to lie naked with him. His warm trim body fit perfectly with mine. Eventually, I thrust my tongue in his mouth. The sex was fast, disappointing and over in an instant. He apologized. I held him tighter and told him it would take time to get used to one another.

The following day, he took me to his brother Jack's house to meet "the gang." The gang consisted of Jack, Jack's girlfriend Aliza, Luke's best friend Steve, and Steve's girlfriend Sue. All four of them were doctors, as was Jack's housemate, Ted. They were all slightly older than I with established careers. I loved being with this professional, ambitious, people-oriented group. They were warm and welcoming and seemed genuinely happy to meet me. Despite the fact that I was uncomfortable with food-centric activities, I immediately felt at ease in this close-knit group of friends. Nobody seemed to notice that I only ate salad or if I snuck off to have a quick smoke.

On the way home, Luke told me how thrilled he was that I was with him. "They all really liked you. You get along with everyone and socialize so well. I was very relieved that you could do your own thing and didn't need to hang on to me the whole time. You looked like you were having a really good time. I felt proud to be with you."

I did have a really good time. Meeting these people was exciting. I was thrilled to be a couple with Luke. I hoped to see a lot more of "the gang."

What pleased Luke the most about "my performance" was that I didn't hang onto him. My mother valued the same thing about me. I didn't "need" her, or anything else for that matter. Luke wanted that exact same thing from me. He would only be able to tolerate being in a relationship if I was independent, self-reliant, and need-free where he was concerned. Feeling high from connecting with the gang, and starry-eyed toward Luke, I let down my guard. All I heard was, "I felt proud and happy to be with you."

After that weekend, our relationship progressed quickly. The holidays were upon us and there was no doubt we'd attend each other's work parties and family gatherings. His party was before mine; it was the first time he saw me dressed up. I'd gone to Mom's house to change because that's where most of my clothes were. Luke picked me up there and they met.

I knew Mom would like Luke. What was there not to like? He was a handsome doctor who was polite, warm, and bright. They chatted while I got ready. When I entered the room, Luke could not stop smiling. "You look beautiful," he said. "Can you believe how beautiful she is?" he asked my mother.

He handed Mom his camera. "Jean, would you take our picture?" This was the first picture of us together, possibly the first of a lifetime of photos that would fill volumes of our family albums.

As we drove to the party, Luke kept looking at me. "I'm so happy to be with you," he kept repeating. "I can't wait to introduce you to my colleagues." I felt the same way.

When we danced, it felt as though we were the only ones in the room. (In fact there were at least a hundred people.) While talking to others, I felt Luke admiring me from across the room. When we were together, I felt excited. I felt like an "us," which I loved.

On the way home, Luke again complimented me on how socially poised I was, how beautiful I looked, and how comfortable and easy it was to be with me. "It's so great that you can talk to other people and not hang all over me," he said.

Later that night, he looked lovingly at me. "My family adores you, my colleagues think you're great, and so do I. I think this is truly the beginning of the rest of our lives together."

I felt exactly the same way. For the first time in my life, I was sure I had met "Mr. Right." I had no doubt that I wanted to spend the rest of my life with him. Then he asked me to move in with him! I was shocked. He was a seemingly rational, deliberate man who, in my estimation, lacked passion, asking me to make this huge commitment only six weeks after we'd met.

I had planned to move out of the city at the end of December into an apartment on the campus of the hospital where I worked. Luke thought it made more sense for me to move in with him since he had a house that was close to my work. And it seemed we were in this for the long haul. Since we both worked so much, it would insure that we'd see each other most nights. Also, he'd charge me a low rent, so I'd save money. In his mind, it was a no-brainer.

I had looked forward to having my own apartment. Moving in with Luke was not in my plans. I told him I had to think about it. *Isn't this ironic? I'm usually the one in a relationship to jump in feet first.*

Luke usually took things very slowly. He had never lived with anyone before. I had lived with several boyfriends, but always ended up wanting out. The shoe was on the other foot, and I didn't know what to do. He was clearly hurt that I wasn't enthusiastic about his proposal. A few days later, I decided to move in with him and also rent a small apartment on campus "just in case." "My dog comes with me," I told him.

"Of course she does," he replied. He was thrilled with my decision and immediately called Jack and Steve to tell them. I called Dani, but insisted we wait a few days to tell my mom. Later Luke informed me that my mother had cautioned him against it.

I moved into his house on New Year's Day, 1991. Luke was so sweet about making room for my stuff in the closet and drawers. He gave me a room downstairs for my office, and suggested we go furniture shopping so we could make it "our" place. We bought a loveseat, couch, washer/dryer, and a bookcase. We split the cost of everything.

Once I was all settled in, he threw me a moving-in party. We invited our friends and family. It was a blast.

The transition from dating to living together was simple. Even though we'd known one another less than two months, living together felt natural and comfortable. We both worked long hours, but we ate dinner together almost every night. Then we'd watch TV or listen to music, read, and go to bed. We'd lie in bed holding each other and talk for hours.

If I got home first, I threw together some dinner for us and waited for him. I loved preparing food for him, even though I didn't eat much. The minute he walked in the door, I draped my arms around his neck, climbed up him and wrapped my legs around his waist. He'd hold me like that while we laughed or had a quick chat. I'd go upstairs with him and watch him change out of his work clothes into jeans. We talked and laughed the whole time. Sometimes he let me pull him on the bed for a make-out session. Occasionally he wanted to make a phone call or something before we ate, but he was always affectionate and glad to see me. That was when I felt the happiest.

We took our first vacation together on Valentine's Day, three months after we met. As we waited for the taxi to take us to the airport, I read and re-read the card Luke had slipped into my suitcase moments earlier.

This is the happiest Valentine's Day of my life, that's for sure! Flying off to Mexico with you, who I'm so in love with. You are what I've been looking for my whole life. It's hard to believe it's really here. Here's to our last Valentine's Day as single people, and our first together.
I love you. Luke

The vacation felt like a honeymoon. We held hands, laughed, kissed, walked on the beach, lay by the side of the pool reading, swam in the ocean and played tennis. At night we dressed up and went out for romantic dinners. The only time we spent apart was early in the morning when I went running and for an hour or two each day when Luke "needed" time alone. He made me promise I wouldn't interrupt him or even come near the room during that time. That was fine with me. I had no problem entertaining myself. When I asked him what he was doing, he told me, "It's private, but it's my form of therapy." His need for time alone did not send up red flags for me. I felt excluded only because he was keeping a secret, not because he needed space. I occasionally teased him about it. He found my teasing kind of amusing. We let it go at that.

CHAPTER 4

Five months into our relationship, Luke and I had our first fight. I had been staying in the city for a pediatric rotation because I was working fifteen-hour days in a hospital there. One week I had to work all-night shifts. That week, I asked Luke to visit me on his day off. He refused, saying he had set the time aside to study and write a paper for a class he was taking. I reacted angrily, saying he had all the time he could possibly need when I was working. Feeling exhausted, neglected, and abandoned, I argued and pleaded with him until he agreed to come see me for an hour or so. When he arrived, we continued arguing. I became so hysterical that I started punching him. He remained calm, holding my wrists so I couldn't strike him. He restrained me in a bear hug until I calmed down. When I did settle down, we tore off each other's clothes and made love. It was the best sex we'd ever had.

This fight was the turning point in our relationship. Whether my rage frightened him or what he perceived as my neediness set off his sirens, I can't say, but from that day forward, instead of laughing and holding me when I jumped into his arms to greet him, he told me to "quit it," in an annoyed tone of voice. Before the incident, if Jack or Steve called during dinner, he'd tell them he had to call them back after we finished eating. If he had to take the call, he'd apologize to me and talk in front of me. Now, he took calls more often than not and went upstairs to his office, his "sacred space," to talk. He talked for a long time without acknowledging me. Before, if I called him during the day, which I did infrequently, he was happy to hear from me. Now, he said I was too dependent on him, even if I just called to say "Hi" or to tell him something funny. He began finding fault with me about petty things, like misplacing receipts. I reacted to this change, although it was subtle at first, immediately. When I sensed him pulling away from me, regardless of how it manifested, I started to panic. I became increasingly anxious and obsessed with trying to placate him. It took months for me to recognize that I wasn't totally at fault, and even longer to confront him.

I completed my internship at the end of June and started the second year of my psychiatric residency in July. This year is called PGYII, (post graduate year two). As a PGYII, I worked on a psychiatric inpatient unit. My workload decreased dramatically. I only spent ten hours a day in the hospital and had overnight call every fourth night. I was much happier and more relaxed than I had been as an intern. My schedule was easier and I was doing something I loved. I looked forward to spending more time with Luke, but as I became more available, Luke became less so. He enrolled in more night classes, took on more patients and secluded himself more frequently in his home office. He accepted more paid overnight calls and demanded more time with Jack and Steve.

Whenever I complained about our lack of time together, he told me to "grow up," or that I was "too dependent" on him. He became a relationship barometer, giving me daily reports on how he felt about "us." He'd say, "Today I feel pessimistic about the relationship." On a good day, he might say, "Today I feel optimistic about us." Hearing these prognostications, I felt increasingly anxious. Often, they seemed unrelated to anything I had done. Rather, they reflected his internal moods. One day when he was feeling particularly hopeful about the relationship, he promised me we'd go away on vacation. "I'll make it up to you then," he said. I clung to that promise like a lifeline.

Though he had distanced himself, we had a terrific summer overall. Luke, Jack, Steve, and their girlfriends, planned to buy land together, build three separate houses and create a kind of commune. Luke now included me in these plans. He and I looked for prospective land together. We constantly talked about what kind of house we'd build. We went away with the gang on several weekends. One weekend, we visited his brother and sister-in-law in Boston. They'd just had their first baby. Luke was so enamored with the baby; he crawled around on the floor with her, held her non-stop and even changed her diaper. Watching him be so tender, playful, and relaxed with his niece, I wanted to have children with him even more. Another great thing about the summer was that Dani began dating Ted. The gang expanded to include Dani and Ted.

In August, Luke told me, "We'll get married when you're a PGYIII. Maybe we can even have a group wedding with Jack and Steve. When you're a PGYIV, we'll start trying to get pregnant. By then we'll be living in our house, you'll have a much easier schedule, and we'll be more financially secure."

We wanted two kids, but Luke wasn't sure he could impregnate me. He produced very little semen. His plan was to mix his sperm with Jack's and use that mix to get me pregnant. "We won't know if the child is mine or his, but it doesn't matter."

I thought this idea was strange on the one hand, but lovely in that it was testimony to how much he loved his brother. I was game.

We planned to go on vacation in September, but it was difficult to schedule. My time off was dictated by my residency program. The time I was allotted overlapped with Luke's birthday, but he wanted to spend his birthday with the gang. I finally convinced him to spend his real birthday with me on vacation. "We can celebrate with everyone else when we get back. What's the big deal if it's a few days later?" I pleaded.

I worried that he would pull the plug on the vacation until we actually got in the car and started driving to Virginia Beach, seven hours away. The drive down was wonderful. I finally had his undivided attention. There were no patients, family, friends, or work to interfere. We had a chance to reconnect. I felt fantastic until he told me that he'd need to spend eight hours a day alone in the hotel room studying and writing a paper for his class.

"All day, everyday?" I asked incredulously. I tried to sound blasé, but I was livid and distraught. I felt betrayed. I'd been looking forward to spending this time with him for months. He'd held out this vacation like a carrot on a stick. Now he was cutting that carrot in half.

"Yes! And don't start. We'll spend the nights together. You know how important this class is to me," he said coldly.

I tried to remain calm, but I felt irate and helpless. Deciding that even a crumb of his time was better than nothing, I told myself to shut up and make the best of it. *If only he'd marry me. At least I'd know we were together. I could give him all the space he needed and not feel so neglected and anxious.*

I gave him the time he requested. I got up early to go running so that my shower and getting ready for the day did not interfere with his studying time. Gathering all the things I needed for the day, I headed to the beach or town, or wherever I was going, alone. I found plenty of things to do, but sitting on the beach, watching other couples all lovey-dovey, and staring at the window of our hotel room where he was sequestered, was unbearable. Sometimes I could tell he was on the phone. I assumed it was with Jack or Steve or one of his precious patients. They couldn't live without him and he couldn't live without them, even for a week. It took all my self-restraint not to burst into the hotel room and beg him to spend time with me. I knew that was out of the question. Even if I returned to our room to retrieve something I forgot, he was angry.

On his birthday, I asked him if he could quit working early. I wanted to go out dancing to celebrate. That pissed him off. I quickly learned the only way to avoid his wrath and have a shot in hell at keeping the relationship going, was to play by his rules without complaining or questioning him. It was worth it to me to suffer this deprivation because I couldn't imagine life without him. By now I wasn't even sure I could live without him. The good times were still oh-so-good. But they became fewer and fewer, and further and further apart. Between the good times, I constantly worried about the next time he'd push me away. The more he pushed me away, the more desperate I became.

CHAPTER 5

On Sunday mornings, Luke and I lay in bed for hours. We cuddled, made love, talked, laughed and cried. Those mornings, vacation planning with him and sitting at the dining room table working on our latest thousand-piece puzzle together, were the intimate times that sustained me. In my mind, they were inviolable unless one of us was on call. My call schedule was out of my control. His was voluntary and paid.

Given the choice between taking an overnight call that paid $2,000 and spending time with me, Luke always chose call. We argued about this a lot. He said I was insane for getting upset. He told me that so many of my reactions were insane that I began to wonder about myself. Then, I started actually doing things that were a bit nuts and out of character. For example, I sneaked a peek at his appointment book every morning. I wanted to know what patients he was seeing that day and what time he'd be home. This was to brace myself for the potential abandonment feelings.

I specifically wanted to know if he was scheduled to meet with any of the female patients with whom he seemed preoccupied. I felt threatened by these women. This included the one he had spoken to me about on our first date. He often videotaped their sessions and spent hours at home watching the tapes. He talked to them on the phone as well. When they called the house, he spent however long it took to help them through their latest crisis. I never felt threatened sexually, but that he devoted so much emotional energy and time to helping them, I felt threatened and jealous. He set limits with me, but not with them. I felt unappreciated, neglected, and incensed. He seemed to care more about them than he did about me. Whenever I broached the subject, he told me I was crazy and that I should know better since I was a psychiatrist, too. If he included me, by asking my advice or describing a situation he was having with a certain patient to teach me something, I loved it. But when he left me out completely, I felt enraged and distraught.

I memorized Luke's call schedule. Sometimes he showed it to me. Other times I'd have to search through his briefcase to find it. Once I knew his schedule, I'd compare it to mine. I loved when we were on call the same night. I wouldn't have to miss him at home alone, and it assured us more time together when we weren't on call. If he was on call when I wasn't, I set up a date ahead of time with my friend Mark, Val, my sister, or one of the women in the gang to ward off the anticipatory dread and loneliness of Luke being gone. Those nights, I slept on his side of the bed, smelled his clothing and fondled his belongings to assure myself that he in fact lived there and would soon be home.

Shortly after returning from the September vacation, it was time to plan our next one. I had a week off at the beginning of December, but he had a long tradition of going away with Jack and Steve around Thanksgiving. He was not about to forego that for me.

We scheduled a date to plan our December vacation on a night in October when neither one of us was on call. We had to plan ahead to make certain we'd have time together. I'd been anticipating our "date" all day. When I came home and found him already there, I was excited. My hopes faded when I realized he was closed in his office and on the phone. Knowing his shut door was a sign that his call was private, I sulked in the bedroom. Half an hour later he was still on the phone. Even though it was "forbidden," I opened the door to his office. His office was his sanctuary. Unlike his bedroom, which was functional and sparse, his office was thoughtfully decorated, comfortable, and inviting. That's where he kept his books, therapy tapes, computer, and I don't know what else. He locked it when he wasn't home and refused to give me a key. I got his attention and mouthed, "Come on."

He waved me away and motioned for me to close the door.

I slammed the door and stormed to the bedroom. It was painful that our time together meant so little to him, but I knew it was futile to complain. Whenever I asked him to get off the phone to pay attention to me, he always said I was too needy and it was giving him a bad feeling about our relationship. The thing that got to me most was that he'd speak at greater length and with more intimacy to his phone buddies than to me.

"Who was that?" I asked when he finally hung up.

"My multiple personality disorder patient."

"You spend more time talking to her than you do to me," I whined.

"She's going through a difficult time."

Interpreting even his terse response as a sign that he might be willing to spend time with me, I asked meekly, "Hey, do you want to play a game of Tetris?" When I was lucky, he'd let me sit on his lap while we played this computer game. I would have been content to sit on his lap, with his chin on my head and his arms around me, for the rest of my life. But even during those times I never felt secure. Whenever he moved, even just to shift my weight from one leg to the other, I'd feel anxious and forlorn, thinking he was going to say he had to do something else. I lived in a dread-filled state of anxiety, anticipating my imminent loss.

"Not now. Let's work out our vacation plans first," he said in a neutral tone.

I climbed onto his lap with trepidation, afraid he would push me away. He neither embraced nor rebuffed me. He seemed so indifferent to me that I may as well have been sitting on a wall. That's how precarious I felt. He could push me over the edge at any moment. I sat very still, hoping he'd forget I was there.

He reiterated that he needed to spend five full days in Cancun with Jack and Steve. Then he gave me the dates. "You can't come down until after the five days"

I was furious. The five days overlapped with my allotted vacation days. I was so pissed off that his vacation with the boys was going to cut into my time with him, I threatened to go to Club Med alone.

"You're being spiteful and immature," he said, and threatened to cancel our plans all together.

He was right, but, so what? He deserved it! While I was trying to contain my hurt and anger, he announced that his brother would be staying on with us for a couple of days.

"But you promised to spend time alone with me!" I pounded on his chest and screamed. "It's not fair! Jack gets to infringe on my time, but your time with him and Steve is sacred!"

"You're crazy," he said calmly. "Anyway, I thought you liked Jack."

"I do like Jack, but I want to be alone with you. I don't see Jack or Steve inviting you along on vacations with their girlfriends."

I felt crazy and enraged. How could he, an astute, talented psychiatrist, not realize he was driving me mad? *Perhaps that's his goal.*

Our time in Mexico hardly felt like a vacation. The only flight I could get arrived two hours before Jack and Steve left. I had to wait in the lobby of the hotel for them to leave before Luke allowed me to come to the room. We were staying at the hotel where we took our first vacation together ten months earlier. This time, Luke was cold and distant. Our conversation was stilted. The tension was palpable. At dinner the first night, he told me Jack and Steve decided to ask their girlfriends to marry them. "I'm nowhere near that with you," he added.

I felt devastated, jealous, and angry. His dream of the six of us together forever had become my dream, too. Now he was taking it away.

I panicked as I watched the relationship slip from my grasp. I'd lie next to him in bed wanting to touch him, but he turned his back to me and went to sleep as if I wasn't even there. I stared at his back for hours each night wanting to reach out to him. Growing more and more fretful, I imagined the probable scenarios: he'd recoil, ignore me or push me away. The pain of his pulling away was becoming so unbearable that I convinced myself it was his way of preparing to ask me to marry him. I knew this defied logic, but it's the scenario my mind concocted to help me deal with the devastating reality that he was preparing to break up with me. I wanted to marry him so badly.

Every time he opened his mouth, I was scared he was going to tell me it was over. I couldn't figure out how to stop him. I'd done everything he'd ever asked of me. Whenever he complained about my behavior — "You're too disorganized," or "You don't return phone calls or save receipts," I admitted he was right and begged for forgiveness. In a matter of days, or weeks at most, I'd fixed whatever it was he'd complained about. He'd acknowledge that I'd gotten much better, and then find something else that needed fixing.

However minor or idiosyncratic my flaws seemed to me, I knew that to him they were egregious. I felt like a dam that sprung a leak. Every time I plugged the hole, two more appeared. It took all my energy to stop the leaks and, no matter how hard I tried, he'd find bigger, more ominous ones. He agreed that I was getting much better, but he also couldn't stop finding more faults and becoming more put off. My salvation was that I knew he was too decent to break up with me over the holidays, which meant I had a few more weeks at least. Like the year before, we went to each other's parties. But this time, he acted cold towards me. When I asked him what he thought I should wear to his party, he said, "I don't care what you do." I flinched. His response was like a slap in the face.

In late December, we began couples therapy. I had been pleading with him to go, to try to work things out. As a last ditch attempt at salvaging the relationship, he finally acquiesced on the condition that he choose the therapist. "I'll go, but don't get your hopes up. I think the relationship is beyond saving." I hung on to the tiniest shred of hope; I was willing to do anything to buy more time with him. Besides, I wanted a trained and objective party to witness our interactions. Surely the therapist would point out to Luke how unreasonable he was being. If nothing else, I would derive a sliver of satisfaction in watching Luke being confronted. We started seeing Josh, a therapist Luke knew from the classes he was taking on a new form of therapy called Accelerated Empathic Therapy (AET). Luke dropped out after two sessions. But that was enough time for Josh to get a handle on the situation, as well as the pathology and futility of it all. Josh had videotaped the sessions. I watched those videotapes until I had them memorized. After Luke quit, I continued going to Josh, as well as my other therapist, Dr. Mikker, for the next few months.

In mid-January we were working on our latest puzzle when Luke said in a foreboding tone of voice, "Hon, I need to go away alone for a while. Even though I love you, I'm depressed being with you. I have to figure out why."

Doing puzzles was the least stressful activity we shared. The puzzle table was where we relaxed, wound down, talked, laughed, problem-solved, had occasional romantic interludes and generally, and genuinely, enjoyed one another. No matter what was going on between us, the puzzle table was a cease-fire zone. That he dropped this bombshell on me here felt like a double betrayal.

My hands started to tremble and my eyes welled up with tears. "For how long?" I tried to keep my voice steady.

"At least two weeks." He fit a piece into the puzzle.

"Can't you go for shorter?" I chewed on the piece in my hand.

"No! I need to go away to think about us."

"I can't stand the thought of being away from you for that long." I staggered out of my chair and wrapped my arms around his neck.

He pried my arms off his neck and went into the kitchen. I followed him. I was desperate to figure out a way to make him stay home or, at least, to go away for a shorter period of time. My anxiety was so overwhelming that my thoughts were jumbled and confused. I felt dizzy. My visual perceptions became distorted. The walls looked like they were melting, becoming liquid, like the background in that famous painting, "The Scream."

I prepared myself for his leaving by making plans to spend time with my closest friends. I was on the verge of a panic attack every time I thought about Luke leaving.

While he was gone, he called to check in every night. The conversation was forced, but amicable. "When are you coming home?" I asked.

"I don't know. I love you, but I still can't figure out why being with you depresses me."

I wanted to scream my head off and tell him he was deranged and being an asshole. If he loved me, why couldn't he be with me? I could have strangled him for giving me mixed messages. Instead, I told him I loved him and missed him and prayed that by some miracle, he would come to his senses. I took solace in the fact that he had promised to visit my father's grave with me in February, on the second anniversary of my father's death. That was a month away. I doubted he'd renege on his promise.

When he returned, I did everything I could to avoid being alone with him. I knew he was still too decent to break up with me over the phone or when we were both running out the door to work. But I could only delay the inevitable for a few days. I was sitting at the puzzle table when he came home from work.

"Hon, I love you more than I've ever loved anyone," Luke said with tears in his eyes. "But, I can't stay with you. Maybe we'll end up together, but for now, I need to break up."

I fell to the floor wailing. "I can't live without you."

"I'm sorry, but I've made up my mind." He walked into the living room, sat on the couch and turned on the TV.

I crawled across the room, grabbed onto his legs and pleaded.

"I don't understand. Why can't you stay with me if you love me?" Kneeling in front of him, I pounded his legs with my fists.

"I don't understand it either." He grabbed my wrists.

"Can't you wait until I finish my PGYII year? Don't forget you promised to go to the cemetery with me."

"I'm sorry, but I made up my mind," he repeated.

I ran upstairs and threw myself on the bed, hysterically crying. I prayed he'd come after me, but I didn't know what I wanted him to do once he got there. The only way he could have helped me was to tell me he'd changed his mind. Through my sobs, I listened for him. It took him a while to come. I felt even worse in his presence as I was reminded that soon he'd be gone for good.

Standing at the foot of the bed, he watched me writhe in pain. I was screaming, crying and emitting sounds I'd never made before. Like a wounded animal, I howled. I screamed for my father. "I want Daddy." I screamed for Luke. "I need you." Soon, I didn't know who I needed, who I was mourning, or even who was in the room with me. Luke and Dad had merged into the same person. They became one and the same agonizing loss. I wanted to die.

Luke didn't try to console me. He cried, too. "I'm not your father," I heard him say through his sobs.

Hours passed. He hadn't moved. My pain was infinite. I did not calm down.

I felt him leave the room, but I didn't look up.

He returned and sat down next to me. "Here," he said, handing me a little yellow pill. "Take this; it will make you feel better." I swallowed the pill. He held a glass to my lips so I could take some water. I hoped it was cyanide, but it was only valium. When I awoke in a fog, it was morning. Luke was gone.

CHAPTER 6

Luke thought he was doing me a favor by breaking up slowly. Or maybe he was taking care of his own needs by doing it that way. But breaking up is like pulling off a bandage The slower you do it, the more it hurts.

To be "fair and honorable," he let me stay in the house. He stayed somewhere else. "You can take all the time you need to move out, within reason." It was the dead of winter.

I gradually moved some of my things to my apartment on campus, which was practically too small to live in.

He called every day and told me he missed me, but that we could not get back together. He did, however, concede to spending a few nights together each week "to make the transition easier."

"We can do a taper," he said.

Like getting off an addictive drug.

"You can sleep over with me four nights a week for the first two weeks. Then we'll make it three nights. Then two, one, and then, no more. It should take about five weeks."

I was thrilled with his proposal. Even a minute with him would be better than nothing. At least that's what I thought at first.

Once we started the taper, I stayed at my Mom's or Mark's house on the off nights, but I missed Luke like crazy. I was not ready to stay alone. I lived like a vagabond, dragging my stuff all over the fucking place. I was so disorganized that I kept misplacing and breaking things. I felt scattered and overwhelmed. Work was really busy; I was on call a lot. Everything was slipping out of my control.

I was alone. Luke was moving on with his life. He was biding his time until I left. I was sure he'd meet someone else the minute I was out of his hair.

I didn't know why I kept hanging onto him. It didn't even feel good. I wondered if I was trying to hold on to Luke, my dad, or some fantasy of what my life was going to be like. I was freefalling. I couldn't connect to people. I felt cut off, isolated, and empty.

Our last night together was agony. All I could think about was that I'd never see him again. I stayed awake all night watching him sleep. Finally, I decided I'd be better off dead, so I snuck into his office and stole his medication samples. I pocketed enough pills to kill myself. Knowing I had them was a great relief.

I'd seen the pills when I was in his office playing Tetris with Luke. Even after he had broken up with me, he asked me to sit on his lap and play with him. "Having you on my lap makes me feel so calm," he said.

That was all I really wanted -- to sit on someone's lap and be held. Whether it was Luke or my dad didn't matter. I could barely tell the difference. I'd gone to Dad's grave with Luke on the first anniversary of his death. Luke held me while I cried and told Dad how much I missed him and how angry I was at him for leaving me. Luke cried, too. It was so similar the way they loved me, but didn't want me.

I was jealous of Luke. He had so much to keep his mind off things and I had nothing. He really enjoyed Tetris, which was a pretty addictive game. He also had the gang. I hated him for that. I wanted him to suffer and feel lonely. It didn't seem fair that I wanted to die while he was excited about living and moving forward.

My pain was boundless. I was exhausted. My saving grace was that I had the pills, the videotape of our last therapy sessions together, and all the notes he'd left me, as recently as the day before. They all said, "Hon, I love you."

I told Josh about the pills and the plan. The plan came to me as I was leaving Luke's house for what was supposed to be the last time. "I'd go to a hotel to overdose, and then call either you or Luke. I wouldn't make the call until it was too late to save me, and I wouldn't tell you where I was."

"Are you serious about this plan?" asked Josh.

"I don't know. The thing that scares me is that I don't care who I hurt in the process. I don't care about upsetting Mom, Dani, or even my dog. Usually, that would be foremost in my mind."

"Maybe you're not really serious then," he said. "It doesn't make sense that you wouldn't care about hurting the people you love the most. It sounds more like a way to get back at Luke for hurting you so badly. That your fantasy is to kill yourself with his pills sounds more like revenge than about really wanting to die. Not to mention it's the same way his mother killed herself."

I thought about that and decided he was probably right. I was furious at Luke. Not only did he hurt me and betray me by reneging on his promises about our future together, I was also angry because he never allowed me to take care of him. Instead of letting me comfort him in times of distress, or even confiding in me, he secluded himself in his office or the bedroom for his "scream therapy." I wasn't supposed to be in the house when he did this, but one time I pretended to leave the house and instead snuck upstairs and listened outside his door. What I heard terrified me. He was yelling and crying and pounding the wall. The only words I could make out had something to do with his mother. It seemed like an exorcism of some kind.

Josh made me promise to call him if I decided to hurt myself. I also promised to return the pills to Luke's.

Josh suggested I start taking Prozac.

"I don't want to take medication," I replied.

"Just try it for a couple of weeks," he urged. "If you don't like it, you can stop taking it."

"Okay," I said. I was less than enthused.

CHAPTER 7

The following day, I told Luke about the pills. He pleaded with me to return them, but I refused. He insisted I spend the night at his house so he could keep an eye on me.

I was thrilled that he was worried about me. Once I realized he still cared about me, I did not need to see him. I declined his invitation. This seemed to make him worry even more. He started calling me a few times a day to check in on me. I was glad I had him on edge. After all, I thought he deserved it.

After two weeks on Prozac, I started to feel better. It was as though I had had trouble seeing and then suddenly I had glasses. As the days progressed, I felt so much better it bordered on miraculous. I stopped thinking about suicide.

Luke continued calling me a few times a day. He suggested we go out for dinner. Having dinner together became a weekly ritual for us. I experienced an emotional setback each time I saw him. I still loved him and wanted to marry him. I was torn apart over the break-up. The pain dissipated slightly when I didn't see him, but came back in full force every time I was with him and again had to leave him. Still, I could not forego these dinners.

A month after I moved out, Luke came to visit me at the hospital where I was on call. My beeper went off while he was there, so I had to tend to a patient. Before I left, he threw his arms around me and held me so tight I could barely breathe. "I feel closer to you than anybody I've ever known. I love you so much, but I still can't be with you. Maybe some day, but not now. You have no idea how hard this is for me," he said tearfully.

I wanted to rip his head off. Instead, I calmly said, "I guess you'll just have to figure it out." I was gratified to know he was suffering, but I was also infuriated with him. Jack's girlfriend's words resonated in my head. When I had gone to her crying about the breakup, she'd told me, "Luke will always be alone. He has too many intimacy issues to be with someone. It's not you; it's him." It was small solace, but it was better than nothing.

Every time I had this type of interaction with Luke, it sent me into a tailspin. It upset me so much that Josh and I decided to increase my Prozac from 20 mg a day, to 40, figuring if 20 mg made me feel better, then 40 mg would help even more. It did. So did talking to my friend Mark, a fourth-year resident who had supervised my work with several patients. I spent a lot of time at his apartment and, when I felt too distraught to be alone, I even slept there. Our relationship was purely platonic. Mark was gay.

Mark was more irate with Luke than I was. "How dare he play you like this!" he'd say with so much intensity and passion that he sounded like the spurned lover. "He hurts you over and over and you let him get away with it."

"He only hurts me because I let him," I said in Luke's defense.

I ran to Mark every time Luke hurt me. I had done the same thing with my mother whenever my father hurt me. Before Dad got sick, I asked Mom what she thought Dad would do when I graduated medical school. We were sitting on the deck in Mom's backyard. She said, "Daddy loves you, but his feelings toward you are so ambivalent. He wants you to fail and he wants you to succeed. In his mind, your success is a reflection on him, but at the same time, he wants you to be totally dependent on him. When you're not dependent on him, he almost can't tolerate it." Regarding my graduating medical school, she said, "I don't know if he'll be able to have a relationship with you anymore. It may be too difficult for him."

That my success threatened my relationship with my father tormented me. I needed both, but realized that may be impossible. Would I have to spend the rest of my life fucking up in order to keep my father? Was it the prospect of my imminent success that killed him? I would never know.

In early April, Luke told me he was going to his father's wedding in California. His father had become engaged around the same time as Jack and Aliza, and Steve and Sue. I pleaded with Luke to take me with him, but he refused. "You're not part of the family anymore."

He might as well have kicked me in the stomach. How could he be so cruel? He was going to my favorite place in the world, but I was not welcome.

"Fuck him," Mark said when I told him about this latest devastation in what had become a long string of devastations. "You should teach him a lesson."

"I don't want to teach him a lesson. I just want him back," I cried.

"He's such an asshole," he said fervently. "All he does is fuck with you. It's time to get revenge." He suggested I put sugar in Luke's gas tank so he couldn't drive to his office to see his "precious" patients.

I thought that was a bad idea and I said so. But a seed was planted that had not been there before. Before then, I only fantasized about hurting *myself*.

I knew he was right about Luke treating me badly, but I still loved him and fantasized about making a future with him. I maintained friendships with the gang, but it was getting harder and harder for me to relate to them from outside the loop. I'd seen Jack and Aliza at a psychology conference that I went to with Luke in early March. Aliza showed me her engagement ring and excitedly related the details of their wedding plans. It was so painful to see the two of them so happy and embarking on the life I yearned for with Luke.

Luke called me from California and regaled me with stories of the wedding. Thinking of Luke and the gang at his father's wedding without me, I felt so bad that I again wanted to die. I jacked the

Prozac up to 60 mg.

A few weeks later, Luke canceled a dinner date with me at the last minute. "I'm sorry, Hon," he said. "We found the land we want to buy and tonight is the only time we can all get together with the lawyer."

This threw me right over the edge. I became hysterical. How could he buy the land without me? It wasn't supposed to happen like that. He was supposed to realize how much he missed me and wanted to be with me. I had to be part of this deal. I couldn't let him build "our" house without me. But how was I going to stop him?

"I think we should take a breather," he said. "I shouldn't have told you about the land. It's becoming too difficult for me to keep seeing you and try to move on with my life at the same time. Besides, it's hurtful for you, too. I love you, but this is the way it has to be."

He might as well have put a gun to my head and pulled the trigger. My world exploded into darkness. The despair swallowed me. I was falling into a dark, bottomless pit. I increased my Prozac to 80 mg and became totally obsessed with getting Luke back.

I was torn. On the one hand, I wanted Luke to tell me where the land was, what it looked like, and about the meeting with the lawyer. But I couldn't bear to hear the details. If he didn't tell me, I didn't have to believe it was real. I could believe whatever I wanted. Maybe the lawyer never showed up. Maybe the sellers changed their mind. Maybe the gang couldn't agree on the terms. Anything was better than knowing for sure that they went through with it.

I couldn't stop imagining the meeting that I was not part of. I tried to visualize them all at Luke's house sitting around the puzzle table. I couldn't picture the lawyer. Was it a he or a she? Did I really want to know?

This is what I was thinking about when I took a patient for an ECT treatment the following day. I was standing in the ECT room watching the nurse prepare the patient for her treatment, and looking around the room. My gaze settled on the vials of medicine sitting on the counter. The nurse lifted one of the bottles off the counter. She stuck a syringe into it and slowly pulled back the plunger, filling the syringe with clear sodium pentathol, a short-acting anesthetic.

As I watched her insert the needle into the catheter in the patient's arm, everything started to happen in slow motion. Suddenly it hit me. If I could somehow induce Luke into another state, a state where he realized how much he wanted me, I could get him back. I felt euphoric at my epiphany. Now I just had to figure out how to do it.

I told Mark about my revelation that evening. "What a great idea," he said excitedly "You still have a key to his house, don't you?"

I did have the key. In fact, Luke was allowing me to use his VCR to dub some of the tapes for my Grand Rounds presentation in mid-June. Luke and I had arranged that I call him before using his VCR, and I would do it when he wasn't home. I had been going to his house around lunchtime to work on the tapes.

"It's as though he wants you to fuck with him," Mark said when I told him about our arrangement. "And it's perfect, because you have access to the drinks in his refrigerator and the neighbors won't think anything of your being there."

Mark jumped up and grabbed a book on psychiatric medications from his bookshelf. Thumbing through the index, he rattled off names of drugs. "You need a clear, tasteless, odorless liquid." He was more animated than I'd ever seen him.

Mark knew much more about psychiatric medications than I did because he was three years ahead of me in his training. "Are you sure you just want to make him sick, not kill him?" he asked, looking up at me with a conspiratorial smile. "If it were me, I'd want to kill him."

I said sternly. "I want to marry him, not bury him."

"I'll never understand that after what he's done to you," he said, repeating what he'd been saying to me all along.

"You don't have to understand it," I replied. "You just have to help me figure out how to make him sick enough to stay home from work for a while. It has to be long enough for him to realize he wants me back."

CHAPTER 8

While writing a note in a patient's chart, my beeper went off. I slammed my fist on the counter and continued writing.

The nurse sitting next to me gave me an exasperated look.

"It's probably someone from medical records hounding me about delinquent paperwork," I explained. "How the hell do they expect me to get it done if they keep interrupting me? Besides," I said disdainfully, "My contract's been terminated already, so what are they going to do – fire me twice?"

It was no secret that I'd been struggling ever since Luke broke up with me. My colleagues and the hospital staff were aware of my devastation. They'd witnessed my behavior becoming more erratic. They'd seen me cry, show up late for unit meetings, curse at my beeper and blow off resident lectures.

I glanced at my pager. It was Luke! I hadn't spoken with him since he told me about the land deal two weeks earlier, except to tell him I was going to his house to use the VCR. I missed him terribly. I sprinted to my office and dialed his number. His answering machine — *our* answering machine — came on with the message we recorded together. He was still using it. I interpreted this as a sign that he still wanted to be with me. I thought longingly about how happy we were when we chose the Bob Marley song and how fun it was to get the recording just right: *"One love, one heart, let's get together and feel all right."*

"Hon, I feel awful. I don't know what's wrong with me," he stammered when he answered the phone.

Warmth surrounded my heart when he called me "hon."

"Do you want me to come over?" *Please want me!*

Twenty minutes later, I was pulling into Luke's driveway. I slid my key into the side door of the yellow Cape Cod I'd recently called home and entered through the kitchen. Following the din of the TV, I found him curled in a fetal position on the floral print loveseat we purchased together.

Without waking him, I tiptoed upstairs to get a blanket. In the bedroom, I couldn't resist snooping for signs of another woman. To my great relief the dresser drawers he allocated to me were still empty. Some of my clothes, including ones he bought for me, were still hanging on "my side" of the closet.

I draped the blanket over him, kissed the top of his head and set about evaluating his physical state. A month shy of completing my second year as a resident, I'd performed scores of physical exams and was well versed in assessing patients. I loved looking at him! I studied the face of this man I hoped to build my future with. The usual fret-filled creases across his forehead were practically erased by slumber. So many times I wished I could ease his torment from inner demons. Leaning my head on his chest, I watched the second hand on my watch. His heart rate and breathing were normal. I brushed my fingers through his hair. When I touched my cheek to his forehead to feel for a fever, I had to stop myself from lying down next to him and holding him. I felt so at peace finally being with him without worrying that he'd push me away. Letting down my guard, I gave into the comfort and the fantasy about our future together — yet again.

Luke started to moan.

"Sweetie, I'm right here," I said, softly caressing his hand. I focused on my fingers stroking his wrist. I prayed I'd be able to touch him for the rest of my life.

"It was so strange." He struggled to sit up. "I felt fine when I went to work, but about mid-morning my body started aching everywhere. My hands were trembling. I felt so weird that I canceled my afternoon appointments." His hands were still unsteady.

Sounding concerned, I said, "You never cancel your patients."

What I really felt was the stirring of the familiar jealousy. *You live for your patients.* "Maybe you have the flu or some type of twenty-four-hour virus," I said, working my fingers up to his forearm.

"Yeah, maybe." He shrugged his shoulders, grimaced, and rolled his head from side to side.

I kneeled beside him, eased his arm around my neck and hoisted him to his feet. I was thrilled that he asked me to help him. I felt elated that, for a change, I was in a position of strength to his vulnerability. I wanted to take care of him.

Easing him onto the bed, I heaved his legs onto the mattress, rolled him onto his side and covered him with a blanket.

"Hon, I have to go back to work. I'll be back in a few hours." I brushed my lips against his cheek as he drifted off to sleep.

I hesitated before calling Jack. I didn't want to share Luke with anyone. I finally made the call and, when I returned a few hours later, Jack and Steve greeted me at Luke's front door.

"I'm so glad you're here," I tried to sound genuine. "How is he?"

"He had a rough few hours, but we gave him something to help him sleep. He should be okay for awhile." Steve fidgeted with the stethoscope coiled in his hand as he spoke. "His vital signs were normal, so we're going to wait until the morning to take him to a doctor."

It never occurred to me Luke would need to see a doctor. This was just supposed to be between the two of us. I quickly brushed such thoughts aside and tried to look composed.

"Can you sleep here?" Jack asked. "He shouldn't be alone tonight."

"Sure," I fought to hide the enthusiasm in my voice.

In the morning, Jack and Steve relieved me so I could go to work. "How can you be so calm when Luke is so ill?" Steve asked me on the fifth day.

"I've learned to detach emotionally in order to function. Besides,

I think he's going to be fine." It never occurred to me that he might not recover. I couldn't even fathom why everyone was making such a big deal about Luke's illness. I knew it would run its course and he'd be okay. I just hoped he'd stay sick long enough to figure out he needed me.

I stayed with him every night that week. It was one of the best weeks of my life. While I tended to his personal needs, Jack and Steve took him to a neurologist, an infectious disease specialist, and an endocrinologist. The results of his spinal tap were inconclusive, as were the blood tests and CT Scans. Nobody knew what was wrong with him, but there was no denying he was gravely ill.

On the seventh day, I found a note taped to Luke's door stating Jack and Steve had taken Luke to the hospital.

Panicked, I called Jack immediately. Before he had a chance to say goodbye, I was in my car heading downtown to the hospital. I needed Luke to be home so I could take care of him. Why did they have to go and ruin everything?

CHAPTER 9

Every evening after work I rushed to Luke's hospital room. I *needed* to be with him, to look at him and touch him, even if he slept through the entire visit.

Over the first two weeks, his health deteriorated a little each day. Baffled, the doctors ordered every high-tech test imaginable. They performed a brain biopsy as a last resort. This invasive diagnostic procedure, much more serious and potentially dangerous than any of the others, involved removing a piece of brain tissue. One little mistake could destroy cognitive functions, lead to brain swelling or infection. But I was unfazed. In part, the weeks of tests desensitized me to the gravity of the procedure. The bigger part was my deluded state of mind, which had me think, *so they removed a teeny tiny piece of his brain. No big deal.*

Somehow I managed to convince myself that Luke's condition was unrelated to what I'd done. I thought maybe I'd triggered the initial symptoms, but that then some obscure and virulent pathogen had taken over and gone haywire. I believed it was merely a coincidence that he'd become so ill. As his illness worsened, I all but "forgot" that I had any part in it — except for a few isolated moments when the memory and possible connection broke through to my consciousness. In those moments I became so panicked that I quickly pushed it out of my mind.

After the brain biopsy, Luke's condition began to improve. I was relieved to see him getting better. Only now I worried he'd no longer want me around him. The fact that we'd broken up was relevant again. My role felt more ambiguous and my anxiety about our relationship intensified.

As he grew stronger, we went for walks. Because he was still unsteady on his feet, I pushed him in a wheelchair. During one such outing, we went to the hospital courtyard. I positioned Luke beside a wooden bench and sat down next to him. When I stroked his hand, he pulled away and maneuvered the wheelchair to face me.

"What are we going to do about us?" he asked plaintively.

My whole body tensed in response to the tone of apology and resolution in his voice, the same tone he'd used when he broke up with me. My chest burned and I felt faint. Fighting the impulse to throw myself into his arms, I looked into his eyes and quipped, "We can go to the hospital chapel right now and get married!" Making light of the situation seemed the only way not to suffocate under its horrifying weight.

Luke backed the wheelchair further away. His eyes clouded over as though he was about to cry. "I was afraid this would happen. You've been wonderful, but my feelings haven't changed. Unfortunately now I'm indebted to you. I feel even guiltier about breaking up than I did before."

I still couldn't understand. If he'd said he didn't love me, perhaps I could have accepted a hopeless situation and walked away. The tremendous inconsistency between his professed feelings and his aversion to being with me confused and infuriated me.

In the late day humidity of the hospital courtyard, rage and tears caught in my throat. "Can I still visit you?" I asked, choking them back.

The fret-filled creases returned to his forehead. "I enjoy your company and appreciate your visits," he said haltingly, resting his chin in his hands. "As long as you understand that my feelings haven't changed, of course you can still visit me." He was only a few feet away from me, but I felt as though we were separated by a thick pane of glass, and eternity.

I left the hospital, shaken. If my selfless care taking didn't make him want to marry me, what would? To fight my anxiety, I met a friend for a drink. While I chatted with her, a burly man with dark hair in a ponytail sidled next to me and introduced himself.

"I'm Scott. I've seen you in the electronics store where I work. I've been watching you for the past half-hour. Would you like to dance?" His deep baritone voice was commensurate with his size.

I felt vulnerable and unattractive after Luke's rejection. Scott's attention was a welcome diversion. I was tipsy and intrigued by his confidence.

As he led me around the dance floor, the overwhelming chemistry between us was all-consuming. I couldn't take my eyes and, soon, my hands off him. By the second dance, I stopped thinking about what happened with Luke. By dance number three, it was a given we'd be going home together.

A few days later, the moment I walked out of the elevator on Luke's floor, I knew something was terribly wrong. The usually friendly nurses actually turned away from me when I said hello. I considered leaving, but my compulsion to see Luke outweighed my better judgment.

In his room, family and friends stood around the bed where he sat leaning on a pillow. When I walked in, all conversation stopped. Normally everyone offered warm greetings and embraces, but tonight they glared at me. Suddenly I realized they *knew.* I knew, too. *This had been my fault all along.* My vision blurred, my heart raced and I couldn't catch my breath. My heart pounded wildly as my legs began to give. I stopped just inside the doorway and begged my brain to recall the location of the red exit signs.

"We need to talk," Luke said. Jack supported him as he stumbled out of bed and lurched toward me. Weaving a bit, he directed me down the hallway into a vacant conference room, the same conference room where I attended medical lectures the year before. Every other time I visited, Luke used my shoulder for support, but tonight he used the wall to brace himself, confirming my worst nightmare.

I slowly lowered myself into a chair. I could hear the second hand of my watch tick loudly, underscoring what was about to happen. Luke leaned against the back of the chair next to mine. He gazed at me with his melancholy eyes and, choking back a sob, said, "I know you tried to kill me."

Although his voice was barely audible, his words reverberated through my skull. Unable to look at him, I stared at the floor. The room seemed to darken as my thoughts raced. Was he bluffing or did he really know? Should I confess or could I spin a believable tale? If I told him, would he still love me? Could what I had done really have had all these consequences? Maybe it *was* just a coincidence that he became sick around the same time. It was too horrible to believe. My denial was so great during his entire illness that I had never even considered that I might be confronted. *Was I really responsible?*

I carried on this internal debate for a few seconds before whispering, "Not exactly."

Later that night, Luke called me to ask if I was all right and what I was going to do now.

"I guess I'll have to kill myself, just like your mother did," I replied before dropping the phone.

CHAPTER 10

July 1, 1992
The staccato beep of the telephone receiver beside my head kept tempo with the throbbing in my temples. Stabbing pain in my eyes alerted me that I'd fallen asleep without removing my contact lenses. Prying my eyes open, I realized I was under a coffee table, fully clothed. As I shook off sleep, images from the previous night exploded in my brain like shrapnel. I wanted to believe it was only a dream, but my panic told me otherwise. *I know you tried to kill me,* Luke's voice echoed over and over.

I glanced around the unfamiliar room at a desk spray-painted black, an unmade futon bed, and the unpacked moving cartons strewn about the floor. My gaze settled on Brin, my Old English sheepdog, sleeping on a black bathmat in the far corner. Suddenly, I understood. I was in my new apartment down the street from my new hospital, and this was the first day of my job as a third-year resident.

Stumbling to my feet, I flopped onto the couch. My head was pounding. Brin needed to go for a walk, and I was starting my new job in a couple of hours. Yet, only a few hours earlier, I'd essentially confessed to nearly killing Luke. Not knowing what to do, I decided to do what I always did to alleviate stress, go running.

I'd been running ten miles a day since my junior year in high school. When my parents fought or my own rage boiled up, I put on running shoes and took off. Within minutes, my thoughts about what I was escaping were gone. By the end of the first mile, the intensity of my emotions began to wane. I'd observe, but not process, the things around me. I'd count footfalls, think about which block I'd turn down, how far it was from here to there, and whether passersby thought I was skinny. Once I discovered the escape element of running, I went out two or three times a day just to get away from things.

This morning, as I ran through intersections, around idling taxis and buses and past storefronts, I barely thought about the previous night's horror. Feeling much calmer, I showered, donned a conservative summer dress and walked to the psychiatric clinic to see Jim, my first scheduled patient.

Jim was a nineteen-year-old college dropout I'd treated for the past three months on my inpatient service. The police brought him to the psychiatric hospital on a stretcher in four-point restraints. He had threatened to kill his father. He'd fought against hospitalization for the first month, denying that anything was wrong with him. I'd worked hard to understand him and to help him recognize the inconsistencies between his perceptions and reality. Ultimately, he grew to trust me and cooperate with treatment. He ended up doing better than anyone expected. At the time of his discharge, he agreed to outpatient treatment, but only with me.

Following our appointment, I attended to a number of walk-in patients and went to several meetings. Aside from fleeting episodes of panic, my day was unremarkable.

After work, I put Brin in my car and drove to my weekly therapy session with Dr. Mikker, a colleague of Luke's I'd been seeing for the past year. I'd stopped going to Josh in April. I'd been in therapy on and off for over ten years. I'd struggled with depression and anorexia since junior high.

I had no intention of telling Dr. Mikker about the previous night. In fact, I had plans to meet Scott, the man I met the week before, after my session. I was stunned when Dr. Mikker leaned forward in his chair and said, "I know what you did to Luke. What are you going to do now?"

I looked at him dully as I felt all energy drain out of me. "What else can I do but kill myself?" I slid from my chair to the floor and crawled across the room to the couch. Dragging myself onto it, I lay down on my back and sobbed.

Through my hysteria, I heard him say, "I'm going to admit you to a psychiatric hospital."

At first, images of Johnny in rehab flashed through my mind. A montage of memories of my father collided with images of my own patients. My dad had been in and out of institutions during much of my life for depression, mania, and multiple suicide attempts. His first suicide attempt came after a girl he was in love with broke up with him. Dad ranted about crazy conspiracies, complained about the food and didn't bother to shower or shave. Johnny spent his days doing calisthenics in his hospital room.

"I'd rather die than be hospitalized!" I screeched. "People will think I'm crazy! I need to go running — I can't be locked inside! Besides, I'm fine. I just need Luke. Oh, my God, my life is ruined!"

As an inpatient psychiatrist, I derived comfort from knowing I was psychologically healthier than my patients. It seemed that what separated them from me, given that I identified with a lot of the things they experienced, was that I'd never been hospitalized. In my mind, being a psychiatric outpatient was one thing, but being hospitalized meant crossing the line into the land of no return.

Dr. Mikker spoke sternly. "The only input I want from you is which hospital you prefer."

As a medical student and resident I'd rotated through almost every psychiatric hospital in the area so, wherever I went, I was bound to run into someone I knew. The prospect of being locked inside the loony bin, combined with the potential for humiliation and shame I would feel if I met anyone I knew-especially patients I had treated, or worse, former colleagues of mine, was too much to bear. Visualizing these possibilities, I felt even more despondent. "Send me to the morgue," I wailed.

"Have you ever worked at St. Francis?" he shot back impatiently.

"No, but I attended lectures there." I recalled walking through the halls of St. Francis with my fellow residents. I liked the quaint, casual feel of the place and thought I might like to work there someday. In contrast, the psychiatric hospital where I'd been working had an air of aristocracy that made me uncomfortable. My hospital and I were not a good match, and I most definitely did not want to be there as a patient. If I had to go somewhere, St. Francis was the best option.

"Good. I'll admit you to Dr. Lancet's service. He's the best."

I buried my face in my arms and cried while he talked to Dr. Lancet on the phone. I must have fallen asleep, because the next thing I heard was Dr. Mikker talking to Dani and my mother. I was horrified that this had gone beyond Luke, Dr. Mikker, and me.

"What are they doing here?" I was too ashamed to look at them.

"I called them."

"Hi, Mel," said my mother from across the room.

"Hi, Mom," I mumbled without looking up. She had been so supportive while I was in the throes of despair over the breakup. She had even taken care of Brin a few times so I could go straight from work to visit Luke in the hospital. How could I face her now?

I was relieved that Dani was there to serve as a buffer between Mom and me. "Hi, Mel," said Dani. She was standing next to me. I raised my head to look at her.

"Come on. I'll drive you to the hospital," she said.

Too exhausted to get up, I asked her to help me.

She draped my arm around her shoulder and eased me to my feet. She wrapped an arm around my waist and led me out to my car.

"We have to wait for Mommy and Dr. Mikker. They're going to

follow us," she said hesitantly.

"I don't want to go to the hospital." I looked at her imploringly, wondering if I could convince her to take me somewhere else.

"I'm sorry Mel, but you have no choice," she said softly.

CHAPTER 11

The fifteen-minute drive to St. Francis seemed too short. I'd barely registered the implications of where we were going. Suddenly we were turning into the entrance. We drove down a long, winding road and around the three-story red brick hospital. Through the fading daylight, I noticed a large, freshly mowed field and two tennis courts. In an affluent suburb about thirty minutes north of New York City, this psychiatric hospital was about fifteen minutes from my mother's home and the hospital where I'd done the first two years of my residency, and Luke's house.

We parked in front of the entrance. An officious looking security guard hurried out, waving his hands. "You're not allowed to park there."

"We're here to admit her," said Dani, pointing at me. "Her psychiatrist arranged everything with Dr. Lancet."

He backed off. "Oh, I'm sorry. We're expecting you."

I walked Brin toward the field and down a little path, following what sounded like a waterfall. We came upon a statue of the Virgin Mary. When I noticed my mother and Dr. Mikker park their cars next to mine, we headed back toward the building. Silently, and without looking at any of them, I put Brin in my car, kissed her nose and walked toward the entrance. I was terrified about what was happening. I kept telling myself I'd only be here for a few days.

Dr. Mikker said something to the security guard, who pointed to a door about twenty feet past the security desk. That all these people had put aside whatever it was they were supposed to be doing to take care of me touched a deep longing I'd had my entire life, to feel important enough for people to come through for.

Dr. Mikker opened the door to a large waiting room and gestured for us to enter. He instructed me to empty my pockets. He took my keys, money, and the Dexedrine pills I had snuck into my shorts while I was in the car.

"You two can wait here while your mother and I go into the office. You'll be able to see us from the waiting room."

Like an avalanche, it hit me that I was going to be locked in. I felt dizzy with anxiety and overwhelmed with fear and rage at the thought of being trapped. The sheer terror of what was happening to me made my heart race and my knees buckle.

"I can't stay here," I screamed. Frantic, I pulled a mop out of a cleaning bucket, put it on my head to simulate a wig and danced around frenetically. Squishing my face against the window that separated my mother and Dr. Mikker from me, I licked the glass and studied my mother. I didn't *want* to act like a lunatic, but I couldn't stop myself. My lack of control frightened me. So did the fact that I knew my mother would be livid at my inappropriate behavior. If only I could explain to Mom that some alien being had taken over my body and mind. Watching her tense face through the window, with her shoulders hunched and her skin pallid and drawn, I knew that would be impossible. She was so rigid that she didn't comprehend the concept of being out of control. She couldn't even stand that I got up and down constantly while working or looking for things or when I shook my leg, which was a nervous habit. My behaving like a nut job would really piss her off. That was the last thing I wanted to do. I was terrified of her anger. *Is this how it feels to go crazy, right before full-blown psychosis sets in?* I knew I'd rather be dead than psychotic. Just the thought of becoming psychotic was enough to give me heart palpitations.

After about twenty minutes, they emerged from their meeting. I locked eyes with my mother momentarily and was shocked and frightened to see her eyes brimming with tears. I'd only see her cry three times. Once was when I was about seven when her finger got stuck in Dani's stroller. The other time was when I was in college and we put her dog to sleep. The third was at Dad's deathbed.

I quickly looked away from her and glared accusatorily at Dr. Mikker.

"We're all set to go to the unit," he said to Dani.

"I want to go home!" I cried.

"You can't. We admitted you involuntarily," he said, looking at my mother, not at me.

Fuck you, at least I could have talked my way out of the hospital if I had been admitted on a voluntary status. You're such a piece of shit you didn't even know what I did to Luke. What kind of therapist are you, believing everything I tell you. You don't deserve to be in charge of me. Who are you anyway, in your big house, with your cushy office and aloof style? I have no idea why anyone recommended you in the first place.

Dani gently pulled me into the hallway. I didn't resist because I felt she was my one true ally. Besides, I knew I had to go along with the game plan until I could figure out a way to escape. We took the elevator to the Women's Issues Unit, a specialized area created by Dr. Lancet to treat women with eating disorders, personality disorders, and accompanying psychiatric diagnoses.

The night nurse unlocked the unit door. While Dr. Mikker talked to her, I grabbed my mother's hand. "Please don't leave me here!" I couldn't believe what was happening to me. I wanted to claw at the door or jump out a window. I felt so terrified and claustrophobic that I wanted to shriek at the top of my lungs and never stop shrieking.

My mother jerked her hand away as though she'd touched something disgusting. "It's okay, Mel. Soon you'll be asleep. I'll visit you tomorrow." She handed the nurse my confiscated belongings. I stared at the brown paper bag. *I have to get my keys. Maybe one from the other hospital will work here.*

The nurse unlocked the unit door for Dani, my mother, and Dr. Mikker, then quickly re-locked it. I knew trying to run away would be useless. Someone would grab me before I got out of the building.

I'd have to be patient and methodical in planning my getaway. My body felt like one giant cramp as though all my organs twisted in on themselves. As they disappeared from view. I felt desperately lonely.

"Let's get you settled in your room before your doctor gets here. You can go to sleep after he leaves," said the nurse dispassionately.

I followed her robotically. Halfway down the hallway, she knocked on and opened a door in one fluid motion. We entered a large room with hardwood floors, two pine beds tucked into opposite corners, and matching built-in dressers, desks, and bureaus. A girl I judged to be in her late teens lay on the bed to my right reading a paperback.

The nurse pointed to the empty bed. "That's yours. You can relax until Dr. Lancet arrives."

I dumped the contents of my backpack on the bed and rummaged through the pile. I was looking for a cigarette. Instead, I discovered one of Brin's rawhides, a book titled *Psychiatric Disorders*, and some wrinkled papers. I was so hungry I sucked on the rawhide.

My roommate asked me if I was anorexic or bulimic.

Relieved for the distraction, I replied, "Anorexic, but I'm not here for that."

She put her book on the nightstand next to her bed. "Then you won't mind the unit rules. We're not allowed to leave the dining room until we eat everything on our plate, and we can't exercise."

"I can't follow those rules!" I squealed in panic. "What are you here for?"

"Anorexia." She slipped a plastic retainer into her mouth. "I've gained fifteen pounds since I was admitted. At first I was really scared to eat, especially because they lock the bathroom doors for an hour after every meal so you can't even throw up. After a week or so, I started eating because they threatened to force-feed me. Surprisingly though, as I gained weight, I started to feel better.

Thanks to Dr. Lancet, now I can eat without obsessing over calories and exercise. I'm being discharged in a couple of days."

I couldn't imagine being cured of my preoccupation with exercise, calories, and weight. I hated the way my body felt unless I was at least ten pounds underweight. I certainly couldn't go without running. I hadn't missed a day in fifteen years. Plus, there was no way I'd eat a normal amount of regular food! I'd limited myself to vegetables, salads, dry cereal, diet ice cream, and diet soda for as long as I could remember.

My mother had threatened to have me hospitalized for my eating disorder, but never followed through with it. I was incredulous that nearly twenty years later, I'd accidentally landed on *this* unit. Even in my state of despair, I could appreciate the irony. But I'd be damned if I'd allow them to mess with my weight. "Dr. Lancet must really be something," I said, dropping my backpack on the floor.

"Yeah, he's the best. He's really strict, but he saved my life." She turned off her lamp again.

Dejected, I thought, *nobody can save me.*

CHAPTER 12

Fifteen, sixteen…" counting my sit-ups under my breath was helping me feel centered. When I hit fifty, the door cracked open and a tall, balding, fifty-something man with a moustache stuck his head into the room.

"Melanie? I'm Dr. Lancet. Come with me."

Walking briskly on the balls of his feet, Dr. Lancet strode purposefully down the hall. I practically had to jog to keep up with him. His khaki pants were a bit too short, the tail of his white wrinkled shirt hung out over his belt, and his penny loafers were penniless. A ring of brown hair circled his head like a halo.

We stopped at an elegant oak door. It opened into a lavish, book-filled room. I slumped into the corner of the couch clutching a pillow to my chest like a security blanket. He sat in a chair a few feet away.

As he placed a legal pad on his lap, his wedding ring caught my eye. I wondered how many times he'd been married, and if his wife was pretty. The design on his tan socks was different colored soccer balls. Probably a Father's Day present from his children, if he had any. I knew not to ask. All my life, my mother had reprimanded me for probing into things that were none of my business. I didn't see my curiosity as inappropriate, but I knew Dr. Lancet might. In the therapeutic relationship, the patient is supposed to focus on her own issues, not on the therapist's personal life. So I mustered some restraint and waited for him to speak.

"I'm sorry you had to wait so long. I was at a cocktail party when Dr. Mikker called me."

His volunteering this personal information helped me warm up to him. I hated therapists who hid behind the Freudian ideal of remaining a blank slate. That sent the message that the therapist was superior and the patient was not worthy of knowing anything about him.

My therapist in medical school had been like that, which had infuriated me. I decided he was too stupid to figure out how to moderate between an appropriate amount of self-disclosure and the total breakdown of boundaries. So I resolved to "break him down," which I ultimately succeeded in doing.

"Dr. Mikker told me you're a resident in psychiatry. He also informed me about what you did to your ex-boyfriend. I must say, in my twenty years as a psychiatrist, that's a new one on me. We'll explore the whys and wherefores of that in a future session though. Right now, I'm going to do a mental status exam and obtain a brief psychiatric and medical history."

He asked me questions based on the same admission protocol I used. He wanted to get a handle on my diagnosis and assess my state of mind. Most importantly, he needed to know whether I might try to hurt myself or someone else that night. He was clearly experienced and superb at his job, which helped me to be more open with him. One thing that triggered my wariness radar was his dispassionate, almost cold style. I wondered what it would have been like had Luke been interviewing me instead of Dr. Lancet.

Dr. Lancet was forming an opinion of me based on my body language as well as my words. Suddenly, I became extremely self-conscious. I wanted him to like me and to think I was smart, funny, and articulate. Wanting to project an appealing persona, I reminded myself to smile, because people always told me I had a beautiful smile. I worried that if Dr. Lancet didn't find me attractive, he wouldn't care enough about me to really help me.

Using tools from my psychiatric training combined with my intuitive ability, I was sizing Dr. Lancet up as well. I was good at reading people. I had to be in order to deal with my father. He lied to me, more often than not, and could flip from loving to wrathful in the blink of an eye. Years of experience had trained me to become hyper-vigilant in our interactions, picking up on the subtlest change in his inflection, the direction of his gaze, and his overall body language. For instance, the timbre of his voice became defensive and slightly higher pitched when he was about to lie or renege on a promise. I'd never figured out an effective way to protect myself from his sudden cruelty. The best I could do was try to read the situation and not be caught off-guard. Reflexively, I came to approach every situation this way. I never knew when someone was going to turn on me, but I believed it was inevitable.

My major concern regarding Dr. Lancet was that, rather than really listening and seeing me for who I was, he'd be feeling so superior that he'd erase me from the equation. I took it all in--his appearance, body language, and how he phrased his questions and listened to my responses. How strange it was to watch him watch me as we sized each other up.

Taking notice of my scrutiny, and probably tuning into my self-censorship, he put his pen down and looked me in the eye. "I'm sure it's tough for you to be the patient rather than the doctor, but the only way I can help you is if you let me be in charge."

His words jolted me back into reality. While I wanted him to see me as an attractive, appealing woman and a potential colleague, the cold hard fact remained; I was an involuntary psychiatric patient. Earlier that day I'd been treating patients, but now I was one. I was used to being an outpatient, but this was different. As an outpatient, the sessions had been voluntary, circumscribed (fifty minutes one or two times a week) and scheduled at everyone's convenience. In that brief time period, I could control what I revealed to the therapist, decide whether I wanted to show up for the sessions and even plan my outfits based on the impression I wanted to make. Here, I was at a total disadvantage. Dr. Lancet would decide when and if we'd meet, how long I had to stay in the hospital, whether I would have outdoor privileges and even how much I'd be required to eat.

That he was seeing me at my lowest point felt horrible. My attempts to appear cool and entertaining were futile. It took too much effort. Distraught and vulnerable, I was totally dependent on him. As this sunk in, I succumbed to exhaustion. Overwhelmed with anxiety to the point that my thoughts became jumbled and incoherent, I began to whine. I sprawled out on the couch and cried. Despite wanting him to like me, I couldn't stop behaving this way. The more pitiable I acted and felt, the more I longed for him to hold me and make everything better. I yearned to crawl into his lap. Instead, I rolled into a fetal position and buried my head in a pillow. He seemed unfazed by my lack of decorum. He probably saw it as nothing more than a to-be-expected textbook case of regression.

The interview lasted over an hour. He delved into my background, family matters, and my father's extensive psychiatric history. By the end, I was totally spent. Dr. Lancet concluded the interview by asking if I had any questions.

"Could you please transfer me to a different unit? I'm a vegetarian and I need to exercise every day. If I miss one day of exercise, I'll lose my mind." I paused and smiled, realizing how ludicrous this sounded. After all, I'd been hospitalized *for* losing my mind. "What I mean is I'll get anxious and agitated." He looked me up and down, apparently noticing my body for the first time.

"How much do you weigh?" he asked pointedly.

"The scale on this unit read ninety pounds," I volunteered reluctantly. I knew my weight was much too low, and that he would probably start harping on it the same way my mother, friends, and colleagues did. On one hand, I felt relieved when people bothered me about being too skinny because, aside from my clothes feeling loose, that was the only way I knew I was thin. When nobody commented on my weight, I was convinced I was fat and needed to lose weight. Still, I didn't like when people continuously bugged me about it. There was no way I would voluntarily gain weight. Plus, I felt fine physically and was proud of my food and exercise regimen.

It empowered me to feel stronger than other people. I could fast for days on end without giving into the constant hunger pains, and I went running daily, no matter what. Back then it didn't occur to me that I was a slave to my compulsion, or that it might be a sign of weakness, not strength. I was sure people were jealous of me because of my strict self-discipline.

Dr. Lancet raised an eyebrow. "And how tall are you?"

"Five three," I mumbled and quickly added, "I'm thinner than usual because I haven't been eating or sleeping lately with everything that's been going on." This was true, but I had been glad to lose more weight.

He looked skeptical. "I think you should stay on this unit so we can treat your eating disorder."

"But I'm not here for that and I don't want to focus on it." I was on the verge of hysteria. If he forced me to gain weight, I'd have to kill myself. Given the circumstances, my weight seemed like the only thing in my life I had a prayer of controlling.

He sighed. "At this point, Melanie, I'm not too interested in what you do or don't want."

"Can you at least relax the food rules for me, since that's not why I'm here?" I was already plotting ways to circumvent the "no exercise" rule. Maybe I could run laps around my room and do calisthenics between hourly checks. In order to do this, however, I'd have to convince Dr. Lancet that I didn't need constant supervision. If a staff member were assigned to watch me around the clock, I'd have to jog in place in the bathroom while pretending to take a shower and do sit-ups when she turned her back.

"We'll discuss it tomorrow, but what troubles me at the moment is the fact that not wanting to follow rules may be one of your biggest problems."

His astuteness impressed me. This comment and his responses throughout our meeting suggested that he already understood a lot about me. As he slid his chair back, signifying the end of our meeting, the frightening gravity of my situation hit me once again.

"What's going to become of me?" I whimpered.

"For now, you'll go back to your room and go to sleep. After all, it's nearly midnight. I'll see you tomorrow around noon." He stood up and I followed him. Back in the hallway, he hailed the nurse sitting on the couch next to a stack of charts. "I'm done with her."

CHAPTER 13

A woman's voice said, "Time to get up!"

Rubbing sleep from my eyes, I looked around the unfamiliar room. "Why do we have to get up?" I asked my roommate.

"For breakfast. We each have our own tray based on how many calories we have to eat. A nurse watches us eat and you can't leave the dining room until you finish everything on your tray. After breakfast, we get our meds."

"A nurse watches us eat?" I felt nauseous with anxiety. I was so scared of gaining weight that I always skipped breakfast. I'd be damned if I was going to start eating it now. I was furious at myself for getting into this situation. Jogging in place, I said, "I can't stay here!"

She brushed the underside of her long brown hair before whipping her head back toward the ceiling. "Good luck! Nobody gets off this unit unless they gain weight or they're sent to the hospital to be tube-fed. Besides, whatever you did to get here must have been really bad, because normally the resident-on-call would admit you at night, but instead, Dr, Lancet came to see you."

"It was serious all right." I said curtly. I did not feel like telling this stranger my business.

Since attendance at meals was mandatory, the fifteen patients on the unit lined up outside the dining room. The nurse handed me a tray containing a hard-boiled egg, a pint-sized carton of whole milk, a six-ounce box of corn flakes, a glass of orange juice, and two pieces of toast. I knew the caloric content of every food in the universe, but I stalled by pretending to read the nutritional information on the cereal box and glancing discreetly at the other patients. A few seemed to eat without conflict, while others pushed pieces of food around their plates or chopped the food into tiny pieces. I stared at one girl, whose fingers were thinner than the stem of the spoon that she was squeezing so hard I thought it might snap in half. Her skeletal face contorted as she smeared egg over the surface of her cardboard plate, turning the off-white plate dandelion yellow. Even though she looked tortured, I felt jealous of her because she was skinnier than I was.

Sucking on the crust of my toast, I calculated how many jumping jacks I'd have to do to burn off the calories. I ate the white part of my egg and swallowed a few corn flakes. "I'm done," I announced, handing my tray to the nurse.

Maybe because I didn't yet have a formal treatment plan, she allowed me to leave the dining room despite my leftover food.

After breakfast, I went in search of a cigarette. All I cared about was having a smoke, figuring out where I was going to exercise and trying to persuade Dr. Lancet to excuse me from the food rules. We were only allowed to smoke in the TV room. That's where I was headed when I heard my name. "Is there someone here named Melanie? She has a phone call."

Assuming it was my mother, I walked slowly to the only patient phone on the unit. It was a payphone attached to the wall opposite my room. The receiver dangled near the floor.

"Hello," I said tersely. I was pissed at her for signing me into the hospital.

"How are you?" asked Luke.

I was ecstatic when I heard his voice. "How do you think I am? I'm locked in the bin with a bunch of anorexics," I said with a touch of humor. Even though I was surprised he had tracked me down so quickly, I wasn't surprised he wanted to talk to me. I still believed he'd eventually agree we belonged together. In retrospect, I still feel a surge of panic every time I think about how completely I minimized what I did to him. I essentially separated my actions from the "real me" as though it had nothing to do with who I really was.

Ultimately, I came to understand my disconnection between what I did and who I was to be a repetition of how my father behaved towards me. He'd abuse me one day, and then act as though nothing happened the next. I, being the desperate, dutiful daughter, went along with the charade until I ultimately came to view his abusive behavior as totally separate from his complete and utter love for me.

"At least you're safe. That's all that matters." His words sounded rehearsed.

"When you're discharged from the hospital, will you come visit me?" I imagined walking around the unit holding hands with him.

"Actually, I called to tell you that I'll never be able to talk to you again." He sounded preoccupied and like he wanted to hang up. I thought I heard Jack in the background.

I started to tremble. "But you said you still wanted to have a relationship with me. Don't you know I need you?" I leaned against the wall for support. My shrieks drowned out the dial tone. When I realized he'd hung up, I smashed the receiver against the wall and crumbled to the floor weeping.

I remained there like a pile of laundry with the receiver hanging above my head. "If you'd like to make a call, please hang up and dial again," the recording droned as feet passed by me in both directions. Eventually, a passerby stopped to put the phone on the hook. Nobody stopped to quiet me.

CHAPTER 14

I dragged myself to my bed, sprawled on my stomach and burrowed my head under the pillow. Closing my eyes, I listened for Dr. Lancet's footsteps.

As a child, when I heard my father approaching my room to check on me at bedtime, I'd practice my "sleep breathing." Inhale, count to four; exhale, count to five. He'd kiss me on top of my head and straighten my covers before tiptoeing out of my room. Once I heard him step off the carpeted stairs onto the dining room floor, I'd slip out of bed and perch against the banister at the top of the stairs to resume eavesdropping on him and my mother. I couldn't discern what they were saying, but I'd hear enough to know they were fighting. *Please stop*, I'd pray, night after night.

I was so relieved when he arrived.

"Melanie, come with me," Dr. Lancet commanded from the doorway,

I slid off my bed and followed him to the library.

"I see you made it through the night without incident," he said as we sat.

Clutching a pillow against my chest I stared at Dr. Lancet's loafers, still penniless. "I wish I was dead, but I don't have a plan." I let the pillow fall into my lap and massaged my temples with my fingertips. "Luke called to tell me he'll never talk to me again," I added.

"We'll talk about Luke later. First we need to discuss your medications." He spoke authoritatively as he flipped through his notes.

"You're going to continue them all, aren't you?" I pleaded.

"Let's see. You're taking two different types of antidepressants and a stimulant Luke prescribed for you." He looked me in the eye and shook his head.

"Dr. Mikker prescribed the Prozac and after I showed him the literature on Desipramine, saying that, even though it's typically used to treat depression, it's been shown to be helpful with attention deficit disorder, he prescribed that, too. Luke wrote my Dexedrine prescriptions."

Dexedrine was a controlled substance, which made it illegal for him to prescribe to someone he wasn't seeing professionally. "He's such a goody-two-shoes that he must have thought I really needed it, if he was willing to put his career on the line like that. Don't you agree? I mean, he must have agreed that I had ADD. And he would know, since we lived together. Besides, I would have been perfectly happy if he had written a prescription for Ritalin instead, since that helped me a lot in the past." I knew this all sounded bad.

"Cut the crap! You doubled your dose of Prozac without discussing it with Dr. Mikker and persuaded Luke to give you the medication you wanted. Luke could have his license suspended for prescribing a controlled substance for you."

I stared at him defiantly. "Yeah, but —"

"But *nothing,*" he interrupted. "You're not going to get away with your usual crap with me." He remained stone-faced. "I will not allow you to sabotage your treatment, even if that means assigning someone to watch you twenty-four hours a day."

I shrank deeper into the cushion and leaned my head on the arm of the couch. "So what are you going to do about my medication?" My impulse was to put my hands over my ears and sing *I can't hear you,* to drown him out.

"I'm going to discontinue them all for a while. Once all the drugs are out of your system, I'll reevaluate the situation."

"I thought this unit was for eating disorders, not detoxification,"

I mumbled.

"It's whatever I say it is. I make the rules and you follow them. Do you understand?" Then he spoke softly. "Melanie, you've been headed for disaster for a very long time. It was just a question of whether you'd hurt yourself or somebody else."

I wanted him to rub my back, the way a parent would comfort a sick child. "You're probably right."

I thought about the recurring dreams I'd been having since I started medical school:

I'm speeding down a highway feeling exhilarated, when suddenly I lose control of the car and head directly into oncoming traffic. In another dream I was a kid on the street where I grew up. I was outside playing in the street when suddenly, my sneakers became jet-propelled and I raced down the street, toward the busy intersection at the bottom of the hill. I was unable to slow down or stop. My father grabbed onto me and I screamed at him to let go because I knew he couldn't stop me, and I didn't want him to cross the intersection with me in case we got hit by a car. He didn't let go and we raced through the intersection into the woods across the street. We didn't stop until we crashed into a tree.

"I'm always right, and don't you forget it," Dr. Lancet said with deep kindness.

"Please don't make me eat everything on my tray. I'm having a hard enough time being here without having to worry about getting fat." Squirming, I tried a different tactic. "Can't we fight one battle at a time? Please, I'm begging you."

"I will make my decisions based on what I think is right for you. I won't give in to your begging, crying, or anything else," he scolded. "Since this is a holiday weekend and I won't be here for the next two days, I'll relax the food rules for you until Monday. You'll probably sleep through most of the meals while you're withdrawing from your medication anyway." He stood and walked toward the door.

"I guess you're done with me," I said as I followed him.

"I'll see you Monday," he said as he closed the door behind him.

I walked toward my room in a daze. As I passed the dining room, a nurse called to me, "Melanie, I kept your lunch tray warm."

"I'm not hungry." I scurried past the door and then turned back. "Would it be possible to get a cigarette?"

A voice came from the dining room. "If you can wait a few minutes, I'll give you one of mine."

I peeked through the door and noticed everyone seated in the same chairs they'd occupied at breakfast. "Who said that?"

"I did," said a tall, thin blond.

I backed out the door, fearing the nurse might force me to eat. "I'll wait for you in my room."

A few minutes later, the woman knocked on my door. I was doing jumping jacks and staring out the window at the field below, becoming increasingly upset about being stuck inside on a beautiful sunny day.

We headed down the hallway, past patient rooms and the library, to the nurses' station. "I'm Robbie," she said as she stood in the doorway, cleared her throat and pantomimed smoking. A nurse pulled a pack of matches out of a drawer and handed them to her.

In the TV room, I glanced at three patients reading magazines on a red leather couch. They looked up at me briefly and went back to reading. I leaned against the wall next to Robbie. As she extracted a pack of cigarettes from the pocket of her sweat pants, I noticed the scars on her wrists. I thought about Luke's girlfriend prior to me. She had slit her wrist in reaction to him canceling a dinner date with her.

"So, what are you in for?" she asked as she handed me a cigarette.

"The usual," I said in a deadpan voice.

She nodded. "I tried to kill myself ... again." She held out her wrists to show me her self-inflicted wounds. "So did Maggie," she said, pointing her cigarette toward one of the women on the couch.

I was getting tired of her show-and-tell session. I also felt intimidated by her bossiness. Then it occurred to me that a few days earlier, she could have been my patient. If she had been one of my patients, I still might have been slightly unsettled by her aggressive, confrontational style, but I would have been clinically removed enough to see her behavior for what it was, defensive bravado. This is meant to keep others at bay and to protect herself from her deep-seated feelings of inadequacy and self-hatred. Had she been my patient, I would have gently pointed this out, and hopefully helped her work through her self-loathing. As a fellow patient, I was in no position to do so. Part of me wanted to tell her to cut the shit but, more than anything, I wanted to get away from her.

At least she wasn't one of my former patients. That would have been the icing on the cake, to be a patient with one of my former patients! I had a fleeting thought about Jim, the patient I had seen the day I was hospitalized. Suddenly, I was overcome by guilt and sorrow at having abandoned him. I would end up thinking about Jim often over the years. I regretted leaving him without explanation and wondered how he was doing.

A nurse popped her head into the room. "Melanie, your mother's here."

Mom was standing in the entryway reading a notice tacked on the wall. Dressed in jeans and sneakers, her brown boyish hair lay flat on her head. She looked tired.

I was surprised at how glad I was to see her. I hurried to her, intending to hug her, but suddenly remembered how angry I was at her.

"Hi, Mel," she said warily. "I wasn't sure what you needed, but I brought you some clothes and toiletries." She eased the duffel bag she'd been carrying to the floor.

"What I really need are aspirin and cigarettes." I was pretty sure Dr. Lancet wouldn't allow the aspirin, but at that moment I didn't much care. I just hoped the same thought wouldn't occur to my mother.

A nurse approached us, telling us to visit in the library. "I'll take your bag to the nurses' station so I can look through it before you take it to your room."

"Don't you want to do a cavity search?" I called after her sarcastically.

Studying the landscape painting hanging on the wall above my mother's head, I asked where Dani was. I felt hurt that she hadn't to come to see me.

"She and Scott went to the city to pack up your apartment." She sat on the edge of the couch rummaging through her purse.

Why they'd be packing up my apartment when I'd need to live there in the next week or two was beyond my comprehension. I told her this.

"Melanie, you don't get it. You're not going back to work anytime soon." She sighed and then handed me a bottle of aspirin and a pack of cigarettes.

"Well, maybe not for a couple weeks, but not much longer." I shoved four aspirin into my mouth.

"You have to call your boss and tell him you're not coming back to work. The papers I signed committed you to the hospital for a minimum of sixty days. I assumed you knew that."

I could barely make sense of what she was saying. Sixty days was two months and I had no intention of staying there for more than a week or two. Surely there must be some mistake. I started to panic and feel very angry. Then the despair set in. "Will you call my boss for me? I'm too ashamed," I said weakly, fighting back tears.

"Sorry, Mel. You have to call him yourself."

I wished she'd make things easier for me, just this once. But she never was the warm, fuzzy mother I sometimes longed for and often sought out in my female friends. I felt like a scared vulnerable child.

"

CHAPTER 15

"Where's Dr. Lancet? I've been rotting here for almost three days." I whined to the nurse in the nurses' station.

"He'll be here shortly," she replied dismissively.

I felt so disgusting. I hadn't even brushed my teeth since I got there and I slept through most of the weekend. I asked her if I could take a shower.

"You'll have to wait until we unlock the bathroom doors at eight-thirty," she said turning the page of her newspaper.

I stormed back to my room and slammed the door. A few minutes later, a psych aide came to my room. "Dr. Lancet wants to see you. He's at the nurses' station."

Dr. Lancet was leaning against the doorframe of the nurses' station, involved in an animated conversation with a nurse. I cleared my throat.

"Melanie, wait in the library. I'll be there in a few minutes," he said without looking at me.

I wanted to scream and grab him by the throat for being so indifferent to me. I was so angry I felt like knocking all the books off the shelves and tearing them to shreds. Instead, I reached for *The Brothers Karazamov* and sat at the desk, pretending to read. I'd read part of it before, and had been meaning to get back to it someday. Besides, Dr. Lancet was sure to be impressed by my interest in Russian literature.

A few minutes later, I sensed him walking into the room. My heart skipped a beat when I realized he was finally there. I wanted so much to see him. Remembering how pissed I was at him, I pretended to finish reading a sentence before turning to look at him.

"You look nice and refreshed," I said jealously. His blue-and-white-striped button-down shirt looked crisp, his khaki pants freshly pressed, and loafers nice and shiny. *And I look wretched, and I stink.*

"That's because I had a relaxing weekend — except for the phone call from your mother." He pulled a chair over to the desk where he may or may not have noticed my book was upside down.

"Why the hell did she call you?" I felt left out and suspicious.

"She wanted to make sure you call the director of your residency program to tell him you won't be returning to work." He scribbled something in my chart.

"I said I'd call him – what's wrong with her?" I felt indignant. That he was writing in the chart instead of listening attentively bothered me also. I worried that he had written something derogatory about me. In actuality, he probably wrote something like, "discussed calling patient's boss" or possibly something about my intense level of denial regarding my illness. But given how I felt at the time it wouldn't have surprised me if he'd written, "patient is loathsome and I feel like messing with her brain." Perhaps what he'd written wasn't even about me. Maybe he was so indifferent toward me that he was thinking and writing about something else.

"Would *you* trust you after what you did?" he asked, shielding the chart with his body.

Even though I was getting bent out of shape, I knew he had a point. I meekly asked him how long I'd be out of work. I hoped he'd say a week or two.

"I'm sorry to tell you this, but you may never be able to work as a doctor again." His declaration shocked me, but I thought he was probably just trying to rattle me.

On our way to the nurses' station, I asked in my sweetest voice if he would transfer me off this unit. "It's so hard for me to be surrounded by borderlines and anorexics."

When I became anorexic the summer before eighth grade, I quickly realized I had built-in radar for spotting other anorexics.

Anorexics are in their own little secret society. There's a tacit competition between them/us. Each anorexic wants to be the *most* emaciated.

Being surrounded by anorexics thrust me back into this mindset. I had to get away from them before I became more obsessed with their weight and mine. As for the borderlines, (people with borderline personality disorder, BPD, of which Robbie definitely was one), the worst of the worst are those who get hospitalized (wrist slitting is almost sine qua non of a "bad" borderline). Borderlines are notoriously manipulative, needy, crisis-oriented, and emotionally labile. They have no respect for boundaries and often threaten suicide when they feel frustrated or angry. Although these behaviors are manifestations of their illness, they can be so obnoxious it's often harder to sympathize with them than it is to dislike them.

Surprising me, he said, "I'm transferring you to 2 South, an acute unit this afternoon. But Melanie, we aren't going to ignore the fact that you have an eating disorder."

I was so ecstatic that I almost forgot how upset I was about having to call my boss. As a resident, I'd spent the previous year working on acute units, which is where every patient not on a specialized unit is admitted. The patient population is diverse and co-ed, with pathologies ranging from depression to schizophrenia to bipolar disorder. I'd still be locked in and subject to the whims of Dr. Lancet and the staff, but rules regarding eating and exercising were non-existent. At the moment, that was all I cared about.

"I think you'll do better on the acute unit because you won't spend every second trying to circumvent the rules. It's very important for you to focus on how you became desperate enough to do what you did. Besides, I'm going to assign you to Susan, a wonderful nurse and therapist. She's trained to work with people like you."

What the hell did he mean "people like me?" Didn't he know I was unique and in a class of my own? We'd see how wonderful she was. I was sure she'd never seen the likes of me before.

I left a message for my boss. Then Dr. Lancet told me he'd see me later.

"When's later?" I asked. On an inpatient psychiatry unit, patient-doctor meetings are rarely "scheduled." In-patient psychiatrists are constantly faced with unexpected admissions, emergencies, and meetings. Their time seeing patients is catch-as-catch-can. The lack of a precise time for my sessions with Dr. Lancet perturbed me.

"Later," he said with annoyance.

As I walked away, I caught a whiff of my body odor. Sticking my head back into the nurses' station, I asked to take a shower.

"You'll have to wait," said the nurse in the room. "All staff members are busy."

I stomped to my room to get my cigarettes and some aspirin. Jessie stood beside her bed, stuffing her clothes into a suitcase.

"You're going home today?" I asked as I shoved six aspirin into my mouth. Coming off my meds was giving me intense headaches.

"Yeah, and I can't wait."

"I'm being transferred to 2 South. I can't wait for that, either."

"That unit is like a zoo."

"I'd rather be in a zoo than with a bunch of women bragging about their suicide attempts." I took a cigarette out of my pack and left the room. *At least I don't have to write her discharge note.* For me, the worst thing about working on an inpatient unit was doing the paperwork for the admissions and discharges. I was always delinquent with my discharge notes. For every patient discharged, there was a new admission almost immediately. Partly due to my ADD, and partly because I was acting out in resentment at being so overworked, I found it close to impossible to keep up.

On my way to smoke, the psychiatric aide handed me a towel, soap, razor, and shampoo. "You have to sign the razor out and return it when you're done," she explained as we walked to the nurses' station.

I turned the water as hot as I could stand and stood under its stream, soaping my protruding ribs, hipbones, and shoulder blades.

When I finished, I put my dirty clothes back on, wrapped my socks and sneakers in the wet towel and walked barefoot to the nurses' station.

"I'm back," I announced, waving the razor over my head.

The same nurse who'd been looking through charts earlier was now talking on the phone and drinking coffee. "You can't walk around without shoes."

I handed her the razor and looked down at my feet. Flexing my toes, I watched the tendons bulge. *Even my feet look skinny. I must be close to my favorite weight, eighty-five pounds.* I walked away without putting on my sneakers.

Soon the psychiatric aide came to escort me to 2 South.

I slung my backpack and duffel bag over my shoulder and shuffled down the hall with my shoelaces untied. The straps of my bags were digging into my flesh and my shorts were hanging off my hips.

"You aren't planning to bolt, are you?" she asked as she unlocked the unit door.

Not yet. I twisted my waistband and held onto it to keep my shorts from falling off. "Of course not," I said emphatically.

CHAPTER 16

When my escort opened the second of two locked doors onto 2 South, I noticed the unit broke into a right angle, with a long hallway straight ahead and another to the left. We turned left and walked past a medication room the size of a large closet, and then past the dining room before stopping at the nurses' station.

I dropped my bags on the gray linoleum–tiled floor. The walls were off-white and devoid of artwork, and the fluorescent lights in the ceiling were flickering. "This unit is like the ones I worked on. It feels like a psych ward. The women's unit felt more like a floor in a five-star hotel."

My escort smiled. "Most of our units look like this. There's actually a waiting list for the women's unit. Frankly, I'm surprised you wanted to leave that cushy environment."

We were standing in front of a glass partition that separated the nurses' station from the hallway. She walked to the back of the station, opened a door and went into a room I couldn't see. *That must be the secret chamber where the staff gathers to discuss the patients.* I shuddered to think what the staff would say about me behind closed doors.

Through the glass, I saw three metal carts in the middle of the room where patients' charts were shelved. Their blue bindings, upon which the patient's last name was written in large, bold, capital letters, faced outward. I strained to read the names, fearing that one or more of them had been patients of mine.

My chart had been tossed indifferently amidst Dunkin Donut coffee cups and partially eaten donuts on the speckled Formica counter that wrapped around the perimeter of the room. I wanted to shatter the glass and abscond with it. I worried that one of the psych aides would read my chart and tell her friends about me while they all got drunk and laughed.

Suddenly, a handsome young man with long, brown, wavy hair and cut-off jean shorts started skipping around me singing, *"I'm too sexy for 2 South."* After a few choruses, he changed the words to, *"You're too skinny for 2 South."*

I recognized he was manic. I found him amusing and refreshing, especially after having come from such a serious, depressed environment. I was glad that he noticed I was skinny. But I began to feel self-conscious, realizing he might find me repulsive. Knowing that manic people blurt out whatever's on their mind, I feared he might start calling me a dog, or something worse.

An attractive forty-something woman with bobbed, blond-highlighted hair emerged from the nurses' station and ran over to us. "Michael, how many times have I told you not to bother people?"

"He's not bothering me." I leaned over and whispered in her ear, "Maybe his doctor should increase his Lithium." I felt conflicted about offering my medical opinion, but I knew what I was talking about and wanted her to know I wasn't just your run-of-the mill psychiatric patient.

I knew my need to broadcast that I was a doctor was a way of trying to keep her from messing with me. She probably saw right through me and may have felt even more inclined to put me in my place. If I had to do it over again, I would have kept a lower profile. It would have been useful to me to identify the situations that prompted me to feel like bragging, and then examine what that need was about in order to gain greater self-awareness.

"I'll take you to your room." We passed patient rooms on the left and therapy rooms on the right. "I'm Susan. I'll be your 'primary,' which is just a fancy way of saying I'm the nurse in charge of your case. If you need anything, ask for me."

The cold impersonality of the word "case" sent a chill of disappointment down my spine. I needed to be special!

"I'll serve as the liaison between you and Dr. Lancet." She pointed out the laundry room and then opened a door just beyond it, the last door on the corridor. "This is your room." She placed my bags on the floor between twin beds about an arm's length from one another. "That's yours." She waved toward the metal-framed bed closest to the window.

"I guess I have a roommate," I said, pointing at the stuffed animals on the other bed.

"Yes. Terry. She'll be back from occupational therapy soon. Come on, I'll show you around." Pointing to the large sparse room across the hall, she said, "That's where we have community meetings and other meetings that include the entire unit."

We walked back down the hallway and stopped right before we reached the nurses' station. On our left were three phone booths and to our right was the TV room.

"You're allowed to smoke in there." The TV room had worn orange carpet, large wooden chairs with orange upholstery, and a television suspended from the ceiling on the far wall. The TV was turned on, but the sound was muted. Smoke permeated the air, stained the walls and wafted into the hallway. The room was dim.

Fondling the nearly empty pack of cigarettes in my shorts pocket, I asked her if I could stop for a smoke.

She pulled a cigarette lighter out of her back pocket and handed it to me. "I'll show you the rest of the unit later."

Rushing into the TV room, I chose a seat under one of five huge windows along the far wall. The windows, which were filthy, looked out over a courtyard with two wooden benches, uneven rows of flowers that I assumed had been planted by patients in occupational therapy, and a few trees whose leaves shaded the benches from the blazing sun. Directly across the courtyard was the brick wall of another wing of the hospital, and to both sides were glass-enclosed corridors with doors leading to the courtyard. I quickly turned away from the windows. Knowing I was not allowed outside only increased my frustration and anger.

From where I sat, I could see the entire room as well as a slice of the hallway. A man sleeping in the corner was slumped in the chair with his neck extended backward; his head rested against the wall. His mouth was agape, his hands lay in his lap, and cigarette butts and an overturned ashtray littered the floor at his feet. I assumed that he was a permanent fixture in the room and, more than likely, a burnt-out schizophrenic. As I stared at him, an image of my father sleeping on the couch in front of the television cropped up to haunt me. He'd done this regularly. My mother cursed him under her breath when she swept the pipe ashes from around him. I'd want to wake him, yet feared the inevitable tirade that would follow as my mother shouted, "You lazy bum! Why don't you get a job?"

Susan walked over. "I wanted to say goodbye. I'm leaving for the day, but I'll be back in the morning. The other patients will be back from their activities any minute and dinner is at five. Are you okay?" I was surprised she was spending time talking to me, because the day shift had ended a half-hour earlier. Most staff members in hospitals where I'd worked bolted out the door the second their shift ended. As she left, I felt a sinking feeling in the pit of my stomach. I already feel attached to her, I realized with self-loathing.

A few minutes later, about ten patients barreled into the room. Among them was a large black woman holding her breast like a machine gun, squirting milk at a diminutive Latino man.

Let the games begin.

CHAPTER 17

"Rise and shine," called Susan. "It's seven o'clock, and breakfast's at seven-thirty."

"I saw you with your mother last night," Terry said as she climbed out of bed. She was about five-foot-two, with short, mousy brown hair and pudgy cheeks. "She was a teacher at my elementary school. My doctor's kids went there, too."

"You're kidding! Who's your doctor?"

"Dr. Lancet. He's friendly with my parents." She pulled her nightgown over her head. "He has four sons. Only one is still in elementary school."

I was thrilled to have this new information about Dr. Lancet, but pissed that my mother hadn't mentioned it. I suddenly realized that she must have gotten his number, which I assumed was unlisted, from the school phone book. I wondered what else they had talked about and why neither of them mentioned this to me. Did they think I wouldn't find out? Were they conspiring to lock me up and throw away the key? I was thinking crazy conspiratorial thoughts. That wasn't like me. It was my Dad's mind at work. I shuddered at this realization and decided just to ask Mom point blank.

"I'm going to call my mother right now to ask her." I rifled through my drawer to find a quarter for the payphone.

"You're not allowed to use the phone 'til eight." She sat on her bed tying her shoelaces.

"That figures," I said as I dropped a handful of change into my pocket. All the fucking rules were starting to piss me off!

"Why are you here?" She looked so sad. I wanted to rub her back, but I made my bed instead.

"Dr. Lancet said it's called bipolar disorder. He says so far I just have the manic part."

I stared at her to pick up any signs of mania, but if anything, she seemed a little lethargic, not manic. I wondered if she was on a high dose of Lithium, which could also account for what appeared to be the beginnings of a "beer-belly."

We walked down the hall together. I ducked into the TV room as she continued on to the dining room.

After a few minutes, other patients trickled in and, as they lit up, the room quickly filled with smoke. When a frail woman with a pockmarked face and dirt-caked fingernails sat down next to me, I returned to my room and lay on my bed.

Terry came into the room. "Community meeting's in a few minutes. I'll be right back to get you."

I'd treated several patients around Terry's age. They'd been admitted to my service in the throes of their first manic episode. According to what I learned in bits and pieces from my mother, it seems likely that my father had his first episode at roughly that age. Late teens and early twenties are typically when symptoms of bipolar disorder and schizophrenia begin. Having witnessed this disease from its onset and over the course of time, I was aware of the potential havoc it could wreak. Whereas many people live productive, fulfilling lives with the proper combination of psychopharmacology and talk therapy, it requires extreme commitment and diligence on the part of the patient. Unfortunately, the side effects of the medication can be difficult for patients to tolerate. They often stop taking their meds and then it's only a matter of time before their symptoms reappear.

I felt sorry for Terry. I thought about the genetic component to bipolar disorder and how the genes were always inside her, like a coiled snake waiting to spring at a high-stress time in her life. I wanted to ask if anyone else in her family had it, but I knew it wasn't my place.

We walked across the hall to the meeting room. It fit a hundred people comfortably, yet the only furnishings were thirty or so orange plastic chairs arranged in a circle in the center of the room. I sat between Susan and Terry.

The staff wore "normal" clothes, as did most of the patients — except for a few wearing winter coats, despite it being the middle of summer. The major distinction between the staff and the patients were their clipboards and, in some instances, name tags. Even though I had neither, I felt more like a staff member than a patient. It seemed ironic at first, then, when it started to sink in, horrifying.

A woman with glasses and acne stood up. "As most of you already know, these meetings are a forum for discussing any issues relevant to the unit. This includes problems such as lack of toilet paper in the bathrooms or who's hoarding the snacks. You must raise your hand if you want to say something. The meeting will commence with each person introducing himself. I'm Mary, the head nurse."

As a resident, I used this time to do menial paperwork. Now I distracted myself by guessing each patient's diagnosis. The depressed ones slumped in their chairs and mumbled their names. The disheveled patients with vacant looks in their eyes, trembling hands, and winter jackets were schizophrenic; the ones who couldn't sit still and shouted out impulsively were manic.

One attractive black woman in her late twenties I recognized, but could not place. When she introduced herself as Wendy, I realized she was a psychiatric resident from Luke's training program.

I recalled Luke telling me one of his residents was bipolar, but I didn't know if it was she. Regardless, I couldn't believe how lucky I was to have someone here with a connection to him. My heart raced and I began squirming in my seat. I wanted to shout out to her as I thought back to the times we'd met. I'd seen her at the Christmas party for Luke's staff and at several other social functions. She'd even attended the party Luke and I threw to celebrate our moving in together! Since she knew me as Luke's girlfriend and a psychiatric resident, I felt that the favorite part of my life, in which I existed in my most proud role as Luke's girlfriend and part of "the gang," was not only validated, but only a stone's throw away. I thought by befriending her, I might be somehow magically transported back into that world, the only one I ever wanted to be part of. The world where, for the first time in my life, I felt loved, connected, and valued. Without those people, I was nothing; with them, I was something. Being nothing made me want to die. Being with them, even just being associated with them, made me want to live. I didn't think I'd be able to live without Luke or the gang.

When the meeting was over, I practically flew out of my seat to talk with Wendy. "Hi! Do you recognize me?" My voice quivered with excitement.

She continued walking. "Yes, but it would be best if we don't have any further contact."

I staggered backward like I'd been pushed hard, right in the chest. Fleeing to my room, I stood staring out the window at the field down below. It had never occurred to me that what I'd done would have repercussions — with Luke or anyone else. Wendy's rejection traumatized me. It was my first inkling that people might hate me for what I'd done.

I bolted up the hallway and rapped on the glass of the nurses' station. "What's up?" Susan asked, sliding the glass panel to the side.

"I need to talk to Dr. Lancet!"

"He's with another patient. I'm sure he'll see you in a little while."

"But I need him now!"

"Unless it's a medical emergency, you'll have to wait. I'd be glad to have a one-on-one with you."

"So if I'm bleeding to death, he'll interrupt the other patient to see me, but if I'm just dying of a broken heart, I'll have to wait?" I felt irate and neglected. "Okay, I guess I'll talk with you." I was settling for second best, but I had to talk to somebody. If I were alone,

I probably would have started destroying things or inflicting pain on myself to help take the edge off. I doubted Susan would have anything worthwhile to say, but maybe by simply expressing some of my torment to her, it would feel more manageable.

She took me to the examination room where the staff did admission physicals, daily weights, and minor medical procedures. I sat on the exam table and shredded the white paper covering it. I knew ripping the paper was extremely juvenile, but I felt like doing it, so I didn't even try to stop myself. *I'm a patient now. I can act like a two-year-old if I want to. I have nothing to prove.*

While I ripped the paper, more violently with each tear, I thought about the scores of admission physicals I'd performed as a resident. In a way, I was glad I didn't have to do that doctor stuff anymore. I had hated the medical side of being a doctor anyway. In medical school, everyone said you start to feel like a "real" doctor once you graduate, but that never happened for me. Sometimes I wonder if I got myself into the mess I did in order to escape having to practice medicine; some twisted way of keeping myself free of taking responsibility for rejecting what my father wanted most for me.

I thought back to the admission physical that got me fired, the one I'd never completed. This happened on Feb 27, 1992 -- a month after Luke broke up with me, and a day before the second anniversary of my father's death.

I was splitting a call with the chief resident's girlfriend because a few weeks earlier, I had covered part of her call as a favor. The normal workday ended at 5 PM, and this particular evening, I had to be back at the hospital at 10:30 to take over the rest of the night call. An admission came in at 5:00. I asked her to take the admission, but she refused. I was really pissed and felt totally resentful, as I had bailed her out a few weeks prior. In any case, I had to take it. I did the entire admission interview, but only part of the admission physical. Coincidentally, Luke had sent the patient to my hospital from his psych ER where he had done a physical on the patient a few hours prior. I told the nurse on the unit that I'd complete the physical when I returned at 10:30. Meanwhile I used Luke's findings to fill in the paperwork as though I had completed the exam. When I returned to the hospital at 10:30, there were a lot of pressing things for me to attend to. I did not get back to the original patient until midnight. In the meantime, the night nurses had replaced the evening nurses, and there was a communication breakdown between shifts. When I returned to the unit to complete the physical, the night nurse saw that I had filled in some information that I had not, in fact, done myself. She promptly reported me to the higher-ups, who decided not to renew my contract based on that transgression. As my unit chief pointed out to me, and to the higher-ups, my mistake was in copying the information from Luke's physical exam temporarily until I was able to complete the exam myself. This created the problem, because the rule is that you only have to do a heart and lung exam at the time of admission (which I had done) and you have twenty-four hours to complete the rest of the physical. There were no consequences for the patient, but it was the beginning of the end for me.

"What's going on?" asked Susan.

"The reality of my situation is starting to hit home. At first, I was so preoccupied with getting off the eating disorder unit, I didn't even think about why I was here. But now, I'm starting to realize I may have destroyed my life. That patient I told you I know … she's from Luke's training program -- he trains residents. She won't even talk to me." I was so distraught I could barely get my words out. "Not only might I lose my medical license, but I may have alienated everybody in my life. I have no idea how things got so crazy. Plus, I can't stand being locked inside. I need to go running."

She moved the wastepaper basket closer to me with her foot. "You can't do anything about your medical license right now or about how other people react to you, so that's neither here nor there. Dr. Lancet is the only one who can change your status to outdoor privileges, but since you were admitted involuntarily, you'll be confined to the unit for a while. The important thing is for you to figure out a way to cope with your negative emotions so you don't self-destruct. Do you keep a journal?"

"Yes, I like to write poetry, too." I felt embarrassed because I thought it was rather audacious of me to call what I wrote poetry.

We talked more about the things I needed to focus on in order to get better. Susan asked if I felt any better. Surprisingly, I did. By the mere fact that she listened and apparently cared about me, I felt less isolated and slightly more connected.

CHAPTER 18

Dr. Lancet led me into a Spartan room about the size of a walk-in closet. A large metal desk took up one wall. Two plastic orange chairs stood flush against one another in the center of the room.

I turned a chair backward and straddled it, trying to act cool and cavalier when what I was really feeling was totally pissed off. Dr. Lancet dropped his keys on the desk and pushed the door shut with his foot.

Before he sat down, I blurted out angrily, "Why didn't you tell me one of Luke's residents is on this unit? First no one told me your kids go to my mom's school, and then this. What will I find out next, Luke is your wife's cousin or something?"

"I'm sorry, Mel, but none of these things are intended to hurt you. I didn't know she worked with Luke. But her being here has nothing to do with you."

I rested my chin on the back of the chair and said dejectedly, "She won't even talk to me."

I told him about the time Luke and I ate lunch with her. It was one of those rare days when he invited me to hang out at the hospital with him when he was on call. We were both studying for exams and he thought it would be nice to study together. I was thrilled that he wanted to spend the day with me. We ended up making love on the floor of his office and then he let me sit on his lap while we both studied. Later, we saw Wendy in the hallway and invited her to join us for lunch. Throughout the meal, all I thought about was how in love I was with Luke.

Dr. Lancet cleared his throat. "It didn't occur to me that you knew one another. I'm sorry about that. However, focusing on her will merely distract you from doing the work you need to do."

Thinking about that day, my heart swelled with the love I felt for Luke and I yearned for him even more.

"At least you thought you loved him, but the bottom line is that supposed love and the loss of it made you almost kill him. We need to figure out *how* that happened, *why* it happened, and make sure nothing like that ever happens again."

My chest felt painfully tight. "How are we going to do that?"

"Through psychological testing, as well as family, group, and individual therapy."

"I don't think my mother will come to therapy. She's very private and defensive. She'll think she's being blamed for what happened." I thought about how angry she got whenever she felt threatened. "Plus, she had a really bad experience with family therapy about ten years ago."

The second I revealed that, I regretted it. I wished I could take it back for my sister's sake, but wondered if I hadn't let it slip on purpose. I felt the need to tell Dr. Lancet about how I had helped Dani. Maybe I could get the acknowledgement I craved from him.

"Whenever I came home from college, Dani and I spent time together. On one of these visits, I became alarmed because I recognized that she was depressed. Neither one of my parents had picked up on it. I convinced her to see a therapist. She agreed, but only if I'd arrange it and take her without involving our parents. So I did."

"She continued in therapy with that psychiatrist for the next five years. I know that's largely why she became a happy and healthy adult...unlike me." It felt good to share this with a good listener.

"So then your parents went into therapy together?"

"They were supposed to, but my father either didn't show up, or showed up late or drunk. Then he spent the entire session berating my mother. After a month or so, he refused to go altogether and my mother ended up going alone for a few months. Then she stopped going."

"I can see why she'd be reluctant to have family sessions with you, but it's imperative that she participate in your treatment." He reached for his keys.

"Okay, but I'll pass on group therapy. Talking to other patients won't help me. Plus, I used to run these groups, so it'll be frustrating for me to have to be in it, rather than in charge."

"Group therapy will be an ideal place to talk about those feelings. The psychologist who leads the group is an expert in analyzing interpersonal dynamics. He'll learn something about you, no matter what." He half-smiled at me in a teasing sort of way, because he knew that I knew that one's silence or resistance to participating in group, is fraught with meaning, often more so than words themselves. "Besides, passing is not an option."

The glare of the sun coming through the window reminded me to ask my most pressing question. "Will I ever be allowed to go outside? I need to go for a run." I tried not to whine.

He ignored my question. "I'm sorry our session was brief, but we'll have to end for today. I'll talk to you tomorrow."

I went to the meeting room to watch for my mother out the window. It was ten minutes before three, but I knew she'd be there any second. She'd go to the bathroom, get a drink of water and arrive on my unit at three o'clock sharp.

She'd been compulsively punctual and a slave to her routines for as long as I could remember. Needing everything around her to be orderly and logical, she adhered to deadlines and rules without question. She could be rigid to the point of irrationality, which seemed incongruous with her intellect. Plus, it was often annoying, especially for someone as disorganized and disregarding of inane rules as I was. She and I had a running joke about my getting more organized. I always resolved to do so, and really wanted to, but seemed incapable of it. Eventually, we just gave my resolution a number. She'd say, "How's 'number four' doing?" I'd answer, "Maybe next year."

I sometimes teased her about her compulsiveness, but only when I knew she was in a good mood and wouldn't get defensive and offended. I understood it was her way of fending off anxiety and feelings of inadequacy. I had also come to value it. Throughout my life, her predictability and reliability had offered me a sense of security that countered the constant chaos my father created. It's not that my father wasn't organized. In fact, he had filing systems for everything and, to this very day, the combination to my bicycle lock from junior high is written in his hand writing on the wall of my mother's garage. It's just that he rarely followed through with anything and was inconsistent, unreliable, and unpredictable.

I sensed Mom's presence before she even reached the hospital. I knew she'd turned on her blinker before she reached the driveway, then slowly approached the entrance. *She drives the same way she approaches life, cautiously and unobtrusively.* I watched from the window as she parked, slung a beige LeSportsac purse over her shoulder, checked the locks and looked around before walking toward the hospital.

Had it been my father coming to visit me, I'd have no idea whether or not he'd even show up. He'd leave the house late, drive so slowly he'd hold up traffic, turn without signaling and park in a restricted area, probably the doctors' parking lot. When I saw him, I'd be so thrilled and relieved he'd shown up, I'd barely be able to contain my joy. Distinguishing between feelings of joy and the absence of anxiety can be difficult. The degree of tension I experienced as a result of wanting him so badly, and never knowing whether he'd come through, was extreme. Eventually I came to prefer being let down by him to being stuck in the limbo state of not knowing what would happen.

After leaving the car, he'd tap the bowl of his pipe on the curb to empty the ashes. I could practically hear the tap, tap, tap against the pavement. He'd pat his pockets to locate his tobacco pouch, think better of refilling his pipe and cup the bowl of the pipe in his right hand. While visiting me, he'd fondle his pipe with one hand, pick at the cuticles of his thumb with the fingers of his other hand and suck one hard candy after another.

I did twenty-five jumping jacks before sprinting to the nurses' station. An adorable, college-aged psychiatric aide named Chris looked up at me from behind the glass.

"My mother's here. Can you let her in?" I mouthed. I was excited to see her.

Pressing my face against the glass surrounding the first locked door off the unit, I said, "I don't see her, but it's exactly three, so I'm sure she's here."

Just then, Mom appeared at the outer door to the unit. I grabbed her hand and led her to the community meeting room. I dragged three chairs to the far wall and lined them up facing the window.

"I need to talk to you about something." I looked out the window at the woods beyond the parking lot.

"What now?" she asked warily.

"Dr. Lancet wants us to meet with a social worker together. Think about it for a couple of minutes before you respond."

I knew her first reaction would be anger. She perceived situations where she had to discuss her feelings as threatening and personal questions as attacks. Usually when I asked her one or tried to understand her feelings about something, she'd angrily tell me to stop interrogating her. Much of her sensitivity could be attributed to her mother's and my father's constant criticism of her. Even though she was tenured in a very prestigious elementary school, her mother always asked her when she was going to get "a real job." She scowled. "You know how I feel about being put on the spot."

I'd anticipated this reaction, but I still felt disappointed. I didn't want to have to beg for her help or feel guilty for needing her. I was mentally ill, but I knew I had to make her feel safe and valued and convince her that her input was critical.

"This isn't about putting you on the spot or blaming you," I said in an ingratiating tone. "We need your input to help us understand how I became so disturbed. You're the only one who can help with information about our family." I wanted to scream at her to get past her shit for a minute to see how desperate I was, but I knew if I didn't approach her with kid gloves, I would turn her off completely.

"Do I have a choice?"

"Of course you do. I was just hoping you'd choose to help me."

"You know how uncomfortable this makes me," she sighed. "But if Dr. Lancet thinks it's necessary, I'll do it."

I smiled. "Thanks, Mom. If it's terrible for you, we can stop. I know it seems unfair that you're still picking up the pieces from the damage Daddy did to us, but think about how much worse off we would have been without you."

"Enough. I said I'd do it!"

We made small talk for a while, and then she started shifting in her seat. "Aren't visiting hours over?"

"Don't worry, Mom. They won't punish you for staying a little longer."

Though clearly agitated, she stayed until an obese woman I'd never seen before came into the room. "Melanie? I'm Nancy, the evening nurse. Visiting hours are over. I'll let your visitor out."

My mother jumped up from her chair. "I was just getting ready to leave," she said apologetically.

As Nancy unlocked the unit door, I reached for my mother tentatively. I felt close to her and scared of her at the same time. I was afraid she'd act cold towards me or reject me entirely.

I didn't tell her Scott was coming to visit that evening. She'd be furious if she knew I was still seeing him.

Scott was shocked when I was admitted to the hospital. Even though we'd only known one another for a couple of weeks, he said he loved me and wanted to be with me no matter what. He said, I was "the complete package: smart, sexy, ambitious, athletic, and funny." He'd been calling every day and already visited twice. If I had allowed him to, he would have come everyday. I knew my mother would not approve of my getting involved with yet another man. I didn't want to risk alienating her or put myself in a position where I'd have to lie. I told Scott repeatedly to forget about me and walk away before he got in over his head. I was proud of myself for putting his interests before my own. I didn't really want him to forget me. His support and devotion comforted and flattered me. Also, I genuinely liked him and was attracted to him.

Juggling my relationships with Scott and my mother was challenging. It felt like the dynamic I'd had with my parents. I had suffered enormously because of dual loyalties with them. Here it was again, and I was right in the middle. But I had created the situation. If I had been less needy and ambivalent about wanting Scott to hang around, I would have been more adamant about him leaving me alone entirely.

CHAPTER 19

After mom left, I went to my room to work out. A few minutes later, Terry came in. "You missed a fun session of art therapy!"

"I'm not allowed off the unit yet. Besides, I don't want to go to any of the activities except gym." I knew I could not stand to sit through art therapy, occupational therapy, dance therapy, or any of the other inane therapies. The instructors were always too perky and enthusiastic for my taste. These outlets were useful for some patients, but I was having enough trouble accepting that nurses and psychiatric aides had input into "my case." I'd be damned if I would expose myself to any of these other people.

We talked for a while longer before going to dinner. Squeezing through the aisle between two tables where a dozen or so patients sat shoveling food into their mouths, we sat at the far end of a table.

"Don't look now," she nudged me with her elbow, "but Nancy's on her way over here."

"Your social worker wants to talk to you," sputtered Nancy as she approached us.

Nancy pointed to a man studying a chart in the nurses' station. He looked like a thirty-something version of Robert Redford, with gorgeous, thick, salt-and-pepper hair. Seeing how handsome he was, I felt hideously unattractive.

He approached me with his arm extended. "Melanie, I'm Richie. I believe Dr. Lancet told you I'd be coming to meet you?" He smelled freshly showered.

"Yes, but he didn't mention you'd be taking me to dinner."

He grinned. "Some days I have to work late to keep up. Sorry I interrupted your meal." He was so handsome and warm, I wouldn't have minded if he'd shown up in the middle of the night and woken me up. Besides, I knew what it was like trying to squeeze patients in between all the mandatory meetings, paperwork, and whatnot. Sometimes there were so many obligatory conferences, lectures, and phone-calls, it seemed as if the patients came last.

"I won't take too much of your time. I just wanted to introduce myself and talk to you a bit about family therapy." He gestured toward the conference room on the other side of the hallway.

I wish I didn't look like a mental patient.

The conference room was about three times the size of the therapy room. There was a round white table in the center. Orange metal chairs surrounded the table at odd angles.

He waited for me to sit. He sat next to me and opened my chart. "Dr. Lancet asked me to meet with you and your mother together. How do you feel about that?"

"It's fine with me, but she's less than thrilled." I strained to look at my chart.

"You have a sister?" he asked, dragging his index finger across the page.

"She's in law school. I doubt she'll have time to come to any meetings." I focused on the page he was looking at. "My father's dead," I added, anticipating his next question.

"I'm sorry." He closed the chart and looked at me.

"We're all better off." I wasn't in the mood to talk about my father.

"I'd like to meet with you and your mother tomorrow at two. She can talk to me alone before you join us if that would make it easier for her." He handed me his card and we walked out of the room together. "See you tomorrow."

Since many of the diners had relocated to the TV room, the air was thick with smoke and B.O. I loped to an empty chair under the window and stared at the empty courtyard below. After awhile, Nancy tapped me on the shoulder.

"Your boyfriend's here. Remember, visiting hours are over at eight sharp."

Scott stood in front of the unit door, scanning the hallway as though looking for a sniper. He looked like a gang member in his jeans, sandals, and gray Harley Davidson t-shirt. His massive physique practically obscured the door behind him. He wrapped his arms around me and crushed me against his chest. "How are you?"

"Not good," I replied, as I led him to the lounge. "Let's sit over there." I pointed to an orange couch at the far wall next to the piano.

When he pulled me to him, I stiffened. I suddenly felt so angry with him that I was repulsed by his touch. It was as though I had internalized my mother's anger at *me* for my dual loyalties.

"What's wrong?" he asked, caressing my knee.

I lifted his hand off my knee.

"I can't even touch you?" He sounded hurt.

"Don't you get it?" I snapped. "This isn't a hotel – it's a nuthouse. I'm all fucked up." My mother's rage had reached full force inside me to the point where I started to hate him. "I think you should leave."

He rose slowly. "Did I do something wrong?"

My inner criticism of him came fast and furious. He didn't finish college; he couldn't hold his marriage together (Scott was divorced and the father of two young boys), and on and on. I knew that the anger behind these thoughts was my mother's, not mine, but I couldn't stop it. I felt guilty.

"It's not you, it's me. I have a lot of things to work out." I tried to sound kind, but knew that if he didn't leave soon, I would launch into a completely undeserved tirade.

Before Scott got through the second door, I ran to call my mother. "Mom!" I frantically blurted out.

"Are you all right?" She sounded alarmed.

"No, I feel like killing myself." I started to sob. My feelings were so intense and my thoughts so confused regarding them, I didn't know what I wanted or needed at that moment. I knew my rage at Scott was displaced and the anger was really directed towards my mother for making me choose between them, and historically, between her and my father. It was much safer to be angry at Scott, than at her, because I needed her so much. My telling her I felt like killing myself was my way of getting her to worry about me. I knew the degree of anger I felt toward Scott equaled the level of rage she felt towards me.

"Is there anybody there you can talk to?" she asked in a tone of urgency.

"No, only Nancy, the fat slob, and some aides I don't know." I tried to catch my breath. "The social worker visited me tonight. He wants to meet us tomorrow at two. Is that okay for you?"

"Yes, that's fine." I heard her open the squeaky drawer of her desk and rattle around some pens.

"You have to write it down?" I teased.

"You know me, I can't remember anything," she said jokingly. "No, I was going to write down the directions to his office. What's his name?"

"Richie. He's really cute." I smiled into the phone. "Oh, and Mom…"

"Yes?"

"You know I told Scott to forget about me?" I bit my upper lip.

"Yes …" she said warily.

"Well, he insists he's in love with me and he visited me tonight. I made him leave early." I felt the need to spin things in a way least likely to anger her. Anyway, what I said was mostly honest; I just didn't elaborate on the extent of my inner conflict. I wanted Scott to love me and be there for me despite knowing I had little to offer in return. This was complicated by my fear that our relationship would distract me from dealing with my current problems and knowing that it would interfere with my relationship with her. At this point, I knew honesty with my mother was imperative, so I felt uneasy about not sharing my inner feelings with her. Simultaneously, I resented how her behavior compelled me to lie to her. She could be so quick to judge, criticize and get angry.

"You know how I feel about you and men," she said coldly. "You use them, abuse them, then discard them when you no longer need them."

There was a long history of her disapproving of my relationships. I hated how she saw me, yet couldn't deny my problematic track record. The four relationships I'd had before I met Luke all followed the same pattern. I'd quickly fall head-over-heels. Within a couple of weeks we became intimately and intensely involved. The more he professed his love for me, the more I'd start hating and resenting him. Each of these men had asked me to marry them but, by that time, I had devalued them to the point of seeing them as hardly human. In fact, I could barely stand being near them.

There was no doubt in my mind that I loved Luke, but I couldn't deny that, every time I got involved with someone, I'd felt the same way in the beginning. My sadistic devaluing always took me by surprise, but once it started, it was all over. I could not recapture the feeling I'd identified as love, and the feeling of dislike quickly turned into one of contempt. My mother was not a disinterested party either. She always ended up fielding the calls of the heartbroken men I left in my wake for weeks after I'd moved on.

"We can talk about it tomorrow with Richie."

"Fine," she said sharply.

I pulled his business card out of my pocket. "His last name is

Sabini. You can ask the guard at the front desk for directions to his office. He said you could talk to him alone before I join you. Do you want his number?"

"No, I don't need it." I heard her desk drawer close. "I'll see you tomorrow."

CHAPTER 20

I stood in line with the other patients for morning meds. The nurse handing out pills in little white cups looked at me empty-handed. "You don't have any meds."

"I know, but I'm totally constipated. I need a laxative." Having abused laxatives for at least ten years, I could not go to the bathroom without them. I felt crampy, headachy and bothered by the little bulge in my abdomen. All I wanted was to take a crap, which was hard enough given there were group bathrooms. I wanted to scream at my lack of control over my treatment. Talking about being constipated was embarrassing enough, but now I would have to beg Dr. Lancet for a laxative!

"Your doctor didn't write an order for anything. You'll have to talk to him." She looked past me to the next patient.

I stormed down the hall, then turned around and marched back down the entire length of the floor. I watched the other patients leave the unit for their various activities. The nurses wrote notes in their charts; other staff members walked around. I counted the tiles on the floor, the ones on the ceiling, the dents in the wall.

I'd been pacing for roughly an hour when a dark-haired man wearing wire-rimmed glasses and a blue polka-dotted bow tie approached me.

"Melanie? I'm the psychologist, Dr. O'Riley. Do you have a minute?"

"Yes." I continued walking in place.

He opened the door to the conference room and went in ahead of me. Sitting in the chair closest to the door, he put his briefcase in front of him on the table. "Dr. Lancet asked me to conduct a full battery of psychological tests on you. Do you know anything about psychological testing?"

"Yes, I'm a psychiatrist." I stared at the floor and whispered, "Was."

"So you understand we use psychological testing to aid in making diagnoses as well as to rule out any neurological irregularities?"

"Yes, I used these tests in research after college, and also when I did my psychiatry rotation in medical school. I've seen all the tests and know how to score some of them, but I've never been tested myself."

He shuffled a stack of papers. "As long as you're truthful and spontaneous in your responses, that shouldn't affect anything. I'm going to leave a few questionnaires with you to fill out by tomorrow. Then I'll schedule you for the subjective testing." He put the papers in a manila folder and handed it to me. "Incidentally, I assigned you to my group therapy session this afternoon."

"I'm busy this afternoon." I formed a negative opinion of him initially because of his bow tie, which I associated with snobbery, and because he was making me go to group, something I absolutely did not want to do!

"You have to come to group," he said matter-of-factly.

"I don't want to talk to the other patients. Would you?" I thumbed through the test papers in the folder.

"That's not relevant. You *are* a patient and I'm not."

I almost expected him to sing a taunting *"nah nah, nah nah nah."* I leered at him. *Just you wait until you have a nervous breakdown and wind up in the hospital, asshole. Then you'll see how it feels.*

He snapped the clasps of his briefcase closed. "If your meeting ends before group is over, I'll make an exception and allow you to come in late today. Normally I lock the door once group starts and nobody is allowed to enter."

"Gee, thanks," I shot back sarcastically.

I slunk into the TV room, sat in the far corner, opened the folder and perused the questionnaires. The longest one was the MMPI, used to diagnose personality disorders, then the symptom checklist, a depression inventory, a personality assessment inventory, and a sentence completion worksheet.

"Melanie," beckoned Dr. Lancet from across the room, "Come with me."

I followed him to the therapy room. "I don't have much time, but wanted to touch base."

Pressing on my abdomen and grimacing, I asked, "Would you write me an order for a laxative? I have the worst cramps."

"I told you we weren't going to ignore your eating disorder. Besides, you told me you have a history of abusing laxatives."

I had told him that, but had omitted the extent of abuse. Just as alcoholics are notorious for underreporting how much they drink, I had lied about how many laxatives I used.

"You're a doctor, so you know the physiology of withdrawal. It will take your body a couple of weeks to adjust. I'm going to hold off giving you a laxative for at least a few days. Try eating more fiber. Enough said. I saw in your chart that you have a meeting with Richie this afternoon. So your mom agreed to come after all?"

"Yes, but not without pulling the martyr routine," I chuckled. "You know, poor me, I have to make so many sacrifices, la, la la. Anyway, thank goodness she's coming. It means I'll get out of going to group, or at least miss most of it. I'd rather put up with Mom's crap than go to group any day."

"Okay, well, let me know how it goes." He stood, signaling the end of the session. "It's time for lunch."

After lunch, we had to stay in our rooms for an hour of "quiet time." I used this time to exercise.

Following quiet time that afternoon, I rapped on the window of the nurses' station to get the attention of a pretty psych aide I had never seen before.

"I have an appointment," I shouted through the glass. "I have to go now!" I was so sick of having to wait for everything and being dependent on these stupid young people to give me what I needed. I felt like ramming my hand through the partition, grabbing a set of keys and letting myself off the unit.

She must have seen my face getting red with anger and recognized that I was about to explode. "I'll take you."

We walked through a maze of hallways and down a flight of stairs to Richie's office. He was sitting in a brown leather chair at a big mahogany desk. My mother sat on a matching leather couch across from him. Her purse was pressed against her leg like a clingy child.

I sank into the couch about three feet away from her and held a decorative pillow against myself like a shield. She clutched her purse even closer to her leg and gave me a half-smile.

"Hi, Mel," said Richie. "I was just asking your mother if she has a support system to help her through this difficult time." He swiveled his chair a few degrees to face me.

"She doesn't feel comfortable asking people for help," I offered, putting my feet on the glass coffee table in front of me. "But the minute her friend Jan gets wind that there's a problem, she'll go to my mother's despite her protests. She talks on the phone to her sister and friend Barbara a lot, but I doubt she's called either of them."

"That's exactly what she said. You know your mother very well." He turned toward her. "As a psychiatrist, I'm sure Melanie knows a lot about family therapy. Jean, what about you?"

She looked at my feet on the table, gave me the "Geller look," a frightening glare we named after her mother, then looked at Richie. "Melanie's father, Len, and I attended a few sessions after we were divorced to figure out how to help Mel's sister through her depression. But Len stopped coming because he was too busy with his 'whore' to invest anything in his daughter." Her jaw twitched.

"Whore?" Richie raised his eyebrows.

"He married a gold-digger half his age. Don't get me started."

Don't even go there.

She still resented my father. He never supported our family; he wrote bad checks, and collectors were constantly chasing after him. He was fired from all his jobs, and often was simply too depressed to work at all. Mom spent three years trying to kick him out of the house. He finally left the week I went to college. After a long drawn-out court battle, she'd had to pay him off in order to finalize the divorce.

A few years later, Dad's father died. He was very wealthy, and left my father a lot of money. This newfound wealth pulled Dad out of his depression. He quickly found a girlfriend, Pam. She was a foreign-born citizen fifteen years his junior. Soon after they met, she moved in with him. He started flaunting his money, and her, around town — the town where my mother also lived. He bought a fancy car and went on extravagant vacations, but refused to pay child support or help with my college tuition. When he married Pam, a year or so later, he insisted she stop working and go back to school, while he fully supported her.

Mom was outraged. She was also convinced Pam used him for his money and to obtain U.S. citizenship. I didn't trust her either, but I was more worried that she'd end up hurting my father than I was angry with him. I did think Pam was a phony, but if she was making him happy, who was I to interfere? So, even though my mother pressured me to ally with her, I reminded her that *she* was the one who threw him out

It also bothered me that underneath her anger, Mom seemed to want to get back together with him once he had money. She used my college graduation as an excuse to spend an extended amount of time with him and even sort of flirted with him. I did sympathize with her, but I also felt used. I was also angry that she hadn't wanted him or tried to help him when he was down and out.

A couple of days before Dad died, while he was delirious and incoherent, Pam brought an attorney into his hospital room and changed his will, making herself the major benefactress. That's when I started hating her, too. Regardless of whether Mom and I agreed about all this or not, it seemed to me the urgency of current events was more important for us to discuss with Richie.

"Hopefully your experience here will be better," he said with a gentle smile. "It's important that you have a safe place where you can discuss your feelings. Do you have any questions?" He looked at my mother and then at me.

She shook her head no.

"Are we going to discuss our relationship?" I blurted out.

She winced as though bracing for a blow. I hadn't wanted to make her feel that I was blaming her. I'd just hoped that we could work on our relationship as we worked through what had happened. We might as well get everything out in the open.

"Inevitably," Richie said, "but we don't have to do it all right now." He leaned toward my mother and asked her in a kind voice, "How do you understand what Melanie did?"

She inhaled deeply. "I warned Luke to be careful when he asked her to move in with him. She's like a black widow spider, luring men into her web and then destroying them when they profess their love for her."

Richie glanced at me. I nodded.

"Luke turned the tables on her. She wanted to marry him, but he broke up with her. When he ended the relationship, she became very depressed and suicidal. I think a lot of it had to do with the fact that her father had died recently. She was angry at her father for leaving her. She has major abandonment issues. So she took all that out on Luke, and, ultimately, herself."

The compassion in her voice and the accuracy of her assessment surprised me. Sometimes she put things in such a mean, accusatory way that I immediately became defensive and antagonistic. Now she seemed sympathetic toward me.

Richie turned to me. "Melanie, what do you think about what

your mother said?"

"She's probably right," I mumbled. "I was furious at my father for coercing me into going to medical school and then dying right before I graduated."

She interjected, "Then she punished me by refusing to attend her own graduation ceremony."

My mother had never told me how she felt about my becoming a doctor, although my sister told me that Mom was proud of me. Thinking about it now, I can see that it was more important to her than I realized. She must have imagined how she'd feel watching me get my diploma, knowing that her daughter had achieved what, in her mind, all parents dream of for their children. I also think my "success" may have mitigated the pain of some of her other wounds. While she'd never have the money or social standing of her friends, she had something they would envy, a child who was a doctor. My depriving her of her "day in the sun" was a cruel blow to her. It was the type of thing Dad did repeatedly. He'd give us something to look forward to, then take it away. I had not done it to hurt her; maybe he didn't either.

"So she punished everyone except the person she was really mad at," said Richie.

"That's always been the case. Whenever her father hurt her, she'd hurt herself even more. She couldn't hurt him back because she needed his love so much she'd do anything to win his approval." She rooted around in her purse and pulled out a pink wrinkled tissue. "But she knew, on some deep level, that it was her success that hurt him the most. I sometimes think she failed in order to protect him, and her relationship with him."

Richie leaned toward my mother. "I'd like to cut the session short so I can spend some time talking to you alone."

"Why, so you can talk about me?" I regretted it the minute I said it. It sounded paranoid and defensive.

"Actually, I want to talk to your mother about maybe getting some individual counseling for herself."

"Oh," I said contritely. I'd been encouraging her to go into therapy for years, but she always resisted. I thought it would be good for her to have someone objective and supportive to talk to. I hoped my crisis would lower her resistance and that Richie could convince her to seek help for herself.

CHAPTER 21

I cracked open the door to the conference room, squeezed through the opening, and leaned against the wall. Five patients sat in metal chairs arranged in a circle. Dr. O'Riley sat nearest the door. A man on the opposite side of the circle from where I stood was talking softly.

Dr. O'Riley introduced me to the group. "Here's Melanie. She'll be joining us from now on. Sit over there, next to David," he said, pointing to the only empty chair in the circle. "Let's go around the circle and introduce ourselves." He nodded at Wendy, who was sitting to his right.

"Wendy," she said looking directly at me. "I'm being discharged tomorrow." She didn't add that she was a resident in Luke's training program and that she and I already knew each other.

"Dr. O'Riley, group leader and head psychologist for the hospital. Welcome to the group."

It bothered me that he said "head" psychologist, when he could have just said "psychologist." I had a feeling he was trying to put me in my place and assuage his own ego, because psychologists (Ph.D.s) are paid less and shown less respect than medical doctors (M.D.s). *How long will I be able to tolerate his competitive, narcissistic bullshit?*

"Bruce. I'm bipolar," said an attractive man in his forties. *He must attend AA meetings where the members introduce themselves as alcoholics.*

"David," said the gangly young man sitting to my right.

"I'm Tanya. I have a dual diagnosis," announced the woman sitting to my left. *You also have dual-colored hair.*

"I'm, uh, James," said the man who'd been speaking when I

walked into the room. His voice was soft and kind. I noticed he was slightly effeminate, handsome in an oblique sort of way, and roughly my age. His diagnosis eluded me, so I was curious to know more about him.

"We were talking about the stigma attached to being a psychiatric patient," said Dr. O'Riley. "Melanie, are you concerned about people knowing you're a patient here?" He stared at me with his beady eyes.

"I'd prefer it not be on the front page of the newspapers, but right now I'm more worried about getting to go outside than I am about my reputation." I looked at Wendy.

"What does the group think about what Melanie said?" Dr. O'Riley queried as though reading from a Group Therapy 101 textbook.

The group leader's primary role is to keep bringing the topic back to the group, to facilitate the participants' interaction and to interpret or, depending upon their sophistication, to encourage them to interpret the group dynamic. The impact of having group members confront one another is much stronger than having the leader do it. Presumably, when a patient is confronted with the effect he has on his peers, it increases his awareness of how he contributes to his difficulties in his relationships outside the group. Being a successful group leader requires a high level of intuitive finesse. When the leader is facile, his influence is hardly noticeable. Group members are much more comfortable participating in the process. Gentle pushes and savvy, well-timed interpretations can mean the difference between a productive therapeutic group and a waste of time.

Ideally, the leader remains objective and neutral, using his feelings as a gauge as opposed to a hammer. For instance, if I had been running the group and Dr. O'Riley were a participant, I'd pay attention to the fact that he got my hackles up with his boastful introduction. Knowing my reaction was based on my own personal triggers, I'd only make a mental note of it, waiting to see if the rest of the group found him arrogant. If they did, I'd let them confront him. I might ask what each person thought about the introduction, but wouldn't reveal my reaction. I'd try to be subtle yet directive, so as not to call attention to myself and detract from the interaction of the group members with one another.

My knowledge and proficiency in running groups was working against me. I felt antagonistic and resistant because I resented having to be in a group with a leader I didn't respect and patients who I assumed (perhaps incorrectly) were less sophisticated than I. If this had been a group of my peers, I would have been more amenable because I respected my colleagues' observations and opinions of me, even though I often got slammed in those groups and felt ashamed at having my weaknesses brought to light. In *this* group I wasn't willing to expose myself if I could help it.

"Maybe she's focusing on her frustration about not being allowed to go outside in order to avoid dealing with her real problems," said Wendy.

I made eye contact with her briefly, then telepathically implored her to talk to me outside of group.

"What do you think about what Wendy said?" Dr. O'Riley asked me.

I wanted to shout back, "I think you're an asshole who lacks any originality or spontaneity." Instead, I meekly replied, "She's probably right." *Luke taught her well.*

Looking at his watch, Dr. O'Riley said, "We have to stop for today. We'll resume this conversation next time. Does any one have anything to say to Wendy?"

"Good luck," everyone mumbled in unison.

Please tell Luke I'm sorry and that I love him.

After dinner, I dropped the folder Dr. O'Riley had given to me along with a No. 2 pencil onto my pillow. Sprawling out on my bed, I propped myself on my elbows. The first questionnaire, Beck's Depression Inventory, contained twenty-five statements, each followed by two blank circles, one for yes, and the other for no. Each statement alluded to some aspect of clinical depression. For example: "I no longer enjoy the things I used to" and "My appetite is worse than usual."

When I was done with the inventory, I started working on the symptoms checklist. Midway through the third questionnaire, my eyes started burning and my head ached. I kept staring at the question, "Sometimes I feel angry at people in authority positions." The words began to blur. I put my pencil under the pillow and rested my head on the folder.

"Did you finish your algebra homework?" my father demands as he barges into my bedroom.

"Hold on," I say to my cousin Eddie, who I'm talking to on the phone. He's in all of my classes. "Yes," I tell my father.

"Let me see it." He grabs the notebook from my bed.

"I'll call you back," I say, and hang up the phone. We replay this scenario almost every night. With tears streaming down my face, I climb through my window onto the roof above the kitchen and knock on the skylight to get my mother's attention. She looks up sympathetically, but that's all she can do before I hear his footsteps coming back toward my door. I hurry back inside and sit at my desk, pretending to read. He storms into my room.

"You had two answers wrong," he bellows.

"I'm sorry," I whimper.

"You'll never get into a good college if you don't ace algebra. I brought you a hundred practice problems. Call me when you finish them." He pulls my phone line out of the wall and drops a folder full of algebra problems on my bed.

"I'm only in eighth grade," I shout. "I don't care about college."

I lifted my head off the folder, darkened the "yes" circle and went on to the next question. The next two tests were pure drudgery. The fifth, the Minnesota Multiphasic Personality Inventory (MMPI), consisted of a few hundred questions, many of which were redundant.

As I suffered through it, I scribbled lines through my answers and pierced holes in the paper with the point of my pencil. At one point, I threw the test on the floor and stomped on it while cursing Dr. O'Riley. In the midst of the tantrum, I realized I was projecting my anger at my father -- and at my whole situation -- onto Dr. O'Riley.

CHAPTER 22

Susan came into the laundry room where I was doing jumping jacks. "Dr. Lancet wants to talk to you. He has good news."

She walked me to the therapy room and gave me the thumbs up.

Dr. Lancet glanced at me and motioned toward the chair across from his. "I have a couple of things to discuss with you. First, the staff and I decided to move you into your own room because you're playing therapist to your roommate."

It was true. Terry often talked to me about her problems and, although I always told her to bring it up later with Dr. Lancet, I gave her my best professional feedback.

"Can you blame me?" I snapped. "I *am* a therapist!"

"That wasn't a criticism. We just think you'll be better off concentrating on your own situation." His gentle tone diffused my anger immediately.

"Okay," I said contritely. "What else?"

"Since you've been here a week and haven't acted out in any significant way, the staff and I agreed to increase your status so you can attend activities off the unit."

I wanted to jump up and down from excitement. "You mean I can go outside?"

"Let's see how you do in structured activities. And Melanie … going off unit is a privilege, not a right. If you act out or do anything to jeopardize your increased status, I'll confine you to the unit immediately and ask questions later. Do you understand?" he asked pointedly.

"Yes." I felt as grateful to him for setting limits as for allowing me privileges.

"You're scheduled for Phys Ed this afternoon."

After quiet time, I rushed to the unit door and paced in front of it. The other patients trudged down the hallway, less than enthused.

A psych aide herded us into the alcove between the two locked doors.

"We all have to stay together on the way to the gym. Once we get there, you can do whatever you want except leave the gym. Got it?" She waited for us to mumble "yes" before unlocking the door. I scooted through the door and marched in place.

We took the elevator two floors down and walked through the bowels of the building, past the central laundry room, vending machines, and the huge institutional kitchen. I burst into the gym, grabbed a basketball and sprinted back and forth, shooting lay-ups. Several groups of patients stood around talking, while the psych aides chatted among themselves near the exercise equipment. Soon I became oblivious to all of them and started hearing my father's voice in my head.

"Come on, Mel. Shoot the ball ... You're the best one out there. Act like it! What's the Matter with you? Don't dribble -- shoot! What happened to you out there? You looked like you were half-asleep."

"I am half-asleep. I'm only in ninth grade, yet I have insomnia, I'm starving myself to death, and I'm pulling out clumps of my hair while I huddle in the corner of my room, wishing I were dead. Besides, I'm not and never will be the best. That's your fantasy, not mine." That's what I want to say to him. Instead, I shrug and say, "I guess I just had an off-day."

"Well, don't let it happen again," he admonishes.

I love playing on the basketball and tennis teams, but it seems that everything I enjoy for its own sake, my father sees as my potential claim to fame. I enjoy playing sports because I naturally excel, but I don't aspire to be the best.

At age eleven I learn to play tennis in sleep-away camp. I am such a natural, that I wind up winning the camp tournament. I am proud of that, but my father wants me to take it further. He immediately enrolls me in winter tennis lessons and tries to convince me to go on tour. I have no desire to do so. To me it is just a hobby, but his message — that good is never good enough — makes me feel as if I have failed him

"Your mother's in the lounge," said Cheryl when I returned to the unit.

I'd forgotten to call her to tell her I wouldn't be on the unit at three. I knew she had a book with her though because she takes one wherever she goes. I hurried to the lounge where Mom sat on the piano bench reading her latest detective novel.

"Dr. Lancet let me go to the gym. It felt so good to exercise." I said excitedly before collapsing onto the couch.

She closed the book and slipped it into her purse. "Don't you think it's strange that you're in the hospital because you nearly killed someone, yet all you seem to care about is exercise?"

"Exercise isn't the only thing I care about." I was on the defensive.

"What else concerns you, being skinny?" She glared at me.

"When I don't get enough exercise I feel jittery and anxious." Ever since I had first begun to lose weight, my mother yelled at me to eat and disapproved of all my exercising. She was concerned about my health, but I always suspected she was enraged by her lack of control over me.

"You need to focus less on your discomfort and more on the reality of your situation. Has it occurred to you that you need a lawyer?" she asked angrily.

"Of course not; Luke said he wasn't going to file charges." I had no idea where she was coming from.

"Well, *somebody* did. I don't know whether or not it was Luke." Her tone became less aggressive.

"When were you planning to tell me, right before the guillotine decapitated me?" I leaned my head on the arm of the couch and closed my eyes. I felt exhausted by this news.

"I'm sorry, Mel. I wanted to talk to Dr. Lancet before I told you, but you got me so angry I let it slip. I called him earlier and left a message."

I couldn't believe this was happening.

"I've already contacted a lawyer." She stood. "Let's get a drink of water and a washcloth for your face."

"Mom?" I leaned against her. "Why didn't Daddy come to any of my varsity basketball games or tennis matches?"

"Oh, Mel," she said with so much compassion in her voice, I wanted to cry. "Don't you remember? He was so depressed he couldn't get out of bed."

When my mother left, Cheryl told me I should move my stuff to my new room. "It's the last one on the right, all the way at the other end of the hall. If you need help, just holler."

Aside from some clothes, the only things I'd asked my mother to bring were some of my psychiatry books and most treasured novels. Among my favorites were Tolstoy's *War and Peace*, Hermann Hesse's *Siddhartha*, and Somerset Maugham's *Of Human Bondage*. I gathered them up and put them on the butcher-block desk in my new room. A matching armoire and wood-framed bed were the only other furnishings. There was also a closet and a tall, rectangular, slatted window facing the parking lot. I bolted to the nurse's station to get the little crank to open the slats in the window. On the way, I nearly crashed into Dr. Lancet.

"I just talked to your mother." He pointed to the therapy room. "She told me about the charges."

I slumped in a chair.

"I'm very concerned about how you're taking the news." The gravity of his tone frightened me.

"Well, I'm kind of scared, not to mention shocked. My original fear was that Luke would be angry with me if he found out what I'd done. It never occurred to me there's be all these other consequences."

"He's angry all right. So are a lot of other people." He continued to scrutinize me.

I blinked back tears.

"I'm going to put you on constant observation overnight."

"Why? I'm not a danger to myself or others," I deliberately used the psychiatric jargon.

"I want to be on the safe side. You've just received some horrifying news and we don't know how you're going to react when it starts to sink in."

"Does this mean I can't go off the unit tomorrow?" I wiped my eyes with my sleeve thinking how cruel it would be for him to increase my status and then decrease it when I hadn't done anything wrong.

"We'll talk about it tomorrow," he said kindly. "This is not a punishment; it's a precautionary measure."

A few minutes later, Chris, the cute psych aide, approached me. "I'll be your observation person for awhile." He helped me carry the rest of my stuff to my new room, but didn't enter because male staff can't go into female patients' rooms. He reminded me it was dinnertime. "The staff member assigned to the dining room will keep an eye on you."

"So if I stab myself with a plastic knife, the cafeteria monitor will be held responsible?" I asked sarcastically and nudged him gently with my elbow.

After dinner, Chris was waiting for me outside the dining room. "We have a little problem," he whispered. "While you were eating, we searched your room. Nancy found your suppositories." He wagged his index finger at me.

"Fuck!" I exclaimed loudly. My mother had just brought them for me. I hadn't even used them yet. "Is she going to put me into solitary confinement or something?"

"No, she'll give you a lecture, that's all." He rolled his eyes. "She already called the doctor-on-call to confiscate the suppositories."

I couldn't stand the fact I had no privacy. What got to me even more was that this big, fat, disgusting turd was in charge of me. She reminded me of the some of the nurses I'd worked with-- especially the one that turned me in for not completing that fateful physical exam. She and others like her were power-hungry, self-righteous individuals. They were always going tête-à-tête' with the staff. I couldn't stand being on the receiving end of her tyranny.

Nancy approached, waving the plastic bag with the suppositories in front of my face. "Where did you get these?"

I stared at the little hairs sprouting from the mole on her cheek. I wanted to pluck them out of her goddam face one by one, making her beg for mercy.

"Are you hiding anything else in your room?" Her face was bright red and the veins were popping on her forehead.

"Get away from me!" I shouted as I stormed to my room, slammed the door behind me and dove onto my bed.

CHAPTER 23

The following morning, Dr. Lancet approached me before breakfast. "Chase, come with me."

"Why are you here so early?" I asked, following him to the therapy room.

"One of the nurses called me much earlier than I appreciated to tell me about your little incident." He shoved his shoulder against the therapy room door to open it.

I slinked past him, lowered myself into the chair near the wall and hung my head.

"You just can't take no for an answer, can you?" he scowled, but his tone of voice indicated that he was fighting back a grin.

"Isn't that why I'm here?" My smart-aleck side shot back. I could tell he thought the supposed urgency of my transgression was nonsense.

"Actually, I'm surprised it took you so long to show your true colors." He put my chart on his lap and opened it.

"That bitch violated my rights. She searched my room without my permission," I said defiantly.

"Melanie, you're a committed mental patient. You have no rights."

"I don't even have the right to go to the bathroom once in awhile?" I felt exasperated.

"We already talked about this." He sounded bored.

"This couldn't have waited until later? I mean; it's not like I was hiding a stash of cocaine or anything. It was just a few stupid suppositories. I'm surprised she didn't call in the National Guard."

"Nancy was adamant that I see you before she left. Anyway, we need to talk about this," he said, pulling an envelope from his shirt pocket and handing it to me. "It's a letter from Luke."

"Why is it addressed to you?" I couldn't catch my breath -- I felt like I was being strangled. The mere mention of his name shook me up. I missed him so much. Whenever I thought about him, I trembled in the agony of longing for him. Now, seeing his actual handwriting and knowing that not only had he touched the letter, but was thinking about me enough to write it, I felt excited and frightened. *Was it a love letter? Had he finally come to his senses?*

"Luke called me. He wants to make sure you understand that he will never talk to you again. I told him to put it in writing for you." His sharp eagle eyes stayed on me.

"When did he call? Why didn't you tell me?" I stared at the two typewritten paragraphs, but the words seemed to be jumping around the page. In my intense anxiety, my visual perception played tricks on me. I laid the letter on my lap and strained to read it. He took two paragraphs to tell me how much I had hurt him and his family, how frightened he was of me now, that I must have been very angry to do what I had done, and he hoped I get the help I need in the hospital. He reiterated over and over that he would never talk to me again and I was not to contact him or anyone in "the gang" ever again.

The tone of the letter leaned toward cold neutrality. The word choices didn't even sound like Luke's. I wanted to believe that Jack or Steve wrote it and either signed Luke's name or coerced him into signing it. There was no "Love," "Best," "Regards," or even a "Sincerely" before his signature. *He must be conflicted about how he feels about me. Otherwise he would have ended the letter differently.* I still couldn't wrap my mind around the idea that Luke and I were truly over. I chose not to believe most of the letter. Maybe if I destroyed the letter, I could somehow destroy the sentiments Luke expressed in it. I crumpled the letter in my fist.

"How do you feel about it?"

I un-crumpled it and quickly perused it again. "I still don't believe that I'll never see him again." I was shaking uncontrollably.

"The reality is, you will never, ever see him, talk to him, call him, stalk him, or have any kind of contact whatsoever with him again." As harsh as it was, this stern admonishment was exactly what I needed. It was like a slap in the face to bring someone out of shock. If it had been less emphatic, it wouldn't have roused me. If there had been any ambiguity in Dr. Lancet's warning, any inkling that maybe someday I could contact him, I would cling to that rather than set about the excruciating process of trying to let go of Luke.

"Do you understand what I'm saying?"

I read it once again to see if I had missed something. I was sure there must be a hidden message -- something to give me hope about a future for us together, or at least his acknowledgement that he still loved me. "Yes, I understand." I traced Luke's signature with my index finger.

"I'm not convinced you truly understand the gravity of this situation, but let me lay it out for you another way. If you do anything stupid regarding Luke, there will be dire consequences." Dr. Lancet was more resolute than I'd ever seen him.

"I won't," I whispered, feeling like a disobedient child. I thought Dr. Lancet knew I would eventually try to figure out a way around the rules and was punishing me in advance.

"Okay." Dr. Lancet's tone became less formal. "I'm sure we'll talk about this a lot more over the course of your hospitalization. May I please have the letter back?"

"I can't keep it?" I asked. "You know, as a souvenir of the relationship that ruined my life?" I fondled it once more before folding it and stuffing it back in the envelope. As I handed it to him, my sense of loss was unbearable. "But seriously, what would be the harm in *my* keeping it?"

"At best, it would be another way for you to hold onto Luke psychologically. You need to let go of him. If you keep the letter, you'll read and re-read it constantly looking for hidden meanings and you'll be tempted to write back." He tucked the letter into his jacket pocket. "On another note, your attorney's coming here today."

I was distraught at this whole turn of events and walked back to my room dejectedly.

A few minutes later, Susan knocked on my door. "I have something for you," she chirped as she pushed the door open a crack.

"I hope it's an enema."

"No, but I'm sure you'll like it." She waved a rolled-up exercise mat through the partly open door. It was highly unusual that a staff member was giving me a gift. In all my years in therapy and as a therapist, I had never seen this before. Not only that, but I was confused by the mixed message. "We want you to address your eating disorder, but we're giving you something to make your exercising more comfortable." Still, I was thankful for the mat.

I placed it on the floor between the foot of the bed and the closet, laid down on it and started doing sit-ups. "Is it your turn to baby-sit me?"

"Dr. Lancet thought you might want to talk to me." She walked to the desk and put her hands on the back of the chair. "Do you mind if I sit?"

"Be my guest." I rolled onto my stomach to do push-ups.

She sat facing me. Strands of the yellow ribbon that held her little ponytail in place merged with the collar of her yellow polo shirt.

"My lawyer's coming today," I said between sit-ups. "Somebody filed charges. I may go to prison."

"You must be very frightened."

"Not really, I figure I can always kill myself if things get too bad," I said flippantly.

"I can see how that thought would be reassuring."

I wished she'd react more passionately, hugging me and saying how devastated she would be. But I knew that wasn't the case. She might feel bad for a little while or even liable if I did it on her watch, but then she'd go home to her family, get a new patient to replace me, and she wouldn't give me another thought.

"Dr. Lancet told me about the letter," she said, scooting closer to me.

"I'm trying not to think about it." I eased myself onto my back and rocked back and forth in a tucked position. "I'm sure if I try hard enough, I can convince myself it never happened, or at least that someone else coerced him into writing it."

CHAPTER 24

I paced in front of the unit door while Susan welcomed my mother and the lawyer. I was amazed at how much he resembled Tom Cruise in *The Firm.* As they entered the alcove, he said something that made Susan and my mother smile.

"Hi, Mom," I said, feeling left out. "What's so funny?"

Before she could answer, the attorney reached for my hand. "Hi, Melanie. I'm Tom Aiello. I'm sorry to be meeting you under these circumstances."

"I think the conference room is unlocked," Susan said.

Tom and my mother followed Susan, side by side. I lagged a few steps behind. "Dr. Lancet will join you shortly."

I walked around the table, pulled a chair out and sat with my back against the wall. I wanted to sit on the floor, but knew I should try to act like an adult to assure everyone that I was taking this seriously. Mom sat across from me and flashed a look of disgust when I tilted the chair back. *Why can't you sit like a normal person?* She seemed to be restraining herself from asking.

Tom placed his briefcase on the table and sat next to me. Facing me, he said, "I think it's important for your mother to sit in with us. Is that okay with you?"

I was surprised he'd even asked me. It seemed obvious she had to participate. Maybe he sensed the tension between us and, in an effort to show he wasn't fully aligned with her, was letting me feel as if I had a say.

"Yes," I said reluctantly. Even under normal circumstances, I felt awkward in my mother's presence. I craved her approval and feared her criticism.

"If you want to talk privately, we can do so afterwards." He removed a legal pad and pen from his briefcase. "I assume you know you've been charged with assault in the first degree, a felony."

"Oh, shit!" I exclaimed. "No, I didn't know that." I couldn't believe it. The worst thing that had ever happened to me before from a legal point of view was getting a speeding ticket, and that was back in college.

"I've spoken with your mother and Dr. Lancet, both of whom filled me in on your situation. I must say; it's quite a unique story." He said the last part with such a twinkle in his eye that I almost expected him to slap me on the back and say, *"Way to go, kid!"*

"It's unique all right," I mumbled. I hardly needed to be praised for my ingenuity. As resistant as I was to facing the truth, I knew it was more important for me to be confronted with the severity of what I'd done than to have it made light of.

"I'd like you to tell me all the details. When I'm sure I have a firm grasp on the facts, I'll give you my legal recommendations."

"Would you mind if I sat on the floor?" I glanced at my mother, then back at him. I felt so wiped out that I didn't have the energy to fight gravity and focus on my story at the same time. I'd have preferred to be lying down, but knew that was beyond acceptable.

"Not at all." He looked at my mother and put up his hand to stop her from protesting. I sat with my back against the wall, hugging my knees to my chest. I was a foot or so behind Tom, diagonally, and directly across from my mother. I had a clear view of their feet and legs.

"Sometime in mid-May," I began, "I went to Luke's house when he wasn't home and poured Prolixin, an antipsychotic medication, into the drinks in his refrigerator."

"All right, now walk me through it. How'd you pick the drug? How'd you get it? How'd you decide when to go to his place? How'd you get into his house? Tell me all that."

"My friend Mark and I figured out I needed a colorless, tasteless, odorless, non-lethal drug to put in his drinks. He came up with

Prolixin, which totally fit the bill." I thought back to the day Mark and I came to that fateful decision. He was so excited. I was not at all excited. I was, however, relieved that we had a viable plan. "I had access to a lot of psychiatric meds on my unit. They kept all the patients' medications in a cabinet in the nurses' station. I looked in the cabinet to see what was there, and there was a ton of Prolixin. I had to find a time when nobody was going to be in that room, and when the cabinet was unlocked. It took a couple of days to figure that out." I recalled the anxiety leading up to taking the bottle of Prolixin, which I slipped into the pocket of my lab coat, and then quickly took to my office and locked in a drawer.

"Was the bottle full?" asked Tom.

His voice pulled me out of the immediacy of the act. "It was probably two-thirds full."

"And while you're going through this whole process, you're still talking to Luke?"

"Yes, that was the problem. He had just told me that he and the gang were about to sign the papers to purchase the land to build their houses on-the house that I was supposed to build with Luke. That's what pushed me over the edge. After that, we decided to take a breather because we agreed it would be too difficult for me to hear about the progress of the land deal without being part of it, and too hard for him to move on if he remained so involved with me. We were still talking for a few minutes here and there. That was just to figure out when I could go to his house to use his VCR."

"Did you ever think, 'I shouldn't do this'?"

"I had a few moments like that, but the idea of doing it made me feel so relieved. That feeling of relief overrode the doubt. What I was thinking was that I needed to do it when he wasn't going to be home. I had already been fired, or at least my contract was not renewed, but I was the only one of all twelve residents to be asked to give Grand Rounds, which is a presentation to the entire hospital. Luke was proud of me for that and allowed me to use his VCR to make dubs of the tapes for my presentation. I'd been going over to his house on a regular basis when he wasn't home anyway. I still had a key, and it was no big deal for me to be at his house during the day. That's why I wasn't worried about getting in, being seen, or even his knowing I'd been there. I used to tell him whenever I was going over, just to make sure it was a convenient time for him."

He scratched his head. "Did Mark go with you?"

"No, but he knew when I was going. I called him right after I did it, too. He thought it was really funny."

"So you went to the house, and then what?"

"Well, it's like when you're about to do something you know you shouldn't. The anxiety level is so high that you feel like you can literally explode, but it's like being on the verge of an orgasm, too. It's a heady combination -- titillating and frightening. That's what it felt like when I unlocked the door. All I really worried about was that Luke would find out and be really pissed at me. When it turned out the police were involved and there was all the legal stuff, I was like, *WHAT?!?* I'm telling you, it was so far removed from my thought process. I walked in and I remember locking the door behind me, which I didn't usually do. I opened the refrigerator and looked at the drinks. He had the usual suspects -- white wine, ginger ale, and orange juice. He used to drink a glass or two of wine every evening."

"Did you put it in all three?" Tom wanted to know.

"Um hm."

"And how'd you do it? Be specific. Did you take it out of the refrigerator and hold it over the sink...?" He had been writing furiously and only stopped to ask these questions.

"No, the refrigerator was in a corner of the kitchen across from the door and there was a counter next to it. I took the drinks out of the fridge and put each on the counter, one at a time, and poured a third of the bottle into one drink, then replaced it. I repeated this two more times with the other drinks until the bottle was empty. Then I put the bottle back in my pocket."

Tom furrowed his brow, deep in thought. "Right before you did it, did you have a 'wait a minute -- maybe I shouldn't do this' moment, or did you just want to get it done?"

"I just wanted to get it done. Right after I did it, I had a moment of 'Shit, what did I just do?'"

"But after you did it, you could have gone back and taken all the bottles out."

"That never occurred to me."

"At what moment did you think 'oh, shit, what did I do?' How many minutes before you left the house?"

"Probably just before."

"But you left anyway."

"I had a lot of anxiety as I was leaving, locking the door and getting in my car. But once I was a few blocks away, I kind of put it out of my mind. Remember, I wasn't even sure he'd get sick."

"When's the next time you talked to him?"

"Maybe a day or so later, briefly, just about the VCR."

"Were you anxious waiting to find out if he got sick?"

"I don't think so. You know, it was the sort of thing you kind of put out of your mind to the point where you totally deny it."

"How long was it before he got sick?"

"Probably a few days. There was still stuff in his drinks, so it was ongoing." The speckles in the linoleum tiles seemed to be dancing around.

"So when he got sick, what was your feeling...relief? It worked? I have him? What were you thinking?"

"Relief. 'Thank God.'" My head was pounding.

"Not 'Holy Fuck?'"

"No, because it never occurred to me he'd get so sick. I just thought he'd finally realize he needed me and off we'd go into the sunset. The whole problem was that he'd never stop focusing on the external long enough to realize he needed me. He knew he loved me, he kept telling me that. To me it was just a matter of cutting the other shit out of his life so he'd realize he wanted to be with me. I wanted him to need me." Suddenly I felt totally exhausted, as I always became when stressed out.

"Oh, and there's one other thing. A week or so before the poisoning, I went to Luke's in a fit of rage and tried to break his stereo and computer. I ran paper clips along the wires and through the disc drive. I also scratched his favorite CDs and dragged the paper clip along the frets of his electric guitar."

"Oh," he said, as though it barely mattered.

I knew that the ransacking was more significant than his reaction implied. It was part of what had led to the bigger crime, kind of like how marijuana is a gateway drug to heroin. Because I'd never heard from Luke about his property being damaged, I'd assumed I hadn't, in fact, broken anything. While I felt calmer doing the act, that feeling only lasted a day or so. When my agitation came back, it did so with a vengeance. I returned to Luke's house at 2 A.M. a few nights later, when I knew he'd be sound asleep, and poured sugar into his gas tank. Mark was thrilled that I had actually done what he suggested. I never heard if there were consequences to that action, either.

"When did he go to the hospital?"

"A week or so later." I remembered the panic I felt when they took him away from me to take him to the hospital. I wanted to make them bring him home--back to me.

The door opened and Dr. Lancet walked in. He sat down next to my mother. Dr. Lancet looked at me quizzically. I stood up and moved to a chair next to Tom. For reasons I did not understand then, I felt strong enough in Dr. Lancet's presence to pull myself together. Much later, I understood that his clarity about his expectations of me, coupled with his nonjudgmental way of treating me, made me want not only to please him, but also to try harder for myself.

"What happened that made him go to the hospital?" Tom asked.

"The neurologist became alarmed at his condition." I looked at Dr. Lancet, who was whispering something to my mother.

"What was his condition?" asked Tom.

"He was so stiff that he could barely walk, talk or swallow." I felt more and more anxious as the image of Luke in the hospital that first day appeared in my mind. The face in the image suddenly morphed into my father's on his deathbed. In the weeks preceding his death, he'd had a similar look. Fear, helplessness, confusion in his eyes, loss of volitional movement, and, worst of all, the loss of dignity. A strong man turned helpless infant. It was still practically impossible for me to believe that I played any role in his condition, but the longer that image stuck in my mind, the more real it became. This image gradually shape-shifted into that of the first patient I treated as a medical intern -- one who had the same name as my father, and then went on to be a patient during my neurology service. He died about two weeks after I started treating him. He had often referred to me as his daughter.

"How long was he in the hospital?"

"I was hospitalized while he was still there, but Dr. Lancet told me Luke called him from home. That was less than a week after I got here. I guess it was about four weeks." I looked at Dr. Lancet, who nodded in the affirmative.

"What did they do for him while he was there?"

"Lots of blood tests, CT scans, MRIs, PET scans, and a brain biopsy." I mumbled that last word.

"Did you say a *brain biopsy*?" he asked incredulously. "I didn't know about the biopsy. That changes things. Let me think for a minute." He pressed a closed fist to his lips. About thirty seconds later, he asked, "Have you thought about what you want to do regarding court? Specifically, do you want to go to trial, or try to work out a plea bargain?"

I was surprised he'd even ask about a trial. "I definitely don't want a trial," I told him. "Besides, I already confessed."

"That's smart, especially since a jury would most likely hang you. By the way, how did you get caught?" His voice held some morbid curiosity.

I glided off my chair and reoccupied my place on the floor. I wanted to disappear. "Mark, my so-called best friend, called Luke's hospital when I told him about the brain biopsy. He remained a silent co-conspirator until they removed a piece of Luke's brain." I glanced up to see Tom's reaction.

"Hmm," he murmured. "Who is this Mark character?"

I told him all about Mark. I'd felt totally betrayed by him. He made an anonymous phone call to the hospital and didn't disclose who had administered the drug. Mark was the only one who knew what I'd done, so it didn't take Dick Tracy to figure out it was him. It turned out he also told the director of my residency program. I called Mark the minute I got home from the hospital that night and pleaded with him to somehow undo his actions. I told him I was going to have to kill myself if Luke found out, but Mark only grew cold and distant. I'm not sure why he changed his tune. I suspect it had to do with the fact that his father died unexpectedly while Luke was in the hospital. He went home for the funeral and stayed with his mother for a week. When he came back he seemed different.

"You know, legally speaking, Mark could be considered an accomplice. Would you want to pursue that?" asked Tom.

"It hadn't occurred to me, but I doubt it. I don't want to be like my father, who would have made excuses for his behavior and blamed everyone but himself." I'd hated that about my father, and so had my mother.

"Just out of curiosity," asked Tom, "was Luke so good in bed that you couldn't let go of him?"

His forwardness caught me off-guard, but it was really my mother's presence that made me uncomfortable, more than the question. "As a matter of fact, he was terrible." I held up my pinky and bent it suggestively. Actually, the sex sucked, but the closeness of having him on top of me, holding me -- that's what I loved. I wished he would stay attached to me, physically and emotionally, forever.

Tom let out a sigh. "Okay, I'll need to meet with the district attorney and start working out a plea bargain. Your arraignment is scheduled for mid-August."

Mid-August was still a month away. It was far enough away for me not to have to think about it. "By the way, who *did* file the charges against me?"

"One of Luke's doctors. That really doesn't matter, because once the hospital informed the state, charges would have been filed against you automatically." He turned to my mother and Dr. Lancet. "Do either of you have any questions?"

"No," said my mother, looking worn out.

"Nor do I," said Dr. Lancet. "But if you're finished with Melanie, I'd like to talk to her alone for a few minutes."

Tom reached out and shook my hand. "I'll be contacting you in the next week or so."

I watched my mother as she left the room with Tom.

Dr. Lancet walked around the table and sat next to me. "Are you okay?"

"I'm a little shaken up."

"I don't blame you," he said sympathetically. "You've got a tough road ahead of you. There's one other thing."

"What now?" I didn't think I had the strength to hear anymore bad news.

"Mark called me. He wants to visit you. I made it very clear that he was not to contact you under any circumstances," he said sternly.

"What if I want to see him?" I couldn't stop shaking. Despite his betrayal of me, I missed his friendship. That he had encouraged me, and made light of the whole thing, fed into my distorted way of thinking that somehow it was okay. In retrospect, I think he must have been vicariously living out his own revenge fantasies through me, knowing he didn't have the courage to carry them out himself. Mark was very concerned with projecting a certain image -- being calm, cool, collected, and in control of any situation. He had very pretty features and dressed meticulously. He spoke quietly, but with an air of authority, and he really knew his stuff. That was his public persona. But I knew his other side, as well. He had a caustic, almost sadistic, sense of humor and felt superior to most people. Whenever I was mad at Luke, he came up with ideas for revenge and encouraged me to carry them out. He also tried to fuel my anger at other people, but he cautioned me to stay in control at work. He was a good therapist, but lacked empathy. That's the reason he wanted to be a "traveling shrink," doing three-month stints filling in for other therapists all over the country. He had no desire to have his own patients and, truth be told, he would have preferred to be an Olympic figure skater more than anything else. I also suspect he was a closet borderline. My suspicions were bolstered by the fact that he was intensely interested in and even won awards for the research he did on Borderline Personality Disorder.

"Absolutely NOT!" Dr. Lancet pounded the table with his fist. "I think he's scared of being considered an accomplice and probably wants to feel you out on that. He's done enough damage to you already." He walked around the table to retrieve his briefcase. "Melanie, I still don't know if you understand how serious all this is, so I'm going to continue your constant observation status through the weekend."

"Just to be on the safe side, right?" I pantomimed slitting my throat.

"Correct," he said as he held the door open for me. "It's time for lunch. After lunch you have psych testing."

"Dr. Lancet?" I said as we left the conference room. "About the accomplice thing -- not that I would ever pursue it, but don't you think there's something to it?"

He stared at me. "That's right, you'll never pursue it. But yes, it would seem as though there's something to it."

CHAPTER 25

Susan joined me in the dining room. "Dr. Lancet told me about the meeting. Do you want to talk about it?"

"Yeah, that would be great."

When we arrived at my room, I dove onto my bed and scrunched my pillow against my chest. Susan sat at the door so she could watch the hallway. "I'm probably going to prison, but that's not what's upsetting me the most." I wanted to talk to her, but suddenly worried that she might just be listening because she had to or, even worse, because of the prurient appeal of my story.

"What is?" she asked so compassionately that I felt more inclined to trust her.

"When I told my lawyer the details of what I did to Luke, I felt nothing. It was like telling him about a book I'd read, not like describing something I lived through. It's not that I don't want to care about what happened, but more like it happened to someone else. I just can't connect to the whole thing."

"When the truth is too awful to bear, our mind blocks out our emotions," she said gently.

"I didn't feel anything when Luke was sick, either." I was exhausted. The effort involved in beating down the agonizing longing I felt for Luke had literally burned me out. I could think of him and feel nothing, the same way I had learned to live amidst the battlefield of my parents' marriage and feel nothing.

"It will come to you in bite-size pieces when you're strong enough to handle it. Why don't you sleep for a bit and I'll wake you when quiet time is over?" Her voice was as soothing as a lullaby.

"Okay," I whispered, already falling asleep.

I awakened sometime later to find Susan standing over me. "You have to go for psych testing."

We made small talk until we arrived at Dr. O'Riley's office. His office was about half the size of Richie's, with a rectangular table in the middle of the room, a large oak desk against the far wall, and an Impressionist painting on the wall above his desk.

He took a seat at the table and directed me to the chair across from him, closest to the door.

"I'm going to give you a full battery of psychological tests over the course of several sessions. Today we'll try to get through the figure drawings, both parts of the Bender-Gestalt, and part of the WAIS-R. We'll start with the figure drawing." He slid a piece of blank paper along with a pencil across the table to me. "Draw a person, then a woman, then a man, then yourself."

"I hate this shit," I said as I chewed on the pencil. "First of all, I can't draw to save my life. Second of all, I know how these tests are interpreted, so it's hard for me not to censor myself." Supposedly, the figures would represent my family, and how I drew them relative to one another and myself had significance. How I drew myself (i.e., the size and placement of my figure relative to the other figures, and what features I chose to detail or omit) would provide information about how I felt about myself in the context of my family. I believed in the merit of these tests, but given the circumstances, it was hard to be spontaneous. Then I realized I didn't even know what I wanted the test results to reveal. I quickly drew four stick figures and shoved the paper toward him, as though getting it out of my sight allowed me to disown it.

He put my drawing in the folder and handed me another blank piece of paper. "Now I'm going to show you some shapes and I want you to copy them exactly on your paper." He held up a white index card with a square on it. Then he showed me nine more cards, one at a time. He probably noticed I copied the shapes very deliberately, trying to get them perfect.

"Now I'm going to test your memory." These tests of concentration,

143

visual-spatial ability, and memory help pinpoint neurological deficits. None of them stand alone, but in combination, they provide great insight into psychological diagnoses and neurological deficits. "I'm going to recite a string of numbers and I want you to give them back to me." He read off a piece of paper.

I started chewing on my nails and recited the numbers back to him with my fingers in my mouth.

He wrote something on the paper. "Now do the same thing with these words." He read the names of objects in progressively longer groups.

"That's fine." He put the paper back into the folder and straightened the pile, squaring the edges. "Do you feel up to doing any more, or do you want to stop for today?"

"I'm pretty tired, but I could do one more test." By now I was struggling to keep my eyes open. Even though we'd only been at it for a little over an hour, I felt wiped out. It took a lot of energy to ward off all my interfering thoughts. *You better get the highest score on the planet. If you mess up, you're a failure. Well, of course you're a failure; you're STUPID!* Those, and thoughts about Dr. O. wanting me to fail and thinking I was ugly, vied for my attention. Fighting off at least three different voices inside my head — my mother's, my father's, and mine — made it difficult to pay attention to the task at hand.

"Okay, then we'll do the Rorschach Ink Blot Test. I'll show you one card at a time. Look at the card and tell me what you see. I'm going to write down what you say. When you finish talking, I'll remove the card and place another one in front of you. You'll follow the same instructions for all ten cards."

He placed a stack of five-by-eight cards and a legal pad in front of him, turned over the card on top of the pile and pushed it toward me. A black inkblot stood out against the white background; the bat-like image jumped out at me. As I continued staring at the "bat," I imagined it transformed into something else.

"A butterfly," I said. Then it shape-shifted further and, as it did, my anxiety began to escalate. "Now it's the face of a serial killer." I closed my eyes, no longer able to tolerate the image.

Leaning across the table, he asked, "Can you point to the things that make it look like a face?"

"This is the hair." I dragged my finger along the inkblot. "These are the eyes." I pushed the card toward him. I needed to get it away from me because it was scaring me.

He placed it on the bottom of the pile, scribbled something on his pad and placed the next card in front of me. With all the subsequent cards, I'd start out seeing a benign object, then I'd quickly imagine it had transformed into a dangerous person.

I understood how a projective test is supposed to work, yet I was shocked at my reactions. When you're subject to a lack of structure (the images are not defined, they only resemble other things), your imagination takes over. The ambiguity of the image causes you to tap into your deepest issues and to interpret the image as having to do with whatever feelings have arisen. I'd seen these cards many times before, but I had never looked at them for very long, nor had I been in such a vulnerable emotional state. Now I couldn't help letting the test work on me. I knew my responses indicated I was far from healthy. I still didn't trust Dr. O'Riley, but I couldn't afford to indulge my impulse to sabotage the test. I had begun to realize I needed all the help I could get.

After the eighth and final card, Dr. O. said, "In all my years of testing, I've never seen anyone get as agitated as you." He added, "Your protocol is replete with primitive rage and your responses are the most prolific of anybody I've ever tested."

I rocked back and forth trying to soothe myself. I felt so exposed. "Does that mean that I'm crazy or something?"

He told me he couldn't say anything definitive until he did the official scoring, but my responses indicated a history of severe trauma starting from a very early age.

I slumped so low in my chair that my chin rested on the table. What I really wanted to do was run and hide. I felt so vulnerable. "How early?"

"Very early."

Ever since I'd read about "Original Trauma Theory," which asserts that all our problems stem from a trauma that occurred during our first three years of life and are exacerbated and reinforced whenever we re-experience the trauma or something resembling it, I longed to find that one thing in my life that would explain everything else. Lacking knowledge of any particular culprit, I'd attributed my chronic depression, low self-esteem, and difficulties learning to genetics, and to living with a sort of low-grade ongoing trauma. I was surprised and hopeful that Dr. O might have unmasked an early incident that I hadn't known about.

He said it was clear that I find intimacy incredibly dangerous "to the point of being life-threatening," and I lose touch with reality when I feel threatened by intimacy.

"Do you mean I become psychotic?" I asked with trepidation. I wanted to believe I was sane. To me, psychosis represented the ultimate loss of control and the point of no return. On the other hand, if I had been psychotic when I poisoned Luke, then maybe I could begin to forgive myself and start moving forward. I asked if I could have been psychotic when I did that.

"That's a very complicated question," he said noncommittally as though deciding how much to disclose to me. "Your judgment was certainly impaired, but I'd prefer not to address whether you were psychotic until I score the tests."

CHAPTER 26

I was jogging back and forth in my room when Dr. Lancet appeared at my door. "Chase, get your skinny ass out here!"

I spun around, and saluted him. "Yes sir!"

"We can talk in there." He nodded toward the lounge. "Have you been eating? Your clothes are falling off you."

"A little." I was thrilled my clothes were getting even looser.

"I'm going to order a baseline weight today. Based on that, I'll decide about daily weights."

Oh shit, here we go. They'd weigh me and keep track of my weight every day. I wanted to weigh less than ninety pounds, but knew if I weighed under ninety-five, Dr. Lancet would make a bigger issue out of it. I dug my elbows into my hips to feel my protruding hipbones. Being able to feel them comforted me. I also prided myself on being able to feel the edges of my internal organs. It assured me I was in control of my body, if nothing else.

"Now that you've had time to think about the meeting with your attorney, how are you feeling?"

I shrugged. "Actually, I've been trying *not* to think about it. Frankly, I'm more upset about being on constant for three days in a row and being locked inside on these gorgeous sunny days."

"Melanie, that attitude is what landed you here in the first place. You pushed aside the reality of what you did to Luke while you watched him get sicker and sicker instead of facing up to the fact that you caused his illness." He closed the piano lid and leaned against it. "That's called compartmentalization. It was adaptive when you were younger and living in a difficult environment, but it's very dangerous to you now."

Whenever I used to tell people, particularly my friends in high school, what was going on at home, they would look at me with pity. Once in a while, their reactions gave me a glimpse of how very messed up my home life was. Mostly, it was as though I'd built a fortress between myself and reality. While the walls protected me from the pain, they also prevented me from living in the real world. I felt disconnected from everything and everyone, as though watching life through a tiny hole in one of those walls.

"Part of why you're in the hospital is so we can help you face your pain in a safe environment," he said kindly.

The feelings of distress arising inside me were overpowering. I hadn't been outside for two weeks. I needed fresh air and open space where I could work up some speed and get a decent workout. I asked him if I could go outside.

"Not yet, but I'll allow you to go off the unit with a one-on-one escort."

An hour or so later, Susan popped her head in the door. "Come on, kiddo. We need to weigh you."

I stood on the scale scared to look. I wanted to weigh in the 80s, but knew Dr. Lancet would be all over me if I weighed that little.

"Ninety-one pounds, that's too low." She wrote the weight in my chart. "Starving yourself isn't going to make things better."

I really wanted her to stop talking about it. "I'm going to take a nap before gym."

At the end of quiet hour, a psych aide woke me to take me to the gym.

As I waited for her to sign me off the unit, Dr. O'Riley arrived.

"I'll see you in group in a few minutes," he said as he walked past me.

Whipping around to face him, I told him I was going to gym, not group

"Sorry, but group takes precedence over gym."

That was the final straw. I *needed* to go to the gym. Dr. O's failure to perceive this pulled the trigger on my fury, which exploded with ferocious intensity.

Leaping toward him, I screamed in his face, "I hate you!" I charged down the hallway, knocking over lamps, kicking furniture and punching the walls. Halfway to my room, somebody grabbed my arm. I wrenched it free, continued running and opened my door so forcefully that the doorknob dented the wall. I slammed it so hard it sounded like a gunshot.

A voice called from the other side of the door. "Take it easy! We're going to find Dr. Lancet."

"Go to hell!" I shouted as I rampaged around my room tearing pages out of books and shredding them into tiny pieces, writing curse words on the walls and screaming obscenities at the top of my lungs. I dumped the contents of my drawers on the floor, yanked my clothes off hangers and stomped on them. I ripped the sheets off my bed and, as I was trying to tear a pillow in half, Susan knocked on the door. "May I come in?"

"I don't care."

She eased her way over to me and wrapped her arm around my waist. "I'm sorry you're so upset. I'm going to take you to the quiet room so you can calm down."

I let my body go limp and began to sob. Besieged by shame and horror at my loss of control, I was relieved to be stopped. I was exhausted. Destroying everything within reach had dissipated my rage. Susan's warm, non-threatening touch felt comforting. It was how I imagined a baby feels after throwing a tantrum and being rescued by the loving embrace of a parent.

She pressed a tissue against my nose. "Blow! We don't want you walking around with snot running down your face, do we?"

The hallway was empty as we walked past the nurses' station and veered down a narrow alcove to the "quiet room," a padded room the size of a walk-in closet.

The room was devoid of furniture except for a bare mattress on the floor. "Letting me go for a run would make much more sense than locking me in a two-by-four room like a psycho. All I need now is a straight jacket, and I'm ready for *One Flew Over the Cuckoo's Nest*."

"It's for your own good," said Susan, gently urging me forward.

I grabbed onto the doorframe and dug my heels into the floor, refusing to budge. The prospect of crossing that threshold was traumatic. I thought once I entered the quiet room, I would be irreversibly crossing the line from high-functioning doctor-patient to crazy- patient. The way I saw it, only the real crazies go into the quiet room. It's a slippery slope from there to becoming an eternal patient on the back wards of the State hospital.

"Melanie, please don't make this more difficult than it has to be," Susan pleaded. "Now that you're here, we need a doctor's order to release you."

I went through a mental list of my options. I could break loose and try to escape, I could barricade myself in my room, or I could acquiesce. I realized I really had no options. I took a few steps into the room.

"Why don't you lie down? I'm going to close the door for a minute while I get someone to sit with you." She stepped back.

"I don't want to lie down," I said, leaning against the far wall, facing the door. At least I still had a choice about what to do in there. Thankfully, I hadn't been put into restraints.

She closed the door and peered at me through the small shatterproof window at the top of the door before disappearing.

I pressed my face against the window and tried the doorknob; it was locked. A minute or so later, Chris cracked open the door and leaned his face inside. "Looks like you got yourself into some mess," he said jovially.

"You can say that again." I backed away from the door and sat on the mattress. He sat in a chair at the opening of the door.

No longer at the mercy of my rage, I had momentarily resigned myself to the situation. I knew the better I acted, the sooner I'd be released. I just needed a way to pass the time so I wouldn't have to think about how horrible I felt or about the repercussions of what I'd done. I rolled onto my back and started doing sit-ups "I guess the only way I could hurt myself in here would be to bang my head on the floor. But that would just make my excruciating headache hurt more. Would you tell me when I get to a hundred?" I raced through my first set of sit-ups and started doing push-ups.

"Are you still counting?"

"Yeah, that's ninety."

"Okay, now do the same for the jumping jacks…please?"

During my fourth set of push-ups, I pushed my face into the mattress. Suddenly, the urge to hurt myself became overwhelming. It was as if I needed to feel real physical pain to dissipate the power of the emotional pain that was taking over. I began pulling my hair and banging my head against the padded wall.

"What are you doing?" He jumped to his feet.

Clawing at my face, I felt blood trickling down my cheeks. "Get Dr. Lancet," I screeched. "I need help!"

Susan ran into the room. "We paged Dr. Lancet," she said, pulling my hands away from my face.

"I need something to take the edge off!" I sobbed. "I feel like ripping my face apart!" I watched my tears mixed with blood splat to the floor.

"Dr. Lancet's not in the building," said Chris from the door. "The doctor-on-call will be here any minute."

"I need Dr. Lancet, not some stupid resident!"

"The doctor-on-call will talk to him. He has to authorize any medication orders, anyway."

"May I talk to you?" A man's voice came from the door.

I looked up and recognized the doctor-on-call as a resident from my medical school. "I know him," I whispered to Susan.

"Sure," said Susan as she stepped just outside the door.

I watched them talking. After a few seconds, he walked away

and Susan came back. "He talked to Dr. Lancet. He's writing an order for Ativan." (Ativan is a benzodiazapene, in the same family of drugs as valium.)

"I worked with that guy in the psych ER. He's such a snob."

"You don't have to like him. He's just the temporary liaison between Dr. Lancet and you."

"I hope he doesn't recognize me." I said feeling totally humiliated and mortified.

"Don't worry; he's very professional." She patted the top of my head.

Her skin felt soft and cool as I held her hand against the scratches on my cheek.

"I'm going to get the medication. I'll be right back." She left the door ajar and returned quickly. "This should make you feel better," she said handing me a little yellow pill and a cup of water.

I swallowed the pill and gulped the water.

"Why don't you lie down? I'm going to ask Chris to come back and sit with you."

I curled into a fetal position and waited for Chris to return. "I'm so sleepy," I mumbled as I nodded off. When I awoke, Chris was still there. "Can I go back to room now?"

"That's up to Nancy and the doctor on call," he said.

"That fat fuck?" I said disdainfully before closing my eyes.

"Wake up, the doctor's here to evaluate you. It's already ten o' clock," said Nancy as she rumbled out of the room.

"Melanie, I'm Dr. Shamard. How are you doing?" He stood over me.

"I'm not sure. I just woke up." I turned my face toward the wall so he wouldn't recognize me.

"Do you know why I'm here?" He was holding my chart.

"To see if I'm a danger to myself or others?" I smiled into the mattress at my use of the clinical phraseology.

"Yes. I just need to talk to you for a little while."

I sat cross-legged on the mattress and hung my head toward my chest.

"Do you know where you are?"

"Yes, and I know my name and the date as well. We can skip the mental status exam and move on to the nitty-gritty." I wanted to regain some dignity by letting him know that I knew as much as he did.

"Do you know why you're in the quiet room?"

"Because I flipped out when I wasn't allowed to go to gym." I peeked up at him and was relieved to see he was writing in my chart, not looking at me. Just thinking about Dr. O'Riley telling me I had to go to group was enough to summon the feelings of out-of-control rage. I didn't feel out of control, but knew if I were subject to the same set of circumstances, I would lose it again.

"I'm going to call Dr. Lancet. Then I'll write an order releasing you from the quiet room." He stood. "Do you have any questions?"

"Can you leave a standing order for Ativan as needed?" I asked in my sweetest voice.

"That's what I need to discuss with Dr. Lancet." He walked out of the room and returned a few minutes later. "I talked to Dr. Lancet. I'm going to write the order for Ativan for overnight and discontinue the quiet room."

A few minutes later, a psych aide came to take me to my room.

CHAPTER 27

I cracked open the door and poked my head inside. "Oh, my God!" I stepped over clothes, books, and blankets and righted the chair I'd knocked over. Then I sat and surveyed the damage. I'd never done anything like this before. But my father had.

A week before my father died, he asked Dani and me to come to his apartment. He went over his will with the three of us, explaining he had divided everything into three equal parts. His explanation of the will was interspersed with his showing me the new mitt he had bought for the upcoming softball season, three months away. He discussed some other things he was planning to do in the future. His wife pulled me aside to tell me about their two trips to the emergency room in the past week for falling episodes.

Several hours after leaving his apartment, Dad's wife called to tell me he was in the emergency room again. "Shortly after you left, he took off all his clothes, ran outside, and started bringing handfuls of dirt into the apartment. He broke everything in the cabinets, destroyed some of his books, tried to kill the cats, grabbed his car keys and threatened to drive into the ocean."

"He seemed pretty calm when I saw him," I said. "Did anything happen after I left?"

"Not that I know of," she said.

"Maybe he finally realized he was dying," I said. "Maybe all that talk about his will put him over the top."

Later, the doctor in the emergency room asked me what medications he was taking.

"I'll go to his apartment and find out."

While looking in my father's medicine cabinet, I noticed a pile of human excrement in the bathtub. Gagging, I clasped his pill bottles against my chest (pills for high blood pressure, cholesterol, diabetes, and a bottle of narcotics for pain). I pocketed the bottle of Dexedrine then returned to the bedroom to call the doctor. The apartment had looked like a tornado hit it.

Now I nudged my books into a corner, dropped my clothes in heaps into my closet, laid on my stripped down bed and went to sleep.

It felt like just a few minutes had passed when I heard, Janice say, "Time to get up." Dragging myself out of bed, I looked out the window at the hospital parking lot. Soon I saw Dr. Lancet parking his black Saab. "Dr. Lancet's here early," I said out loud. "I hope he's here to see me."

Soon he appeared at my door. "Chase, come with me."

As we settled into our customary places in the lounge, he said in an annoyed tone of voice, "I had a few more phone conversations with Dr. Shamard than I appreciated last night, so you can imagine how thrilled I am to be here now. The only place I want to be this early in the morning is on the golf course." He pantomimed swinging a golf club.

"How do you think I feel? I know Shamard from medical school. That wasn't too humiliating," I said with dismay.

"So, what happened?" he asked, leaning on the piano.

"I was desperate to get to the gym and run around, but *you know who* informed me that I had to go to group instead. He may as well have told me he just ran over my dog. I wanted to kill him."

"Did you want to kill Dr. O'Riley the way you wanted to kill Luke?" He raised his eyebrows.

"You know I didn't want to kill Luke, or Dr.O, for that matter. I just needed to go to the gym to burn off some steam and he got in the way of my doing that. It had nothing to do with my feelings toward him as a person. It was simply that he caught me totally off guard. I basically went into a spontaneous combustion. It was that straightforward."

"And now?"

"Just thinking about that son of a bitch telling me I had to go to group instead of gym, I feel like punching the wall. I need something to help me get a handle on my rage."

"What do you have in mind?"

"You're the doctor," I said demurely. "However, when I was a doctor, I used a low dose of Stelazine with patients like myself."

"Don't you think it would be kind of ironic to prescribe a drug from the same class of medications you gave to Luke?" he said with a bit of a smirk.

"Yes, but that shouldn't preclude us from using it. I need it. I feel like a loose cannon." Now that the Ativan had worn off, I felt antsy and agitated.

"I'll start you on two milligrams of Stelazine twice a day." He wrote something in my chart. "But I don't want you to think you're in charge of your treatment. I'm only going along with you because I think the medication may in fact help you. Do you understand?"

"Yes, you're the doctor and I'm the patient," I said, bowing my head submissively. "Are you going to write a PRN for Artane in case I develop side effects?"

"No, I'll address your symptoms if and when they arise."

"You want me to experience the side effects like Luke did?" I couldn't believe he would want to punish me, especially now that he had earned my trust.

"No, Melanie, I want to be notified if you develop side effects so I can evaluate you personally."

"Oh," I said contritely. "But what if you're not around?"

"I can always be paged — even on the golf course."

"I remember those days," I said nostalgically.

Standing, he said, "I have to go to morning rounds."

"I remember *those* days, too." I suddenly felt sad. "It seems like only yesterday."

"It practically was," he said, closing the door behind us.

156

I went back to my room, cleared the debris from my exercise mat and started doing sit-ups. A few minutes later, Susan breezed into the room.

"Good morning, Sunshine. Whad'ya say we put your room back together?"

She picked a sheet up off the floor, untangled it and handed me an edge. "Want to talk about what happened yesterday?"

I watched her make a hospital corner and copied her. "Not really, but I guess I should." I went on to explain my father used to make all these promises to me and then renege at the last second, which infuriated me. I felt helpless. "That's exactly how I felt yesterday with Dr. O."

She asked me to elaborate as she fluffed up the pillow.

"Well, all he talked about from eighth grade on was getting into a good college. He made me take honors classes, demanded to see my homework and forced me to pursue any extracurricular activity that would look good on my college application. This started the same year I became anorexic." The more I thought about this stuff, the worse it seemed. "He took me to visit all the Ivy League schools and was really happy when I decided to apply for early decision from one of them." I stared at the ceiling, not wanting to make eye contact because any inkling of emotion I saw in her eyes would distract me from visualizing the scenarios I had lived through.

"That sounds reasonable," she said, almost as a question.

"He insisted on typing my application for me, so I gave him the handwritten copy weeks before the deadline." As I told her the story, I became more and more incredulous and angry at my father. "A week went by, and he hadn't typed it. After two weeks passed, I asked him to give it back to me so I could type it myself. He got furious and told me to stop bothering him."

"That's terrible!"

She was right; it was terrible. "He mailed it the day before the deadline without showing it to me. When he finally gave me a copy a few days later, I saw it was riddled with typos."

"What?" she gasped.

I kind of wished she'd shut up so I could stay involved in the scenario. Every time she spoke, it pulled me back to the present. "When I told him how upset I was about the typos, he told me I was crazy for being upset, and that I was overreacting."

"Overreacting? That sounds familiar."

Ignoring her comment, I went on to tell her that when I was deferred from that school, Dad made every possible excuse for my failure, short of blaming himself. Then, he refused to talk to me.

When I finished talking, I looked at her and shrugged.

"No wonder you got so pissed off yesterday. You did everything you were supposed to so you could go to the gym, and then Dr. O' robbed you of your prize *and* punished you by insisting you go to group, which he knows you hate."

"Yeah, just like Luke. I did everything he asked, but he still dumped me."

She told me I should discuss this further with Dr. Lancet and then informed me it was time for my psych testing.

CHAPTER 28

I was nervous about seeing Dr. O after my outburst, but he started right in on the testing.

"We should be able to complete the WAIS-R as well as the Thematic Apperception Test," he told me.

The WAIS-R is an IQ test with several components, including general knowledge, spatial relationships, and vocabulary. Performance is measured by an overall score as well as by scores for each section. Scores on the component parts are fairly similar to one another and to the overall score. If there's a great disparity in a given individual's scores, it warrants investigation. Since there are only right and wrong answers, the test is considered objective.

The Thematic Apperception Test (TAT) is a projective test along the lines of the Rorschach. There are no right or wrong answers. An individual's responses provide information about the way her mind works and what's going on in her unconscious. The TAT is comprised of thirty black-and-white drawings, each of which is as realistic as a photograph.

"I wish I didn't have to take the IQ test. I don't want concrete evidence of how stupid I am." I felt increasingly anxious about not being able to perform up to snuff.

"Are you aware how distorted that is? Everybody knows you're extremely bright."

I had always felt stupid. I'd gone to ultra-competitive schools, where A's and perfect scores on the SATs were run of the mill. I was not in this high-achieving group because I was so immersed in my own dark world that it was often difficult for me to pay attention or process any information outside of what was in my own head. I often missed school due to depression and exhaustion. I frequently had no idea what was going on in class and fell behind. This sense of inadequacy carried through to college and medical school. It only made matters worse that my father was never satisfied with my grades or test scores.

When I was in tenth grade, my parents and I met with my dean, Mrs. P., to discuss my academic performance and what classes I should take in eleventh grade. My father demanded to see the results of my IQ test as well as my Standardized Achievement tests. Initially, Mrs. P. said "no," but he became so adamant and aggressive that she finally gave in. I felt invisible because Dad was talking about me in the third person.

Most of my scores satisfied my dad. However, my IQ scores were not up to his standards. Based on his reaction, I inferred that my scores were in the borderline retarded range. But it's like an anorexic mindset that slips into thinking one must be fat if she's not far too skinny. My father made excuses for my "less than stellar" scores. He insisted that I must have been tired or not feeling well during those particular tests and that they were not a true reflection of my abilities. He demanded that I re-take these exams.

Mrs. P. told him this was outrageous. He became more and more belligerent until he was standing over her desk, yelling at her. My mother and I just stared at one another in horrified silence. Finally, Mrs. P. called security to have Dad escorted out of the school.

"We'll start with the TAT. I'm going to place one card at a time in front of you. Each card depicts a scene involving people. Describe what's happening in the picture as well as what preceded the scene and what will follow." He removed a stack of five-by-seven cards from the folder, turned the first one over and placed it in front of me.

I stared at the black-and-white drawing of a woman leaning against a fence in the middle of a pasture. "She is forlorn because she just had a fight with her husband and he walked out on her." I rocked back and forth to try to stifle my increasing anxiety. "She's thinking about committing suicide because she doesn't want to go on living without him." I pushed the card toward him. "Her husband is going to come back and kill her."

My answers indicated how preoccupied I was with death and annihilation. I had the impulse to censor them, but I knew they could provide further insights on what had gone so terribly wrong with me. My determination to get better had begun to override my concern with the impression I made on Dr. O'Riley or anyone else. I had spent most of my life hiding behind facades — pretending I was confident and competent when I really felt insecure and inadequate, pretending I wasn't hungry when I really was starving, pretending I didn't want or need anything when in fact I felt completely empty and destitute, hiding behind the title of doctor when I was raging inside and preoccupied with suicide. All these deceptions had only made things worse. It was time to be honest, which in this case meant allowing my thoughts and the articulation of them to flow freely. They were frightening, both in what they were revealing about me and in exposing my vulnerabilities.

Dr. O wrote my responses on his pad and put the next card in front of me. Studying this drawing of an old, witchlike woman standing behind a young attractive woman, I immediately identified the older woman as the mother and the younger woman as the daughter. I started experiencing feelings I would have felt if this were my mother and I. I said the mother was hypercritical and judgmental of the daughter, and the daughter was hypersensitive and despairing at her mother's disapproval. The mother chastised the daughter for her neediness and inability to love. The daughter felt worthless, self-loathing, and hopeless. This scenario, which felt as though it were actually taking place, propelled me into familiar territory, where I felt despondent, despicable, and dependent.

By the time we reached the last card, the voices inside my head, telling me I was an unworthy piece of shit, were so loud I could barely concentrate. Handing him the last card, I again asked if he thought

I was psychotic. He told me he'd have to score the tests before he answered me, but it was obvious already that in my wiring, intimacy led to anger, and danger seemed to be my core issue.

I suddenly felt compelled to apologize for my outburst even though I was scared of how he might react.

To my great relief, he acted like it was no big deal. "I understand you're going through a difficult time. Come on, I'll walk you to the unit."

Walking through the hallway, he spoke without looking up. It dawned on me that he felt uncomfortable outside the context of his role as the authority figure.

"You may have to explain it to the group. They were pretty upset. But that's between you and them."

CHAPTER 29

Back on the unit, Dr. Lancet told me I had to call Dr. Mikker.
"What the hell does he want?" I felt put off by the fact that this man, who was supposed to be so smart and insightful, had been oblivious to what I was up to with Luke. To make matters worse, he abdicated any responsibility for me by forcing me into the hospital, and then had the nerve to send me a bill for $500 for his time. I had no desire to talk to him. In fact, I hadn't given him as much as a second's thought since he'd signed me into the hospital.

Dr. Lancet handed me a quarter and a Post-it note. "Here's his number. Come get me in the nurses' station when you finish talking to him."

As I dialed his number, I noticed my hands were trembling. Since I didn't feel nervous about calling him, I assumed the tremors were a side effect of the medication.

"It's Melanie." I said in a blasé tone when he answered the phone.

"Yes, Melanie." He sounded distant. "I just wanted to tell you I won't be treating you as an outpatient when you're discharged from the hospital."

"Okay."

Dr. Lancet was waiting for me. "How do you feel about what Dr. Mikker told you?"

"I couldn't care less. I figured you'd treat me as an outpatient, anyway."

"I haven't decided yet. A lot could happen between now and the time of your discharge."

That he wasn't committing to treat me shocked me. I felt panicky.

"We'll talk about this another time. Right now, you have to go to your room for quiet time, and I have to write the order to discontinue your constant observation."

An hour later, Susan awakened me to take me to Richie's office. She told me she'd heard about the phone call with Dr. Mikker.

"He dumped me, just like Luke," I said dispassionately. "Only this time, I couldn't care less." I had seen Dr. Mikker for close to a year, but always found him somewhat aloof. He'd been recommended to me by a few people including Luke, who was a colleague of his, as well as a resident friend of mine. It still hadn't occurred to me how angry he must have been at me. I'd completely undermined him and probably humiliated him as well, damaging his credibility and reputation. It gives me no pleasure to think of myself as having harmed him, but the possibility has since occurred to me. After all, who would want to go to a therapist who wasn't even aware that his patient had nearly killed someone while he was treating her?

He must have been very angry to dismiss me like that on the phone. The standard procedure for terminating a therapeutic relationship is that the patient and therapist decide together that the patient no longer needs to be in therapy or can't continue for some reason. They spend at least a few sessions discussing how the patient feels about the relationship being over. Often, the ending of this important relationship brings up all kinds of loss, abandonment, and separation issues that warrant examination.

Through my therapy with Dr. Lancet, I came to understand that I'd been literally dying for someone to come along whom I could not manipulate. He had to be smart enough to see through my machinations and strong enough to confront me. He also had to earn my trust and respect by being honest, consistent, and treating me like I mattered. He had to be a role model to me, someone whose integrity and self-possession inspired me to cultivate those traits in myself. I was extraordinarily fortunate to find those things in Dr. Lancet.

In Richie's office, I sat on the couch, a few feet away from my mother.

Richie positioned his chair equidistant from my mother and me. I envisioned two diagonal lines emanating from Richie's chair to my mother and me. I conjured up the image of being in a boxing ring. I almost expected him to put a whistle in his mouth like a referee.

"I was just asking your mother how things are going." His filling me in on what had preceded my arrival was his way of making me feel safe and included.

"It's been very hard," she said resentfully. "While you were having tantrums about not being allowed to go running, I've been dealing with your lawyer and Luke's family."

I spun around to face her, slamming the pillow against the back of the couch. How dare she not tell me about Luke's family!

"Jack and Steve brought your things to my house." She said "your" as though it were an obscenity.

"What things?" I fought back tears. The idea that Luke actually didn't want any of my belongings in his house made the finality seem too real. He truly was done with me!

"Whatever you left at Luke's house," she replied brusquely. "The boxes are all over my playroom."

"Did you talk to them?" I felt forlorn at the thought that my last ties with Luke were being severed.

"We exchanged pleasantries. That's about it," she said tersely.

Richie rotated his chair toward my mother. "Jean, you sound very angry at Melanie."

"She's always angry at me," I snapped. "She takes her anger at my father out on me. She sees us as one and the same." I hadn't meant to direct the session this way.

"Melanie's being in the hospital brings back a lot of bad memories about Len."

"Memories?" Richie spoke so softly I could barely hear him. I knew he was using that gentle compassionate tone to make us feel comfortable.

She put her purse on her lap. I realized she was using her purse as a sort of protective device. *Like a bulletproof vest.* This surprised me, because it hadn't occurred to me that my mother experienced her anxiety. I thought it automatically transformed into rage, which she didn't try to hide. Her lower lip would tremble, her tone would become icy, and she'd make incisively snide comments. Seeing her vulnerability now made me think twice.

"While we were still dating, Len graduated law school. He refused to take the bar exam though."

"So he never actually practiced?"

"No; he said the law was too corrupt." She faked a smile. "Then, when Melanie was eight months old, he put himself into a psychiatric hospital for a year and a half."

"What?" I jumped up and stood over my mother. "I never knew that."

"Melanie, please sit down." Richie said calmly.

I turned my head to look at him. "What if I don't want to sit down? What if I'm so pissed off that I start punching her?"

"Melanie, please," my mother implored.

I sat on the edge of the coffee table still facing her. "That explains a lot. Dr. O thinks I'm fucked up because I suffered an early trauma. I had no idea what that was until now." I slid my fingers along the top of my nose and sucked my thumb. "You always said I had abandonment issues, like it was my fault. But you never told me Daddy left when I was so young."

Her expression softened. "You used to suck your thumb like that when you were little. We laughed because your nose was always dirty from dragging your wet fingers over it." She practically smiled.

I returned to the couch, leaned back and closed my eyes. Why hadn't she told me this before? It seemed odd that in all the acerbic interactions she'd had with my father in front of me, this had never come out. Come to think of it, I'd never heard her say anything derogatory about his psychiatric hospitalizations or his psychiatric disorder. She'd vilified him for his lack of functioning, but not his mental illness. She must have suffered inordinate hardship when he'd left her alone with an infant, two dogs, and no income. Maybe my early trauma had to do with being left alone with a mother who was overwhelmed and unable to take care of me the way I needed to be taken care of. I knew she became enraged when she felt overwhelmed. What if she had taken it out on me, a helpless infant? What if she didn't want me to know about my father's absence because then I might discover the truth about how she had treated me? Whatever the truth was, and most likely it was a combination of all of these things, I knew I needed to back off.

"Who took care of you and Melanie while Len was in the hospital?" Richie asked kindly.

"My father. Even when Len wasn't in the hospital, my father supported us because Len couldn't hold a job. He bought us our first house and paid for college for both the girls. When Dani was eight, I had to get a full-time job."

"What about Len's parents?"

Her face contorted with rage. "His father was a rich prick who was too busy philandering and playing golf to acknowledge his son was ill and had a family to support. He never even called me."

"But your family came through."

"My father did. My mother wouldn't even talk to me after I married Len." She ripped a tissue into tiny pieces.

"Sort of the reverse of what happened in Melanie's life?" he asked pointedly.

"Melanie was much more attached to her father than to me. But I was always picking up the pieces of that relationship. He constantly let her down, yet she couldn't stay away from him. Every time he hurt her, she came to me for solace," she said sadly.

"What did you do?"

"Wiped away her tears and told her I was sorry he'd hurt her again. I wanted to shake her and tell her to stay away from him, but I knew how it felt to keep hoping he'd change. I did the same thing for a long time."

"But your mother wasn't there for you?"

"She disowned me for three years after we married." She practically whispered this.

I sprang to my feet. "You never told me about your mother!" Dropping onto the couch, I said, "Sorry, I didn't mean to yell."

She finally looked at me. "It had nothing to do with you."

In the past few minutes, I'd gained more insight into my mother than I'd accumulated over my entire lifetime. How could I be angry with her for not telling me these things? Perhaps she really didn't know they were important to me to know. Knowing them gave me a much greater understanding of who she was and why she did what she did. If I had known more about her, her berating me wouldn't have felt as terrible. I would have been able to see that her anger had as much to do with her circumstances and history as it had to do with me. I felt much more sad than angry.

Richie checked his watch. "We have to end soon, but it's important we pick up here next time. Jean, will you take Melanie back to the unit?"

I jogged a few steps ahead of her before stopping. "Why'd you marry Daddy if you knew he was nuts? You knew he had shock therapy before you met him, and that he saw a psychiatrist. I know you were attracted to him and everything, but didn't that send up red flags?"

"Yes." She stopped short and looked into my eyes. "But I was pregnant." She veered around me and walked quickly. "With you."

I felt as though I'd had the wind knocked out of me. I felt guilty, confused, and irate. I needed time to process this bolt from the blue, but I also needed to know one more thing. "Didn't it occur to you I might turn out to be just as nuts as Daddy?"

"Never." She looked away from me.

The obvious parallels between my father's life and mine suddenly struck me as being beyond tragic. It was in my power to help my mother recover from the huge hurts and disappointments my father had caused her, but instead, I was adding to her misery. I suddenly hated myself for what I had done to her, and felt brokenhearted over her losses.

CHAPTER 30

Dr. Lancet walked up behind me. "I received a call from the Medical Board. They want a copy of your medical records. If we refuse to cooperate, they'll subpoena them."

"Am I going to lose my medical license?"

"Probably."

I felt really upset even though I'd expected it.

"How ironic! I'll never practice medicine, just like my father never practiced law." Sadness consumed me.

"That may be true, but let's not jump to conclusions." He kept staring at my hands. "Your hands are shaking. How many doses of Stelazine have you taken?"

"This morning's was my third." I stared at my trembling hands as though they were foreign objects.

"Do you feel stiff?" He looked at my face. "Smile."

I complied.

"Do your cheeks feel tight?" He leaned closer.

I opened my mouth as wide as I could and ran my fingers along my cheeks. "A little."

"Let's go to the exam room." He pointed to the examination table. "Sit and hold your arms out in front of you, palms up. Okay, now bend your elbows to a ninety degree angle." He stood in front of me and gripped my wrists. "I'm going to pull your arms down toward me. Try to resist." After doing this a few times, he said, "You have the slightest signs of cogwheel rigidity."

Although it was very subtle, I felt my arms move, then hitch, move, then hitch, all the way down.

"I'm going to start you on two milligrams of Artane, STAT."

Studying my face in the bathroom mirror, I smiled, frowned,

yawned, puckered, and stuck out my tongue. My facial muscles looked almost frozen, as if I'd received Botox injections. Suddenly, images of Luke's paralyzed face and frightened eyes flashed through my mind. The room began spinning around me. I rushed to my room, collapsed onto my bed, and buried my face in the pillow. I squeezed my eyes shut, but couldn't stop the horrifying images. I recalled spoon-feeding Luke like a baby, changing his catheter and wiping the drool off his chin. The images appeared over and over like a continuous film loop. These images terrified me and I felt sad.

When Luke was at his sickest, he had been unable to feed himself, swallow solid foods, or control his bladder. I worked up the courage to ask his permission to change his catheter. I needed courage because if he had said no, it would have hit me as a total rejection. I attached so much meaning to his allowing me to care for him that I interpreted his permission as his way of saying he wanted me back in his life.

In the process of cognitively separating his illness from what I had done, I'd also minimized the gravity of what was happening to him. I'd only felt frightened twice during Luke's illness. Once was when someone mentioned that he might die, which scared me because I didn't want to lose him, not because I realized I would have been responsible for his death. The other was when it became clear that he was going to recover and no longer need me.

My inability to perceive what was really happening to Luke led me to block out each incident after it was resolved. Having my own symptoms trigger these memories, along with the recognition that I had caused his illness, caught me off-guard. The strength and clarity of the images nearly bowled me over.

Desperate to stop the images, I sprinted to the nurses' station and pounded on the window. "Where's Dr. Lancet? I need to talk to him!"

Susan put her arm around my waist and led me to the conference room.

"It's all right, why don't you sit down?" She pulled a chair away from the table and sat next to me.

"Did you leave the door open intentionally?" I suspected she had, in case I went into a frenzy and she needed to escape quickly. I knew there was a panic button near the door, as in all the therapy rooms.

"Yes." She placed her hand on top of mine. "Tell me what's going on."

I told her and she responded by assuring me that, even though it felt painful, facing reality was the first step in healing.

Tears slid down my nose and soaked my sleeve. "The crazy thing is, I fooled myself into thinking it must be some rare form of encephalitis. Steve and I poured over textbooks and articles trying to figure out what was wrong with him." As I spoke, I felt intense self-loathing over what I had done. "I'm the vilest person on the planet."

"You're not vile — you're sick. That's why you're in the hospital," Susan said gently.

"Now I understand why my mother gets so angry when I talk about wanting to go running. I deserve to be punished, not go outside on a beautiful summer day. I should have been put in solitary confinement so nobody had to be exposed to me." I yanked a clump of hair out of my head. "How could I have watched Luke suffer without doing anything?"

"Please don't hurt yourself. It hurts me to watch you."

"Suffering is the least I can do for Luke." I kept pulling my hair and squeezing my head between my forearms.

"He must have hurt you terribly to drive you to this point." She eased my arm away from my head.

"He did hurt me, but it wasn't intentional. It was just his stuff."

"He preyed on your psychological vulnerabilities," Susan said vehemently. "He's a psychiatrist; he knew exactly what he was doing."

"Yeah, but I could've walked away from the relationship. I chose to stay." In actuality, I couldn't have left. I was too obsessed with him.

"Your own issues made it impossible for you to walk away," she said sympathetically.

"His previous girlfriend slit her wrist because he pushed her too far."

"It sounds like he had a history of driving women crazy, literally."

"I think he actually chose psychologically vulnerable women and then drove them crazy to recreate the relationship he had with his mother. It was a kind of repetition compulsion. He assumed and feared women were crazy because that's what he was used to. Then he confirmed that by recreating the scenario over and over." I folded my hands in my lap and contemplated my analysis.

After a moment or two of silence, she said, "Come on. It's time for lunch."

"Good, I'm starving."

"I'm glad you're starting to eat more."

I chose my usual seat at the end of a table. A few minutes later Bruce, the attractive man from group, sat next to me.

"Where have you been?" he asked as he took a bite of his cheeseburger.

Anorexics like seeing other people eat fattening foods. I used to love making milkshakes and mayonnaise-laden sandwiches for my sister and my father, and watching them eat while I sucked on a stick of celery.

"I've been keeping a low profile since my humiliating temper tantrum. Dr. O'Riley told me the group is really pissed at me." I tried not to think about how much I wanted to eat my fries. "I guess I owe you all an apology."

"No, you don't." Bruce took a few more bites of his burger and then pushed his plate to the edge of his tray. "Anyway, I wanted to make sure you were okay and to tell you I'm around if you need to talk to somebody."

I was amazed at how good it felt to be befriended by him. Until then, nobody on the unit had given me the time of day. Besides, I was physically attracted to him.

" We shoved the empty trays into the warmer. He pulled a lighter out of his back pocket and waved it at me.

"Quiet time in five," called the psych aide from the entrance to the TV room.

"Don't worry about their silly rules," Bruce whispered. "I know how to break all of them."

"Oh, great! That's just what I need." I took a long drag on my cigarette and thought about how much trouble I could get in if I started hanging out with him -- and how distracting and destructive it might be to my progress. But it sure was tempting.

I had been attracted to him since the first time I saw him, but hadn't imagined he felt the same way. I smiled to myself as I entertained the possibility of fooling around with him. The idea titillated me. Not only did he make me feel horny, but I knew that physical contact between patients was taboo. That made the prospect even more exciting.

As we walked down the hallway, he pointed to a door. "That's my room. Feel free to drop in anytime." He winked and bumped me playfully.

I will. And, against my better judgment, a few days later, I did.

CHAPTER 31

Amy, one of your former colleagues, is here to see you," Susan announced as she strode across my room to the window.

Of the twelve residents in my class, I was closest to Amy. We'd worked together on several units and become fast friends and confidantes. We shared an acerbic wit and similar values. We often discussed our difficult cases and had great respect for one another's opinions and insights. Shortly after Luke broke up with me, Amy had been astute enough to recognize the seriousness of my depression and suggested I consider taking a leave of absence. When I moved out of Luke's house and into resident housing, she and I lived down the hall from one another. We often stayed up all night smoking cigarettes and talking. I hadn't spoken to her since I'd been hospitalized, and was too ashamed to want to see her now. Nor did I want to hear about her third year of residency — the third year I'd probably never experience.

"Can you tell her I'm off the unit or something?"

"You're going to have to face people sooner or later, so you might as well do it now. Besides, I thought she's your friend."

I felt a knot forming in the pit of my stomach.

Amy stood in front of the nurses' station chewing on her thumbnail and looking around. She was a pretty woman, but always dressed as though she were on her way to a funeral. I'd seen her nearly every day for the past year, but now she practically looked like a stranger. She seemed bigger than I remembered and, dressed all in black, she seemed to be an apparition, or worse, a witch. In actuality, her looks probably hadn't changed. Our lives had diverged so completely that her "changed" appearance probably had more to do with my feeling that I could no longer relate to her. So many feelings of loss and despair were stirring inside me I could barely stand the thought of being near her. The closer I got to her, the more ashamed and diminutive I felt.

"Hi!" She gave me a hug.

We strolled to the far corner of the TV room. "This is just like the units we worked on together."

"Yeah, but now I'm a patient, not a doctor."

"You're still a doctor. This is just a temporary setback."

"I don't think so. It looks like I'm going to lose my license." I looked imploringly into her light blue eyes. "How'd you know I was here?" I turned halfway around in my chair and looked out the window at the courtyard below.

"Mark told me." She turned to look outside as well.

"Did he tell you *why* I'm here?" I watched a cardinal fly off a branch, making a flash of red.

"Yeah, he did." I felt her looking at me.

"Did he tell you he was an accomplice of sorts?" I turned to watch her reaction.

"He didn't tell me that, but I find it hard to believe."

"It's true, ask him. Does anybody else know?" I braced myself for the answer I thought was inevitable but did not want to hear.

"Yes," she said apologetically. "Everybody knows."

I didn't know how much more of this conversation I could endure.

"Most people couldn't believe it. They'd just watched you give an amazing presentation in grand rounds and, the next thing they knew, you were here." She ran her fingers through her hair. "But don't worry; nobody's talking about it anymore."

Just thinking about my former life, I felt nauseated. I was having enough trouble dealing with my lack of future prospects, the inevitability of court, and perhaps prison. I couldn't tolerate facing all that I'd lost at the same time. Being with Amy was just too overwhelming.

"Aim, would you mind leaving? I'm not feeling too well."

Picking up on the desperation in my voice, she said, "No problem."

She patted my knee then walked away. "Take care of yourself."

I watched her leave and then leaned on the windowsill feeling disconsolate.

"We need to talk," Dr. Lancet said to the back of my head a few minutes later.

I reeled around. "Don't sneak up on me! I'm a bit on edge. Besides, didn't I already see you today?"

Dr. Lancet was pretty strict about keeping our meetings to once a day. If I asked to talk to him outside of the session, he usually told me I had to wait until the next day. This was part of his attempt to train me to deal with delayed gratification and frustration, and to work within the bounds of the established rules.

"You should be on edge for more reasons than you know," he said ominously.

"What's that supposed to mean?" My already high anxiety was beginning to escalate to beyond tolerable.

"What did Amy want?" He sat on the edge of the chair next to mine.

"I guess she wanted to see how I was doing. Why?"

His eyes hardened, his mouth tensed, and he leaned toward me. "Let me spell it out for you. Luke's family is terrified of you, Mark wants to silence you, and the press is hot on your trail."

I was furious that he had not told me this before. "What's that supposed to mean?"

"Luke's brother calls me regularly to make sure you're still here, and Luke calls me as well. They have asked to be given at least a week's notice before you get out of the hospital — even on a pass."

"And Mark?" I slumped in my chair because I felt so defeated by the thought that all these people perceived me as being a monster.

"He wants to be alerted when you're discharged as well." He stared at me as though trying to gauge my reaction. "I've received several calls from reporters. I haven't returned their calls, but it wouldn't surprise me if they tried to spy on you."

"Why didn't you tell me?" I jumped off my chair and got in his face.

He didn't flinch. "I thought it would be an unnecessary distraction."

"What!?" I shouted. "I'm on everybody's radar screen and, for all we know, the paparazzi's holed up just outside my window....and you thought it was an unnecessary distraction?"

"I made it clear to the staff that if anyone besides Scott or your immediate family came to visit you, I was to be paged immediately. That's how I knew about Amy. Since you don't go off the unit alone, I saw no reason to tell you. Maybe I was wrong," he said apologetically.

"Did you say the press is on my trail? Hmm," I said mischievously. "Maybe I could go on the talk show circuit and have a movie made about me." I was so ashamed of what I'd done and so determined to protect Luke and his family, as well as my own, that I hoped it would never even make the police blotter. But two recent local cases had been plastered all over the news and talk shows — Amy Fisher's shooting of her lover's wife, and Caroline Warmus's killing of her lover's wife — so I resorted to sarcasm. It was the least detrimental way I could think of to express my intense anxiety and my anger with Dr. Lancet for his secrecy.

"You will do nothing of the sort," he said sternly. "You need to be remorseful, introspective, and very careful. Do you understand?"

"Yes. Anyway, I was just kidding. You know, using humor as a defense?" I hung my head, feeling ashamed. A cold sweat started at my feet and worked its way up to my hair. "Just so you know, Amy knows Mark pretty well. I told her about the accomplice thing." I knew it was wise to disclose this as I suspected Mark might have even sent Amy to feel me out. I suddenly realized I should not trust anyone.

"That's exactly my point; we can't be too cautious."

"Does this mean I'll never get to go outside?" I stared longingly at the grass and trees in the courtyard. I knew I wouldn't be allowed outside until Dr. Lancet felt completely confident that I wouldn't try to run away or even leave the campus temporarily. Now that I knew he was worried that the press, or one of Mark's or Luke's spies might be lurking on the grounds, even if I was on my best behavior, he wouldn't take that risk.

"Not for a while anyway."

"This whole thing really sucks!" My eyes welled up with tears of regret, rage, and frustration.

"Yes, it does. We can talk about it more tomorrow. Do you think you'll be all right, or do you want to be on constant overnight?"

"I definitely don't want to be on constant. I'm sick of having someone watching me. Besides, my mom's coming tonight, so I'm sure I'll be fine."

"Okay, but you have group in the morning. Please try to be civilized."

CHAPTER 32

Bruce smiled as he sat next to me in group.

Dr. O'Riley asked, "Does the group have anything they want to say to Melanie?"

"It's her business what she does. Are we going to spend the whole time talking about her again," asked Tanya, scowling.

"You sound annoyed," injected Dr. O'Riley.

"Well, yeah! It's like the whole unit revolves around her. If she's not having a temper tantrum, then the staff is busy kissing her ass. Her doctor sees her more times in one day than mine sees me in a week, and Susan follows her around like a puppy dog. Not only that, she's the only who has her own room."

Dr. O'Riley zoomed in on me like a laser. "Melanie, what do you think about what Tanya said?"

"I'm surprised to hear anyone's affected by me in any way whatsoever." The more I thought about this, the more agitated I became. I was unable to pay attention to the group. My inner voices obscured the real ones. A mini-movie began to play over and over in my mind, eclipsing the physical reality of the room.

Luke is lying in his hospital bed crying because he's scared he's going to die. I'm holding his hand and stroking his cheek. It's not only his fear I'm responding to. I'm thinking about how much he'll want me back when he remembers how I made him feel comforted and less afraid.

My father is crying because he knows he's dying. I'm feeling put upon by his neediness. I cannot believe he's ruining the last few months of medical school for me. I'm afraid he's going to place so many demands on my time and energy that I won't be able to study for the board exam.

It's always been about me. I've always been about me. Of course I don't know what's going on with the other patients. All I care about is myself.

"We're all messed up," hissed Tanya, "but we don't go around smashing things in the hallway and destroying our rooms." She pulled an emery board out of her back pocket and began filing her nails. "What exactly is your story?"

I squeezed my eyes shut. "I don't feel well. I think I'm going to throw up." I ran to the nurses' station and rapped on the window before squatting to ease my nausea. A minute or so later, Susan was kneeling next to me. "Why aren't you in group?"

I focused on the hem of her white pants licking the top of her white slip-ons. "I can't stand it anymore. I'm confusing my father and Luke."

Luke always told me to learn to get outside myself enough to see his needs as separate from mine, to respect and honor them even if they ran counter to my needs. How could I, when my needs were so pressing? I did that with my father for most of my life. When he withdrew into himself, even though his neglect of me was so painful, I let it go. I made excuses for his behavior and decided that whatever the reasons, his needs surpassed mine. Ultimately, I could explain it all away by saying he was sick, so it wasn't his fault. Since he was sick, it wasn't about me; it wasn't that I was bad or not worthy of his love. He was limited. End of story.

I had put up with such extreme deprivation for so long, that when I finally could put up with no more, I did a 180. I wanted it to be all about me. I wanted my father to take care of me, love me unconditionally and satisfy my needs without my even having to articulate what they were. I wanted him to compensate for all the previous wrongs I'd endured without asking for anything in return.

By the time I met Luke, I didn't have much left to give anyone. Regardless, I promised him the world and sacrificed my desires and needs until it got to the point that fulfilling his needs (to be left alone, to spend time with Jack and Steve, to spend hours at night talking to his patients on the phone) became just too much of a sacrifice. My rage, anxiety, and sense of entitlement kicked in, and it became all about me. "Come." Susan leaned toward me and extended her hand.

A kaleidoscope of images flashed through my brain: my father on his deathbed, Luke at his sickest, images of the night he broke up with me. I curled into a fetal position on my bed.

"Did I tell you my father forced me to go to medical school, and then died just before I graduated?"

"No, tell me."

"I had wanted to go to graduate school in psychology to be a child psychologist, but Dad pleaded with me to apply to medical school instead. He bribed me by promising to pay for medical school. Even though I hadn't planned to, I spent two years after college taking the pre-med courses and studying for the MCATS. My dad was so happy when I was accepted to medical school that it seemed as though it had been worth the sacrifice. He paid my tuition for part of the first semester. Then he reneged on his promise."

"What?" Susan's eyes nearly popped out of her head.

"During a meeting with a financial aid officer, he announced that he'd no longer be helping me financially. I was in shock. Outside the office, I implored him to tell me why he had changed his mind. At first he wouldn't even tell me. Instead, he screamed at me to get my 'piece-of-shit mother' or her 'piece-of-shit father' to pay for school. I cried and pleaded with him, but he walked away and headed for his car. I chased after him, screaming, 'but you promised!'"

"What did he do?" Susan sounded almost as crushed as I had felt at the time.

"Climbed into his car and slammed the door. I pounded on his window crying, 'I don't understand.' He revved the engine, lowered his window a crack and shouted, 'I'm paying for Pam to go to art school and I can't afford both. Everybody else takes out loans to pay for school, so why shouldn't you?' Then, he drove away. I stood in the parking lot crying and waiting for him to come back to tell me he loved me."

"Did he?"

"No." I did a somersault on my bed and sprang to my feet. "But stay tuned for the next installment."

The experience of eliciting someone's sympathy felt so uncomfortable and embarrassing that I spontaneously did anything possible to divert attention away from both my feelings and the other person's. As often happened when I was feeling either too despondent or too euphoric, intense feelings triggered an automatic impulse to shift the mood in another direction. On the rare occasions when I felt extremely proud of myself, excited about the future, or if I was making a meaningful connection with another human being, I immediately plummeted into despair, and the voices in my head said, *You suck. Nothing good will come to you. You're despicable and worthless.*

Susan picked up on this right away. "I guess it's too much to talk about, right now."

Suddenly feeling exhausted, I plopped back down on the bed. "Yeah, I'm kind of spent. I think I'll nap."

I slept through lunch and quiet hour. Susan came to wake me for the meeting with my attorney.

In the conference room, I sat in my usual chair, leaned back and pressed my knees against the lip of the table. Tom sat next to me. Richie and my mother sat across from me. Dr. Lancet sauntered into the room, dropped my chart on the table and sat between Richie and Tom.

"I met with the D.A. She wants to charge Melanie with attempted homicide," said Tom.

"What?" I shrieked. I was so mortified, my knees slipped off the table and the front legs of my chair crashed to the ground.

"Oh, my God," gasped my mother. The blood drained from her face.

Tom held out both hands in front of him as if to quiet a crowd. "I convinced her to reduce the charge to first-degree assault."

"I specifically chose that drug because it is non-lethal!" I pounded the table with my fist.

"Melanie!" my mother reprimanded.

"Luke broke up with you in January or February, but you didn't poison him until the middle of May?" He looked at me quizzically.

"Yes. That's when the land deal was set in motion."

"And you said you got fired. When was that?" Tom asked as he wrote something on the pad.

"At the end of February, shortly after my unit chief, to whom I was very attached, went away on vacation."

Tom shook his head as though he were coming out of a trance. "What part do you think Prozac played?" he asked Dr. Lancet.

"I'm sure it contributed, but the literature is controversial. I wouldn't go there. The recent death of her father, plus the break up with Luke and getting fired certainly played a role."

Tom told us that Luke's friends and family thought I was evil and manipulative. "It took some smooth talking and lots of promises from me to get them to reduce the charges. They would not take kindly to our trying to attribute Melanie's actions to the Prozac or any other drugs."

At that time, the literature on Prozac leading to suicidal and homicidal behavior was preliminary. Since then, however, these side effects of Prozac have been solidly documented.

Tom returned his pad to his briefcase. "I hate to be the bearer of more bad news, but you should surrender your medical license to preempt the medical board revoking it. The judge will appreciate your accepting responsibility for your actions and therefore might be prone to exacting a lighter sentence. I've already contacted the lawyer who can help you do so. You can meet with him after you're discharged." He handed me the lawyer's business card. "His name is Bill Walsh."

As I studied the card, I started to feel sick to my stomach. I had worked so hard to get the license, which I finally got it in February of 1992. Now, just like that, I had to give it up. It was so painful to think about how I had destroyed my life.

"The arraignment is scheduled for August 14th. We'll meet one more time before that. I apologize, but I have to run." He turned toward my mother and put his hand to his ear to simulate a phone receiver. "Call me if you have any questions!"

"We should start discussing discharge plans," said Richie, angling his chair toward my mother.

She blanched. "When is she being discharged?"

"Don't worry," said Dr. Lancet. "Not until after the arraignment."

"But we should start thinking about it now," Richie resumed. "Specifically, where is she going to live – and who's going to treat her as an outpatient?" He looked at Dr. Lancet and raised his eyebrows.

"Yeah, who's going to treat me?" I looked at Dr. Lancet, too.

The minute I said it, I wished I hadn't. Dr. Lancet had made it clear he would decide about my treatment when he was ready. My bugging him about it was futile and counter-productive. I didn't expect him to answer me or even acknowledge my impulsive outburst, so I wasn't surprised that he blew me off. Part of what he was trying to teach me was how to act like a civilized adult, which meant not interrupting people, respecting other people's boundaries and doing right by other people.

Dr. Lancet said, "I have to go to a meeting." He stepped toward my mother and touched her shoulder. "We'll talk."

"I'll phone you later," I called to his back and smiled.

Richie and my mother smiled as well, which helped to ease the tension--temporarily.

"Jean, would it be possible for Melanie to live with you for a while?"

Her lower lip quivered. "Do I have a choice?"

"We could explore other options."

"Yeah, like prison," I blurted as I twisted my elastic ponytail holder around my wrist and watched the veins bulge on the back of my hand.

"Melanie!" My mother glared at my wrist. "May we continue this discussion another time? I've had enough for one day."

Melanie Cane

CHAPTER 33

Dr. Lancet came into the lunchroom to get me. "I'm leaving early today. We need to talk before I go."

I jammed a plum into my pocket and followed him out the door. "Are you going to your beach house for the weekend or something?" I asked jealously.

Ignoring my snide comment, he asked what I thought of the meeting.

"It sucked!" I tossed the plum above my head. "Luke thinks I tried to kill him, I have to surrender my medical license, and my own mother is freaking out because I may have to live with her." I pretended to throw the plum to him.

I was acting childish and annoying because of the distress I felt over the fact that I wouldn't know where he was over the weekend. On other weekends, I'd assumed he was at his home a couple of miles from the hospital. I derived some comfort from picturing him there. When I'd think about his choosing to be with his family instead of with me, I'd literally feel as if I were disintegrating. That he had a life apart from me threatened my very existence. I tried to assure myself that he was here now, but I couldn't help feeling as if a dark pit was opening beneath my feet waiting to suck me in.

"What did you mean when you said you were fired because your unit chief went on vacation?" he asked, taking the plum from me and placing it on the desk.

"When Luke broke up with me, Judy, my unit chief, lengthened our supervision meetings, talked to me privately after morning rounds each day and sat with me at lunch."

"She was worried about you?"

"Yes; she also believed in me." I thought back to how good I'd

187

felt when I was with Judy. Her praising me or chiding me in her bemused way made me feel understood and appreciated. "She thought I was a talented, empathic therapist. She even got a kick out of the way I acted out sometimes."

"Then she went away for two weeks. At first I was okay, but then I started feeling even more despondent than when Luke broke up with me."

I felt myself falling into that black hole of despair all over again, the same feeling I experienced whenever someone important to me left. At the time, it felt infinite and all-consuming.

"This was in the middle of February?" He tossed me a box of Kleenex. It landed by my feet; I left it there, unaware I was crying.

"Yes, shortly after Luke broke up with me." While talking about this I became absorbed in feelings. I closed my eyes, trying to stay focused on my emotions.

"What did you do when you got fired? I mean, did you call someone or what?" Dr. Lancet's voice began to feel intrusive.

If he had been more attuned to the "feeling" part of therapy, he would have stopped going after the details and focused on my emotions instead. I was actually letting myself feel the pain without jumping around like a banshee to escape it. He should have asked, in a soft, sympathetic and encouraging voice, "What are you feeling?" or "Where are you?" Open questions like that reassure a patient that he's not alone and give him the courage to plunge into the depths of his hell. One of the most frightening aspects of despair is how alone you feel. The isolation fosters a sense of hopelessness. The reassurance that someone else is there with you can make it feel tolerable and allow you to experience and move through it. I wished he realized that and stayed with me in the moment.

"The director of my residency program, who, by the way, had been my therapist many years earlier, broke the news to me in such an apologetic, compassionate manner that I thought he might start crying on the spot. He said he'd tried to protect me, but the head of the hospital was adamant about getting rid of me. He suggested two other programs I should apply to for a job and said that he'd back my application fully. 'Maybe it's all for the best,' he said. 'You were never happy here, anyway. It was a bad match. You'll be a lot happier at either of these other places.' It was a bad match, he was right. But I would have preferred sticking it out over being let go.

"The first person I called was Steve, Luke's best friend. He and I had become very close and he'd been helping me through the break-up. We talked for over an hour and he was very supportive. He even told me I could get a job where he and Luke worked."

"I also called Dani, my mom, and Jack's fiancée with whom I was very friendly. I waited until Luke called later that night to tell him. He was more upset than I was about the firing. Maybe he felt partly responsible, or maybe he was worried that it would push me over the edge. In any case, he offered to come over right away to be with me. I told him that wasn't necessary. He did come by the next day for a few hours. He was so supportive and helpful, saying, 'Come on, I'll help you write a letter to the head of the hospital pleading for your job back.' His concern was touching."

"I had promised Steve I would not mention the word suicide to Luke, and I didn't. The day after I was fired, I called my medical school inquiring over a third year position. I'd been kind of a star in psychiatry there and they offered me a job on the spot. However, they didn't have an opening until November. I applied to two other programs, both of which accepted me." I twirled my finger in the air as if to say, 'Big whoops.'"

Dr. Lancet asked, "But you think all of this might have been avoided if your unit chief hadn't gone away?"

"Definitely. I always freak out and get into some kind of trouble when someone important leaves me or if I feel betrayed."

I told Dr. Lancet about a visit my father paid me at the hospital when I was a third-year medical student: "I was on call and couldn't leave the building, so we met in the cafeteria. I was stressed out and exhausted and I'd nearly fainted on rounds a few times because of the horror of what I was witnessing on a daily basis. Three months earlier, my father had filed a lawsuit against my mother and me to recover the money he'd spent on me after I graduated from college.

"It was a bogus lawsuit, but it devastated me that he would do that, especially because he offered to pay for my premed studies in the first place. *He* was the one who wanted me to go to medical school. If I had been working at the job I wanted, I wouldn't have needed his money. My mom and I met with a lawyer regarding the lawsuit a few times. Those sessions were painful and arduous, requiring us to dredge up in detail all the bad things about my father.

"Despite all that, as I watched my father approach the hospital entrance I could barely contain my delight. His face lit up when he saw me, and he embraced me so tightly I couldn't breathe. Then he held me at arm's length and studied my appearance. 'Look at you, Mel-Mel, in your doctor's outfit. You look fantastic!' I was wearing glasses instead of contacts, using my stethoscope to hold back my out-of-control hair, and my scrubs looked like pajamas. 'I look anything but fantastic.' 'Well, you look adorable to me,' he assured me. We went to the cafeteria, got some coffee and found a table. He opened his briefcase, thrust a pile of papers at me and shouted, 'Did you sign these?'

"On the table in front of me were the affidavits my mother and I had in fact signed. One of them quoted me as saying that my father had volunteered to support me while I pursued my premedical studies and that the amount of money he claimed to have spent on me in his lawsuit was inflated by at least a hundred thousand dollars. I was horrified by the commotion he was causing plus I could hardly make sense of what was happening. I pleaded with him to go outside.

"It was a cold February evening and all I had on were cotton scrubs. My father was wearing a wool overcoat. We stood outside the hospital entrance face to face. 'You're a liar and a bitch, just like your mother!' He shrieked again and again. 'At least I still have one daughter who loves me.' In reality, Dani hadn't spoken to him in over a year because he had hurt her so badly.

"I felt defenseless against the elements and his assault. I ran inside, found a payphone, and called my mother. I was so hysterical she could barely understand what I said. While I was on the phone sobbing, my father came back inside, threw his arms around me and told me he loved me. I wanted to believe him; I was so confused. I went on to fail every exam I took during the next two months. In October of my fourth year of medical school, I threatened to sever all ties with him."

Suddenly I couldn't stop yawning.

Dr Lancet asked, "How long after the incident with the lawsuit was that?"

I counted the months on my fingers. "About nine." I was hoping our session would end soon because I was having trouble staying awake. I didn't realize it upset me so much. "I feel pretty guilty about it now, because he died soon after."

"What happened exactly?"

"I invited my father to meet me for lunch at our favorite deli. Having arrived early, I sat at a table in the back of the restaurant and ordered a cup of tea. We hugged hello. I said, 'You look great, Dad! Is that a new suit?' He shrugged and ordered a cup of coffee for himself and more tea for me. As he stirred milk and sugar into his coffee, I asked him if he knew why I wanted to see him. 'I have no idea, but it's always nice to see you.' His amicable response made me think twice about confronting him. Summoning my courage, I said, 'Do you know how much you've hurt me in the past three years? 'He said, 'I have no idea what you're talking about. But if I did hurt you, it was unintentional and I'm sorry.' He was hardly fazed by my question.

"I continued. 'I don't think you meant to hurt me, but you did. And every time you hurt me, I got so upset I could barely function. First, you reneged on your promise to pay for medical school, and I stopped going to class. Then, you got married without telling me, and I had a horrible car accident.' He said, 'I'm sorry to hear that. I had no idea.' He sounded sincere, but not overly concerned. 'Then you filed your bogus lawsuit.' He jumped to his feet and bellowed, 'That was between your mother and me. It had nothing to do with you. She dragged you into that, not me.'

"I didn't care that everyone in the restaurant turned to look at our table. Staying calm, I looked him in the eye. 'This isn't about blame. The thing is, Dad, no matter how much I love you, I can't continue to have a relationship like this with you. If you hurt me again, I'll sever ties with you completely. It will be as painful for me as having a limb amputated, but I can learn to get around on one leg, whereas I can't stand any more broken promises or major disappointments from you. I no longer need to punish myself.'

"Dad reached across the table, placed his hand on top of mine and started to cry. I stared at our hands, wondering if he'd taken my hand as a loving gesture or in preparation for the amputation."

Dr Lancet said, "I should tell you now that I'm going on vacation for two weeks at the end of August."

Brought back to the reality of the moment, I sucked in my breath. "But you're coming back?"

"Of course!" He wrote in his little book, tore out the page and handed it to me.

I looked at the paper. "Dr. Lancet away August 19 until September 3. Dr. Lancet returns to work September 4." I folded the page into quarters, clutched it in my fist and then held my fist to my heart. My eyes welled up with tears.

"Melanie ..." He scooted forward in his chair. "I want you to listen carefully to what I'm about to say." His voice sounded very gentle. "I planned my vacation way before I met you." He slid off the chair into a crouch. "My trip has nothing to do with you. I'm not leaving because you're bad or because I don't care about you." He paused. "Do you understand?"

"Uh-huh," I muttered as I squeezed the paper harder.

"What did I just say?" He eased into a standing position and rubbed his knees.

"You're not leaving because of me — and you're coming back." I looked at him and forced my mouth into a half smile.

CHAPTER 34

W̲e need to weigh you," said Susan. I followed her to the exam room, stepped onto the scale and shut my eyes.

"Ninety-four." She tore a tiny piece of paper from the exam table and wrote down my weight. "Good, you've gained a few pounds."

"It's the medication." I felt disgusting, but was trying not to think about it. Following her out of the exam room, I said, "By the way, my mom brought my mail and it turns out my insurance runs out at the end of the month." We stopped in front of the tray warmer, which smelled like oatmeal and metal.

"I'll mention it to Dr. Lancet in morning rounds."

After breakfast I went to my room and ran back and forth from the door to the window. Glancing out at the field across the way, I started thinking about a seventeen-year-old patient I'd treated after his parents found him near death from a suicide attempt. His insurance only covered four weeks of inpatient treatment, but at the end of that period he still wanted to die. Despite my spending several hours arguing with his insurance company, they refused to extend his coverage. His parents' income was too high to qualify for Medicaid, so we had no choice but to discharge him or send him to the state hospital. Now, as much as I craved my freedom, I worried that *I'd* be released from the hospital before I was ready.

"Chase!" Dr. Lancet nudged my door open. "Come with me."

I followed him to the lounge, where I sat on the couch under the window and tucked my legs underneath me. Dr. Lancet took a seat on the piano bench a few feet away.

"Susan told me about your insurance. I'm going to call them today." He leafed through my chart. "It's Blue-Cross/Blue Shield?"

"Yup, I'm on the COBRA plan, but that only covered the four weeks since I left my last job. The insurance from my new job never kicked in. Then again, if I hadn't lost my job, I probably wouldn't be here."

"Tell me about that."

"After Luke broke up with me, all I had to hold onto besides my friends was my job. I knew those friendships were tenuous given they were essentially Luke's family. Once I was fired, there was nothing left. When I was with Luke, it was like Mel and Luke, Jack and Aliza, Steve and Sue. I could see my future clearly. There was the big brick house with kids and dogs and the beautiful hospital campus where I went running through the fields. It seemed as though someone took a giant eraser to those scenes from my future and just wiped them out. The only thing left was empty blackness."

"When did the problems between you and Luke come to a head?"

I closed my eyes and concentrated on answering his question. "Shortly after the summer."

In August, we had gone away with Jack, Aliza, Steve, and Sue to stay with Luke's older brother's family at a cabin on the lake. We swam, boated, played tennis, went hiking, made love, sang songs, cooked meals together and had a fantastic time. In the canoe on the last day, Luke turned to Jack and said, "We're the luckiest guys alive. We have beautiful girlfriends and great jobs. I've never been this happy before."

"We spent a wonderful week with the gang and then he started nagging me incessantly."

"What'd you do when he nagged you?"

"Apologized for whatever I was doing that bothered him and promised to correct whatever it was he said I was doing wrong." I shook my head in dismay at the memory of what I'd been willing to put up with. "After awhile, though, I realized he was pushing me away because the intimacy terrified him, and I pointed that out. It took me several weeks to work up the courage to confront him. I was getting angrier and angrier every time he criticized me, which was more and more often. I desperately wanted to appease him so he wouldn't distance himself from me. But I didn't think I deserved all that criticism. I felt totally unappreciated."

"How did he react to your interpretations?"

"He said I was probably right, but that he couldn't help himself. Or else he got mad and said he didn't want to talk about it and went to sleep. I responded to both of his reactions with panic. I was scared to death that he was going to leave me. I couldn't even tolerate him being away overnight for work."

"Go on," Dr. Lancet said in a gentle, encouraging voice.

"Every time Luke worked overnight, I cried and pleaded with him not to go." I shook my head in disapproval of my behavior. In the telling, I realized it was totally irrational. "After he left, I'd look through his closets, smell his clothes and lie on his side of the bed to try to reassure myself that he was coming back. It wasn't even that I minded being alone; it was that he chose to do something else over being with me."

"You know that's part of your illness." Dr. Lancet explained how the threat of being left is unbearably frightening for some people because their sense of self — actually, their sense that they exist at all — depends upon the emotional and physical proximity of their loved one. They get so anxious and desperate at the slightest sign of abandonment that they become irrational enough to be considered psychotic. You fed off each other's pathology. You got whiny and clingy when he distanced himself, which made him distance himself further. It was a vicious cycle. It was some sort of sick dance. You'd approach and he'd retreat, so you'd approach faster and more aggressively, then he'd retreat faster and further. A dance of torture for both of you."

Dr. Lancet wrote something in my chart before closing it. "I'm going to start you on twenty milligrams of Prozac tonight."

"Why? Do you think I'm depressed?" I stretched my t-shirt over the tips of my sneakers, feeling on the verge of acting like an idiot. I was upset.

"You will be when you find out how much this hospital stay is going to cost you." He chuckled and tucked my chart under his arm. "Yes, I think you're depressed and your mood is very labile."

"How much is it going to cost?"

"I'm not sure. We'll have to talk to the accounting office. But I can tell you it's close to a thousand dollars a day. If necessary," he said, moving toward the door, "the finance office will work out a payment plan for you."

I felt so discouraged. "I'll be paying for this for the rest of my life….in every sense of the word."

"Dr. Lancet?" I followed him into the hallway.

"Yes?" He stopped short and turned toward me.

"Is my so-called disease Borderline Personality Disorder?" I tensed as I waited for the answer.

He nodded. "Yes, that's one of them."

"When I was a resident, whenever a borderline came into the hospital we'd say, 'run for your life.' They were so demanding and manipulative, not to mention that one day they worshipped the ground you walked on, and the next day they hated you. Isn't it ironic I never knew I was one?"

His expression became very serious. "Melanie, it's a disease you *have*, not what you *are*."

I barely heard him as I repeated to myself over and over, *"I'm a borderline."*

197

CHAPTER 35

I flung open the door to my room, grabbed the notebook of articles I'd compiled as a resident from the bottom drawer of my desk, opened it to the section labeled "Borderline" and began reading.

Borderlines are often bright and intelligent, and appear warm, friendly and competent. They can maintain this appearance for years until their defense structure crumbles, usually around a stressful event like the breakup of a romantic relationship or the death of a parent.

It's thought that borderlines are born with an innate biological tendency to react more intensely to lower levels of stress than others and take longer to recover. In addition, they were raised in environments in which their beliefs about themselves and their environment were continually devalued and invalidated. Physical, sexual or emotional abuse is usually part of the Borderline's childhood experience. These factors combine to create adults who are uncertain of the truth of their own feelings and who frantically seek an externally elusive stability, though it eternally eludes them
(Losing and Fusing, Roger A. Lewin and Clarence
G. Schultz, year) [1992]

Dr. O'Riley stood in the threshold of my door.
"I'd like to go over the results of your tests with you," he said.
I lumbered after him up the hall to the conference room.
He opened his folder. "Let's see; your IQ is in the superior range."
If the tests had confirmed that my IQ was average or below, I would have believed it. Because the tests indicated I was "smart," I thought it was a fluke and was sure that if I were re-tested, the truth

would come out.

"Well, I was never smart enough for my father — at least not after Dani was born. He used to constantly remind me that my sister was the smart one. 'Dani's going to get a full scholarship to Yale,' he'd say. But when he saw my sad reaction to his comments, he'd add something lame like, 'Melanie will do okay, too.'" I thought about how much it upset me that both my parents seemed to worship my sister, each in their own way. "The only thing I ever felt good about was that I could throw like a boy."

Dr. O. was watching me intently. He shook his head. "If that scenario is indicative of how your father treated you, then your performance on the other tests makes sense."

I steeled myself for his explanation.

"All your responses indicate that your reality testing becomes severely compromised around issues involving intimacy." He leafed through the pages in the folder. "Your thoughts become fluid, your ability to think logically breaks down and you become overwhelmed by fear and anger." He paused. "At the very least, your ability to be rational becomes severely impaired when faced with a stressful situation involving intimacy or when your sense of self is thrown into question."

"By fluid thoughts, you mean my thinking moves back and forth from rational to irrational without my knowing which is which?"

"Yes."

Then I asked the question that had been nagging at me. "Do the test results indicate that I was sexually abused?"

He cocked his head. "That's hard to say unequivocally. Do you have reason to believe you were?"

"When I told Dr. Lancet about the way the director of the residency program had flirted with me at my interview, he said the director's behavior was abusive and sexually exploitative. I was shocked by his reaction, because I had been flattered by the man's come-ons. That was the first time it occurred to me that there might be something wrong with the sexual banter and flirtation I engaged in with men in authority positions.

"Then I started thinking about all the other sexual behavior I engaged in that was inappropriate, I wondered more and more about the possibility of sexual abuse in my background.

"Right after my father's lawsuit, I became promiscuous, jumping from one bed to another, sleeping with a lot of my supervising residents. I always felt unattractive, so I was thrilled to find that I could bed married men, established professors in medical school, and supervising residents on my rotations. I enjoyed the special privileges these liaisons allowed me, like getting to sleep in the residents' call room instead of the students' room, private tutoring, and special access to patients. I was proud of my sexual conquests"

I did not mention I was at it again with Bruce.

"I'd had a few affairs before the lawsuit, but the behavior escalated right after it. I almost had an affair with one of my medical school professors when I was a first year student. I did have an affair with one of my research supervisors, a Swiss physician, before medical school. Then came Charlie, an attending physician. He was my supervisor for the first half of my internal medicine rotation. We'd get together every chance we had. Sometimes he paged me in the middle of the day and I met him in his office, sometimes we went to a motel during lunch, other times he took me to the call room. Once in awhile I stayed overnight in his apartment.

"Shortly before I left for my surgery rotation at a nearby hospital, Charlie asked me to marry him. I thought his proposal was absurd. I was still involved with my boyfriend Johnny. Part of me did find it tempting, because I was intensely physically attracted to him, loved his status and power, and he had been an authority figure to me. Ultimately, I knew the relationship wasn't right for me, or at least that the timing was wrong, so I turned down his proposal and moved onto my next rotation where I immediately seduced the chief resident. For a short period of time, I was sleeping with four men at the same time, including Johnny.

"I knew all along that these liaisons weren't about the sex, which I could have taken or left; rather, they were about my feeling special. It was the attention leading up to and following the sex that I coveted. I'd feel the way I had when my father had doted on me as a child — though, not the way a woman feels with a man who's her equal. The attention I received from these men helped offset the pain my father was causing me.

"After my surgery rotation, I began my fourth year with a two-month elective in ob-gyn at the same hospital where I'd done surgery. Within a week I was sleeping with the chief resident, and within three weeks he had declared his love for me. This affair lasted for the entire rotation, until I 'broke his heart' when he asked me to marry him.

"Next came a pediatric elective and an affair with another resident. This affair lasted the duration of the elective and ended with his heart broken. Oh, and yes, I was still involved with my boyfriend and still sleeping with Charlie, occasionally."

I stared at Dr. O's bowtie. In the stress of revealing these sordid tales my visual perceptions were going awry. It appeared as though the polka dots were jumping around like fleas.

"My father used to stare at my chest and make comments about my breasts. He made lewd comments about other women's breasts and grabbed my mother's in front of me. I don't remember him touching me inappropriately, but my mother was always warning me not to walk around the house in my underwear. At the time, my father's behavior made me very uncomfortable." I started to feel ashamed and hid my face so Dr. O couldn't see my expression. "He also teased me about my period and told me I was unattractive, but that I'd probably grow out of it."

"Your behavior during the testing suggests that you become seductive and sexually provocative at times," Dr. O'Riley said impassively. "However, you do not seem to be aware of what you are doing."

I had no idea what he was referring to.

"Your verbal responses suggest that you were abused and betrayed, but they do not indicate that abuse or betrayal was of an overtly sexual nature."

"In other words, maybe yes and maybe no?" I was frustrated at the ongoing ambiguity.

"Correct." He lowered his glasses to the middle of his nose and looked at me over the top of them. "Your father's behavior was a form of sexual abuse."

"Do the tests suggest that I'm a borderline?" I tried to concentrate on not being seductive or provocative.

He spoke very softly. "Your responses indicate a borderline structure."

"What do you mean?" I felt so ashamed; I wished I could just disappear. I couldn't believe I had missed my own borderline diagnosis. But the worst thing was that I *was* one. The borderlines I had encountered had all been hospitalized, and their diagnoses were obvious because their symptoms were so severe. I had never identified with them.

Diagnosing personality disorders, in general, can be difficult. An official diagnosis requires that a number of criterions be satisfied, as listed in the psychiatric diagnostic manual, and there are many possible combinations of criteria. Due to overlapping features among the thirteen personality disorders, not all affected individuals look — or act — alike. Most "normal" people have traits of one personality disorder or another, but these traits, more stylistic than pathological, don't meet enough of the criteria to make a diagnosis.

Personality disorders are often accompanied by a mood disorder or substance abuse, the severity of which obscures the underlying pathology. Also, borderlines and some of the other personality disordered people act out most of their pathology in the context of an intimate relationship, so people outside their inner circle may not be aware of their illness. Most people with personality disorders are comfortable with the way they are. It's the people around them who find them so difficult.

"Your thoughts are fluid, you have problems with boundaries, and you become easily overwhelmed by the intensity of your emotions, which change very rapidly," Dr. O'Riley continued. "Also, you have great interpersonal conflict and seem to be worried about killing or being killed. A more accurate way of saying that is fear of annihilation. The fear is more one of being erased, rather than literally being killed."

He was describing me to a tee; I felt so humiliated, I wished I *could* be annihilated.

"Your self-image is very unstable and you're preoccupied with the fear of being abandoned." He closed the folder.

I tried to hide my tears. "Is there any hope for me?"

"Of course," he said kindly. "Look how much progress you've made since you were admitted."

"I can't see it." I bowed my head.

"Everybody else can." He smiled and pushed his chair out of the way. "Come on. I'll walk you to your room."

I walked beside him, overcome with shame at having it confirmed for the second time in two days that I was a borderline.

"I'm sorry to tell you this," Dr. O. said outside my room, "but you have group tomorrow."

"No problem," I said, consciously trying not to act like a borderline. Then I lay on my bed and continued reading.

Borderlines typically have poor impulse control, are self-destructive, are highly unstable emotionally and develop wide mood swings and possibly psychotic episodes in response to stressful events. Interpersonal relationships are especially unstable. Typically, borderlines have serious problems with boundaries. They become quickly involved with people, and quickly disappointed with them.

They make great demands on other people, and easily become frightened of being abandoned by them. Their emotional life is a kind of roller coaster.

Borderline personality disorder is one of the most difficult psychiatric illnesses to treat. The road to recovery can take anywhere from three to ten years of intensive psychotherapy.

Or prison, I thought before I fell asleep.

CHAPTER 36

In the medication line, I watched Susan hand out pills. Were my eyes playing tricks on me or did she wink at each patient when she handed them their meds? *Can it be that I'm not her favorite patient? Does she make me feel special because that's her style, but she really treats everybody that way?* I lingered near the front of the line to watch her with a few more patients. She smiled her special smile at each one. My heart sank and I started to feel dizzy.

How could I be so stupid? I bet she doesn't even like me. She's just nice to me because that's her job. I ran back to my room and lay down on my exercise mat. After doing a few unenthusiastic sit-ups, I moved to my bed and pulled out my stack of articles.

An individual with Borderline Personality Disorder has a pattern of unstable and intense relationships. They may idealize a person at one moment, try to spend a lot of time together, and share many intimate details early in a relationship. They may quickly switch from idealizing other people to devaluing them. They may feel that the other person doesn't care, or that the other person sees how "terrible" they are.

Borderline individuals can empathize with and be very nurturing to other people; usually with the hope that the person they are nurturing will be there for them. Some Borderlines have an unusually high degree of interpersonal sensitivity and empathy. These individuals are prone to sudden and dramatic shifts in their perspective of others.

Susan entered the room and playfully untied my shoelace.

I lifted my head to look at her and started to smile, but quickly frowned as I recalled how she'd winked at the other patients. I wanted to reach out and hug her, but instead I rolled away from her to face the wall.

"Do you want to talk now?" she asked as she opened the slats of the window.

Please stay close to me. "Not really."

She sat on the edge of my bed with her back to mine. "Okay," she said softly. "If you decide you do want to talk, I'll be in the nurses' station."

I felt a devastating wave of loneliness when she got up. "I'm a borderline." *Why'd you say that, you idiot?* I glanced at her out of the corner of my eye.

"Meaning what?" Susan sounded as though she had no idea why I was upset.

"Meaning...borderlines are the worst."

She eased the papers out from under my head and looked at them. "Oh!"

"You don't really care about me, right? It's all just an act." Even though I knew about the distorted perceptions and unrealistic expectations borderlines often have when it comes to personal relationships, I was unable to intellectualize my way out of what I was feeling.

She smoothed the pillowcase next to my head. "It couldn't be further from the truth."

"I noticed you're nice to everybody, so I assume it's sort of phony." I hiked my shirt collar up over my face like a veil so she wouldn't see me studying her face.

"That's quite an assumption. Isn't it possible that I care about everybody?" She sounded so compassionate I wanted to cry.

"Not unless you're Jesus," I chuckled despite myself. "I guess it's possible, but I want you to care about me the most." I peeked at her over the top of my shirt. *I'm such a jerk.*

"What would that mean if I cared about you the most?"

I searched her aqua blue eyes for the answer. "I don't know."

As an only child, I had my father all to myself. He played with me, took me to baseball games, read to me, watched television with me, told me bedtime stories and conspired with me against my mother. Then, a month before my sixth birthday, Dani was born.

My father assured me that his love for me would not change. That was the first lie of any consequence that I recall him telling me. I refused to acknowledge Dani for a long time. My playroom became the nursery, but I wouldn't even go in there to get my toys. She was a miserable, colicky baby who screamed and cried constantly. Because she required so much attention, my parents had little time for me. Feeling deprived, I constantly tested my father's love by requesting that he play with me instead of taking care of her. Without fail, he put me off by suggesting that I help with the baby, too. Instead, I'd go to my room and sulk. I blamed my sister for taking my father away from me.

As Dani got older, she continued to encroach on my territory, breaking my toys, diverting my parents' attention from me and insinuating herself in my friendships. Neither of our parents stepped in to protect me, even when she hurt me physically. She threw tantrums and cried until she vomited whenever she didn't get her way. Whenever I complained about Dani, my father defended her, telling me that I was older so I should know better. I did not understand until years later that my father could only love one person at a time.

"If you cared about me the most," my voice trailed off, "I wouldn't disappear." A torrent of tears flowed down my face and I had trouble catching my breath.

"Melanie," Susan said as she put her hand on my shoulder. "You matter to me."

I turned toward her and trapped her hand between my cheek and shoulder. When she left, I went to find Bruce. "Dr. Chase!" exclaimed Dr. Lancet as I passed the nurses' station.

I turned, clicked my heels together, and saluted.

"We need to talk. Now!"

"Aye-aye, Sir." I marched behind him to the therapy room.

Swinging open the door, he pointed to a chair in the center of the room. Mimicking a palace guard, I pivoted and then sat.

"Cut the crap," he said. "Do you know the unit rules, or do you need me to tattoo them on your forehead?" His voice was severe, but I sensed he was suppressing a grin.

I stared at him, trying to gauge the degree of his anger. "Could you really do that?"

"Do what?" He furrowed his brow.

"Tattoo the rules on my forehead," I said, straight-faced.

"This isn't a joke," he reprimanded, and then his voice suddenly softened. "What is it? You look like you saw a ghost."

"Have you always had a moustache?" I squeezed my eyes shut and then opened them.

"At least since you've known me."

"I never picture you with a moustache. I try to picture you in my mind's eye, but can only conjure up pieces of you. Sometimes it's your shoes, other times your hair, but if my life depended on it, I would have never visualized your moustache." I felt like crying, but I didn't know why. "I wish I had a picture of you to carry around with me."

"Melanie, I want you to listen to me very carefully. The fact that you cannot hold onto an image of me is central to your disease." He paused for a few seconds to let his words sink in. "Your father treated you so inconsistently that it was impossible for you to hold onto an image of him that made sense. One minute he loved you with total abandon; the next, he acted as though you didn't exist or as if your very presence caused him pain." Dr. Lancet squatted in front of me. "That this person you loved, needed and trusted treated you so erratically is at the root of your pathology. There was nothing wrong with you. It was his problem. He was a very sick man."

I studied Dr. Lancet's face.

"That's why you can't tolerate it when someone important to

you leaves you, even for a short time."

"What do you mean?" I asked stifling a sob.

"When the person leaves, you can't hold onto the visual image or the emotional feelings of his existence in your life. This causes you to panic and to try to keep him from leaving at all costs. The slightest hint of the person leaving triggers profound anxiety and a loss of your sense of self."

After Luke started pulling away from me, I'd lie next to him, watching him sleep. He slept on his right side. I'd lie on my right side, perfectly aligned yet inches away. I longed to touch him. I abhorred any distance between us; the tiniest space triggered my despair. Like a predator stalking its prey, I sidled toward him one centimeter at a time, holding the blanket away from my body so it didn't move and alert him to my proximity. I'd get so close I could see the peach fuzz on the back of his neck. I stopped breathing as I buried my face in the back of his head and pressed my body against his. I'd panic when he groaned and wouldn't exhale until his snoring resumed. I'd lie awake all night to experience this stolen intimacy, fearing each night would be the last.

"What about my mother?" I slumped forward in my chair, feeling totally depleted.

"She tried her best to take care of you, but she was emotionally vacant. Don't forget, he treated her the same way."

"What rule were you talking about?" I choked back the last of my tears.

"The one about no physical contact between patients. Nancy had a cow about you in morning rounds because you were walking arm in arm with Bruce."

"Oh, that." I rolled my eyes. "She's such an ass!"

"I agree that she overreacts, but because of the situation you're in, you need to be extremely careful to dot your i's and cross your t's. Use her as a yardstick. If your actions will piss her off, don't do them." He leaned against the doorframe stroking his chin. "It would be wise to think about why you insist on breaking the rules all the time."

A few minutes later, I dragged myself to my room and dropped onto my bed and started to read again.

The psychopathology of the borderline patient is a psychopathology at the core. The borderline patient experiences in himself a lack of a sense of his own reliable and predictable ongoingness. At its most basic level, this lack manifests itself in the threat of extinction of the self when approaching emotional closeness with someone else. The threat can burst through with sudden and overwhelming force.

While most people experience closeness to other people that makes the other person available as a source of stimulation and enrichment, as a gain, the borderline experiences this closeness not as a promise, but rather as a threat of a terrible and annihilatory loss. The closeness of the other threatens to bring on the catastrophe of a loss of the self.

"Mel?" my mother whispered as she rubbed my back. "Are you okay?" She sat on the edge of the bed. "Susan said you've been sleeping for hours."

As I rolled toward her, the papers under my head crumpled and the top page stuck to my cheek. I peeled the page off my face and gazed past her at the sunlight coming through the window. "I had a rough session with Dr. Lancet."

She eased the papers out from under me and looked at them. "This reminds me of the tear-stained letters you used to send home from camp. Remember those?"

"I wrote them when I was homesick." I propped my head up on my elbow. "I cried for weeks before I went to camp, and then for weeks when I got to camp. I couldn't stand the thought of being away from Daddy."

"You used to grab onto his arm, drop to the ground and plead with him not to make you go. You'd do the same thing at the end of visiting day, pleading with him not to leave." She shook her head. "You acted as though you were never going to see him again. It was pathetic."

I recalled lying in bed weeks before it was time to go to camp, crying, because I was imagining having to leave my father. "But you did leave."

"Yes, but the camp director had to kick us out." She rolled her eyes at the memory. "Daddy would promise you he'd come back the next day, but the camp didn't allow it."

"So what happened?" I didn't remember.

"He'd get into an argument with the camp director and I'd have to apologize to him and drag Daddy back to the car. It was so humiliating."

I felt disconsolate as I imagined my child-self waiting all day for them to return. I suddenly longed for my father. The intensity of the longing caught me off-guard, but I didn't want to jeopardize this rare moment of closeness with my mother. It felt so good to be talking with her freely and to not feel like she was mad at me. I think we both felt relieved that we could reminisce for a change, rather than talking about our relationship or my current situation.

"You know how he was; he didn't care about rules. He thought he could do whatever he wanted to do."

"Yeah, and he thought I should be able to do whatever I wanted to do also. Remember when I was in fourth grade, and we had dress-up day once a week?"

"You carried on for days because you didn't want to wear a dress to school, so he convinced your teacher to allow you to wear boys' dress-up clothes instead."

"Yeah, and remember those ten-page papers we had to write? We had explicit instructions to do them alone, without our parents help —"

"But he wanted your papers to be scholarly works, so he practically wrote them for you — which is what led to the Pike's

Peak fiasco . . . " We shook our heads at the memory and chuckled. Our chuckles turned into giggles.

"He insisted I write my last paper about the frickin' Peak, but I didn't even know what it was."

"The two of you had books upon books spread out on the basement floor."

"Don't forget the mountains of index cards, maps, and transparencies. The paper never got written because we were so overwhelmed by all the material that we ran out of time to properly organize it, never mind writing the paper." I couldn't stop laughing at the memory of that absurd scenario.

"Then he made up some cockamamie excuse for your teacher."

"He even figured out a way to get around the rules for the Halloween Window Painting Contest, remember? He used to have me trace the picture on oak tag with charcoal and then press it against the window."

"And you won the contest every year." She shook her head in dismay.

"Remember the last visiting day at camp when I was on the verge of becoming anorexic? You were upset because I'd lost so much weight, but Daddy said I looked fine."

"He didn't care that you were on the brink of starvation as long as you were still the best athlete in the camp."

"Why was it so important to him that I was the best at everything?"

She looked me in the eye. "Because the better you were, the better he felt about himself." After she left, I thought about the first time I realized how important it was to my father for me to excel.

About a week after my fifth birthday, my parents and I moved to a new house. Ken, a chubby boy who was my age, lived next door. The first time I met him, he taught me to play knock hockey. We played for a while and I won every game. He showed me his baseball paraphernalia and his bike. I could ride a two-wheeler and wondered why he still had training wheels. We went into his backyard to play catch, and I found that I could throw the ball farther, harder, and straighter than he could.

Later, I asked my father why Ken still had training wheels on his bike. He told me that I was brighter and more athletic than other kids my age and that Ken's father might not let him play with me, because it would make him feel inferior. "A lot of kids and their parents will be jealous of you," he said.

"But I want kids to like me and to want to play with me," I said.

"It's more important to be the best than to be liked," he replied.

From that day on, I became very competitive. I only enjoyed my abilities, however, when other people recognized them. I secretly thought that other kids' parents wished I were their child because I was so outstanding. Yet, if nobody praised me, I assumed I was no good. Ultimately, I lost all faith in my own perceptions, and put all my faith in other peoples' reactions to me.

CHAPTER 37

They denied Dr. Lancet's request for an extension on my insurance coverage," I blurted out in Richie's office. "As of August fifth, I have to pay for everything out of pocket. Dr. Lancet's going to discharge me right after the arraignment, unless something unforeseen happens." I felt my mother's anxiety smothering me from her end of the couch.

"Where are you planning to live?" The words spewed out of her like venom.

"If I can't live with you, I'm sure Scott will let me stay with him and his brother for awhile." I did not want to move in with Scott. I was ambivalent about our so-called relationship. I didn't even know him that well. "Of course Dani said I could live with her in the city."

"Then what, you can destroy Scott's life, too, or sabotage Dani's law school experience?"

"Jean," said Richie with a hint of urgency as he rolled his chair closer to my mother. "I can see why you're upset, but let's discuss this rationally."

"What about me?" I pounded my fist on the couch. "My own mother doesn't want me to live with her."

"Melanie, I know you're hurt and angry." He positioned himself equidistant from my mother and me. "I imagine your mother's feeling the same way."

She glared at me. "I'm angry all right! I raised Melanie to be independent, not to move back home at the age of thirty-one."

"She didn't get bent out of shape when Dani left college and moved back home," I goaded.

"That was different," she practically shouted.

"Because you worship her and hate me!" I said defiantly.

I pictured my mother's house, its walls adorned with pictures of Dani and Dani's artwork. There was not one picture of me. Even Dani acknowledged it, saying it was as though she could do no wrong by our mother, and that Mom was overly critical of me.

"Jean?" Richie whispered, leaning toward her.

"That's absurd; Dani was nineteen when she moved back home, not thirty-one."

"That's not the point! You were glad she came home, even though it meant she dropped out of a prestigious college." Both my parents had pinned their hopes and expectations on me, while they let Dani slide and accepted her for who she was. I assumed there were several factors that contributed to this disparity, the primary one being that I was the oldest, and I had always been an easy and competent child. That Dani was a very difficult child from the get-go must have made them feel less than adequate and overwhelmed. They gave her everything until they were drained, just to keep her from throwing constant, horrendous tantrums. Meanwhile, I fell by the wayside. Perhaps my anorexia was my way of saying I can no longer stand feeling neglected and playing second fiddle, or maybe it was my way of affirming what they already knew -- I did not need anything -- not even food.

Richie looked at his watch. "This an important topic to pursue, but in the interest of time and practicality, we need to talk about where Melanie is going to live after she's discharged."

"Obviously, she's going to live with me," Mom said coldly.

Her overt resentment brought up a painful memory from the end of my senior year in high school. She had been on the verge of getting my father to move out of the house when he had a heart attack. She still planned to follow through, but her friends Jan and Saul, and her sister Jill, told her she had to let him stay. She and I both suspected that my father had deliberately gotten sick to prevent her from making him leave and, during the weeks that followed, her resentment toward him was so great that she treated him terribly. I was certain she now felt similar resentment toward me.

"If you let me live in your house, are you going to give me the finger and make faces behind my back like you did to Daddy after his heart attack?" I looked at Richie and nodded as if to say, *yes, she actually did that*. "A couple of weeks before my eighteenth birthday and my high school graduation, my father, who'd spent practically the last four years in bed, depressed, announced he was going to Montana for an oil deal. It was pretty bizarre, considering he didn't have a job and had never mentioned anything about oil before. Looking back, I realize it must have been one of his many get-rich-quick schemes." I looked at my mother for affirmation. She nodded. "After he'd been gone about a week, we received a call from a nurse in a hospital out there, saying he'd had a massive heart attack and we needed to get there immediately."

Richie looked back and forth between the two of us.

"At first we refused to go. Mom was in the process of getting a legal separation and I didn't want to miss my birthday party, graduation, or the prom." I looked at my mother. "After talking to a few of her friends, my mother realized we had no choice but to go. By that time in my life, I was so sick of him ruining everything. I couldn't believe he was going to mess up these teenage milestones, too. It was so typical of him that it was hard not to think it was deliberate. Part of me wanted him to die because it would make our lives a lot easier."

"And?" Richie leaned so far forward in his chair that it almost tipped over.

"The doctors thought he was going to die, but he didn't. I spent my eighteenth birthday in a Montana hospital, and Mom had to let him come back to our house when he was discharged."

"What about the part about making faces behind his back?" asked Richie, scooting back in his chair.

"It started when we picked him up at the airport and never stopped," I said, my voice trailing off as I remembered our cruelty.

"It's not something I'm proud of," my mother lamented. "But I was so angry at him for trapping me into having to take care of him that I couldn't control myself."

"I did it, too," I said, feeling ashamed to admit it. "All he talked to me about for five years were my grades and college, and then he missed my graduation. I don't even think he knew I left for college."

"The EMS workers were at our house every other night because Len was sure he was having another heart attack. At night he became delirious and psychotic, screaming out crazy things." She looked at me to see if I remembered the nights we'd spent huddled together in the hallway, listening to his delirious rambling. "But at the same time, he did things like mow the lawn, which was completely against doctors' orders. It was as though he was trying to kill himself."

"At least he moved out of your house not long after I left." I massaged my temples with my thumbs to quiet the throbbing in my head. "My high school years were horrible."

By the time I entered ninth grade my father had become so depressed that he stopped working, showering or getting out of bed. When occasionally I missed my ride to school, I'd tiptoe into his room where he lay snoring, wrapped like a mummy in a filthy green blanket. Holding my nose to avoid breathing the stench of decaying hope that oozed from his pores and permeated the air, I'd turn off his television and stand over him whispering, "Daddy, are you awake?" He'd groan as his eyelids fluttered to reveal his glazed-over light green eyes.

"I missed my ride to school. Can you drive me?" I'd cross my fingers hoping this time would be different. But it never was. He'd moan and roll away from me as though he couldn't tolerate my being anywhere near him.

Dejected, I'd stand next to his bed and stare at his back, whispering, "Daddy, Daddy, please drive me to school," before finally giving up.

"Melanie, are you with us?" I suddenly realized my eyes were closed.

"Sorry, I drifted off."

"Jean?" Richie looked over at the crystal clock on his desk.

My mother scowled at me. "I said you could live with me as long as you remain in therapy and agree to certain ground rules."

I opened and closed my eyes rapidly trying to bring her face into focus, yet it appeared to be behind a waterfall. "Don't you think it's ironic that Daddy forced me to do well in school, but he wouldn't even get out of bed to drive me there, no matter how much I begged?"

"Melanie," Richie's voice sounded muted. "Your father was a very sick man."

"Oh," I said without emotion. I turned back to my mother. "What ground rules?"

"You'll have to clean up after yourself, eat like a normal person, be home by eleven each night ..." After that, all I heard was "*blah, blah, blah, blah.*" I *knew* that whether I followed her rules or not, she'd find something to be pissed at me for.

"I'm afraid we're out of time." Richie stood. "Jean, can you walk Melanie back to the unit?"

"Sure." My mother stepped toward me and offered her hand. I looked at it and perceived it as if it were floating in space. The hurt I felt at her attitude gave me a sense of things around me being unreal. The anger that followed the hurt gave me a massive headache. Feeling disoriented by the intensity of my all-too-familiar emotions, I wanted to bite her hand. Instead, I reached for it slowly and let her pull me to my feet.

"Mom," I said, as we walked down the hallway.

"Yes?" she said warily.

"Why'd I have to come home from college to check on Daddy when you lived five minutes from him and I was four hours away?" I wanted to remind her there were actually things about me that she admired and used for her own benefit. I needed to have her recall that I was more than a mental patient who would leave crumbs and dirty dishes in the sink.

"After he moved out, we never heard from him." She looked me up and down. I imagined she was trying to figure out how I, the one who could carry her beloved, but ailing, dog to the vet to be put to sleep and then comfort her, the one who could walk into the apartment of my potentially dead father and take it in stride, had been reduced to being a patient in a mental hospital.

"Yeah, but why did I look in on him instead of you doing it?"

She looked like she was wilting. "You were much braver than I. If one of us had to find him dead, I thought you were the one who could handle it." *At least she knows the truth.*

During my first semester of college, I drove home practically every weekend to check on my father. He lived in a rundown apartment owned by a doctor whose beautiful, grand house was only steps away. I'd pray that neither she nor her kids would be home, because I didn't want to be associated with the "poor crazy man" above the garage.

I'd approach his steep staircase (twenty-five steps, I often counted) filled with trepidation at what I'd find inside. I'd hear the TV coming from his bedroom, but I knew he wasn't watching it. I'd trek through two rooms of squalor to the back bedroom where I'd come upon the familiar scene: a filthy, drooling man tangled in a welter of blankets with his feet sticking out, snoring in the oblivion of sleep. I'd prod him like road kill to see if he was dead or alive. If he was dead, I knew my nightmare would end, but so would my hopes of reviving the father I longed for--that father of my childhood and fantasies, who understood my pain and genuinely cared about me; who taught me to play baseball and took me to games, who ran alongside my bike as I pedaled furiously for the first time without training wheels, and who made up bedtime stories starring my character, "Melanie Call Me Melvin Robin Red Breast."

I'd try to wake him with a soft soothing voice, like a parent waking a child from a nap. He slept so deeply, it was like trying to rouse a patient out of anesthesia. When his hollow eyes opened, he looked past me. I'd pleaded with him to get out of bed to talk to me, but only the slightest shadow of recognition would flicker in his gaze.

On the rare occasions that he did move to get out of bed, I'd avert my gaze from his naked sallow body. I'd rummage through mounds of soiled clothes to find his bathrobe and pass it to him, still looking away — breathing through my mouth to keep out the stench that surrounded him. Trying not to cry, I'd clear old newspapers, dirty tissues, and other debris from the couch so we could sit down together. Tenderly, I'd tell him, "Mommy is worried about you because you never return her phone calls. She asked me to check on you. Are you okay? Can I do anything for you?" He wouldn't look at me or respond. My throat constricted with the awareness that I was talking to the living dead. He had no idea that I'd driven four hours to see him.

After months of this routine, I snapped. One day, after begging him to get out of bed, I grabbed his shoulders and shook him. "Why can't you be a father to me?" I pleaded. "I feel like a charity case because everyone's filling in for you. Saul took me car shopping, Sam played in a parent-child tennis tournament with me and Grandfather is paying my college tuition. Why don't you love me enough to take care of me?"

Dad had sobbed and clutched me to him.

CHAPTER 38

M y mom's going to let me live in her house, but she's going to infantilize me and scrutinize everything I do. She'll probably grade my performance daily, just like Luke did."

"Grade you?" Dr. Lancet cocked his head.

"Yeah, like if I clean all my dishes, sweep the floor and walk the dogs, I'll get a passing grade." I felt the beginnings of a stress headache coming on. "If I leave a glass in the sink or crumbs on the floor, I'll fail."

"What happens if you fail?"

"Then she'll treat me like she treated my father, making snide remarks and talking behind his back." I felt really sad thinking about how she bad-mouthed him. "Dr. Lancet?"

"Yes?"

"What was wrong with my father? Besides being bipolar, I mean."

I held my breath, anticipating his answer. The word I dreaded hearing was "schizophrenia," because that would mean he was even sicker than I'd thought. It also might mean I was genetically predisposed to this dreaded illness. Having gone through so much of my life with no clue as to why my father acted in such a bizarre and upsetting fashion, I longed for whatever insights he might provide.

I was ten when I realized something was wrong with my father. He started becoming irritable, irrational and, as he described it, "claustrophobic." He went on rampages pounding the kitchen table and proclaiming, "The walls are closing in on me! I'm suffocating! We need a bigger house."

Even though we couldn't afford it, we moved to a larger house the summer before I started sixth grade. This impulsive move tested the limits of my parents' marriage. My father insisted on dramatically remodeling the new house, knocking down walls and putting in skylights. We ran out of money midway through the reconstruction and, along with the house, our family was left in total disarray. My parents started fighting over money. Soon their incessant arguments expanded to include other issues.

Walking into my house was like walking into a minefield. We had to avoid stepping on splinters and nails. We never knew when our parents' anger might detonate. Their fighting was vicious. When the screaming started, I slammed my bedroom door and laid on my bed, hugging a pillow over my ears. I dreaded having friends over because the house looked like a construction site and felt like a battlefield.

As my father's torment consumed him, he became increasingly erratic and withdrawn. While he lay rotting in bed, I was my mother's confidante. She talked to me about her venomous hatred toward him and how she believed he had cheated her by failing to provide her with the "American Dream." She expected me to be loyal to her because she was the "good parent" who worked to support our family, went to my sporting events and made sacrifices for me.

My mother perceived my sympathy and need for my father as a betrayal. Since she worked full-time, I often feigned illness to stay home with him, which led to my missing even more school than I already did due to depression and exhaustion. I never attributed my confusion in class to my absence and failure to keep up with homework. Instead, I assumed I was stupid.

Dr. Lancet answered, "Having never met him, it's hard to say, but based on what you and your mother have told me, I'd say he was most likely bipolar, passive-aggressive, and narcissistic. His narcissism is what hurt you the most." He leaned toward me and spoke very softly. "Regardless of his diagnoses, he treated you so abusively that I'm surprised you didn't break down a lot sooner."

"But I did break down a lot sooner. It's just that until now, I've only hurt myself." I peered at him through my hair, which was hanging over my face. "I've been preoccupied with suicide since sixth grade when I went through puberty, and anorexic since eighth grade. During most of high school, I sat on the floor in the corner of my room, rocking back and forth and pulling out clumps of my hair. I was so weak from not eating I could barely move, except of course, to go running." My memories were vivid of sitting in that corner suffering. "Not only that, but I used to storm into my parents' room at night and say I wanted to kill myself."

"But you didn't seek professional help until you were a junior in college?" he asked.

"My mother asked me if I wanted to see a psychiatrist, but I always said no. She sometimes threatened to hospitalize me, especially if I didn't gain weight. I'd throw a tantrum and say if she did, I'd never talk to her again. I guess because I continued to function adequately in school and extracurricular activities, she never pushed it. She probably didn't have the energy to figure out 'the right' thing to do. I thought admitting I needed help was a sign of weakness, and my role in the family was to be strong."

Thinking again about how miserable I had been in high school I asked, "How exactly did my father abuse me?"

I had an image of my father playing catch with me. We shared a love for baseball, just he and I, not my sister or my mother. We played it, talked about it and went to games together. He also coached my softball team. On Sunday mornings I'd go with him to a nearby elementary school to watch him play men's softball.

Dr. Lancet looked at me thoughtfully. "He saw you as an extension of himself; this is the narcissistic component. As such, he demanded you perform in order to please him. Besides that, he was either overly involved with you or behaving as though you didn't exist. He was so erratic, you never knew if you were coming or going." He took a deep breath. "He set you up to fail, and then called you crazy for being upset. Plus, he created a world without rules, boundaries, or cause-and-effect relationships for you."

As a college graduation present, my father bought me Brin, a puppy. He promised to take care of her if I were ever unable to do so. He reiterated this promise when I agreed to go to medical school. "Medical school's four years, you know," I said. "You have no idea where you'll be for that long."

"I'll take care of her even if I move to Europe and have to come back to do it," he assured me. I wanted to believe he'd come through for me even though I knew the chances were slim.

He didn't move to Europe. In fact, he moved to a house on the beach about an hour away from where I lived. So when I called him in my third year of medical school to make good on his promise, I didn't anticipate his response.

"Dad," I said, "I have a month of night calls, so could you take Brin for the month?"

He said no, without explanation.

"But Dad," I cried, "I need your help."

"Get your mother to take her!" he yelled.

"She was never part of this deal. It was you who promised," I choked out between sobs.

"You're acting like a lunatic and a big baby," he exclaimed as he hung up on me.

I had stared at the phone feeling enraged and helpless.

Sucking on the ends of my hair I asked Dr. Lancet, "Am I as sick as my father was?"

Dr. Lancet deliberated over his answer. "That's irrelevant. The question is whether you'll make sure you receive and follow through on the treatment you need."

"Okay," I sniffled, wiping my face with the collar of my shirt. "Does that mean you're going to treat me after I'm discharged?"

"It looks that way." He gave me a reserved smile.

I couldn't believe how nonchalant he sounded. I was ecstatic, relieved, and grateful. I wanted to hug him. Instead, I sat perfectly still and stared at him. He was the only person on the planet who could save me, and he had just agreed to do so.

"

CHAPTER 39

C an we talk?" I asked Susan as she he handed me my morning meds.

"Later, okay?" She craned her neck to see who was behind me in line.

But I need to talk now. I chucked the empty cups at a garbage pail and stormed into the TV room. *Screw her and her stupid pink shirt. Who needs her, anyway?*

About ten minutes later, she breezed into the room and sat next to me. "Okay, I'm all ears."

"Never mind. Mom and my attorney will be here any minute." *Preppy jerk!*

"We can talk until they get here," she suggested cheerfully.

"You're probably relieved I can only talk for a few minutes." I lit a match and intentionally singed the end of my hair.

"Why do you want to hurt yourself," she asked calmly.

I studied her pink polished nails and wished she would dig them into my flesh. "I don't know," I said truthfully.

"Did something happen over the weekend that upset you?"

"No. As a matter of fact, on Friday Dr. Lancet agreed to treat me as an outpatient. I should be happy, not upset. The weekend was the same as always; Mom, Dani, and Scott came to visit."

I was beginning to understand why I often felt deeply depressed or anxious in situations that would make other people feel happy or serene. When something good happened or was promised to me, I expected the good thing would end up hurting me or that the promise of something I desperately wanted would be reneged just when I got my hopes up. My depression and anxiety were in anticipation of the disappointment I believed was inevitable. This convoluted reaction had everything to do with my experiences with my father and often little or nothing to do with the reality of the present situation. In psychological terms, this is called "transference." You literally transfer your experience of people from your past — usually your parents — onto your perceptions of people and circumstances in your present.

"Do you think being mad at me has anything to do with Dr. Lancet making a commitment to you?"

"You're not just another pretty face," I said, half-smiling despite myself. "Maybe I'm afraid Dr. Lancet will change his mind, so I'm taking it out on you. It's that borderline splitting stuff."

"That's worth pursuing."

"Splitting is the hallmark of borderline pathology." I stood on the chair and pretended I was holding a microphone. "One day they idealize their love objects and the next day they devalue them." I took a bow before jumping off the chair.

Splitting is when you divide the people in your life into the good guys and the bad guys by idealizing one and devaluing the other, then pitting them against one another. You can "split" the same person into the "good dad" and the "evil dad" for example. It is an unconscious process. It's also a classic characteristic of the borderline pathology.

Susan clapped. "Okay, professor, it's time for your meeting."

I walked into the conference room and took my usual seat. Tom sat next to me, with my mother, Dr. Lancet, and Richie opposite us. I waved to my mother. She gave me a tentative smile.

"We're here to discuss the final details of Melanie's arraignment," said Tom. "The arraignment's scheduled for Friday morning at nine. Jean, you'll pick Melanie up in the morning and take her. I'll meet you at the courthouse."

Dr. Lancet nodded. "I'll convert her to voluntary status today and write the pass for Friday morning. I'll make the pass from eight to five, just in case. You're not planning to abscond with her are you?" he said lightheartedly to my mother.

"Hardly," she said dryly.

"What should I wear?" I blurted out. I'd worn nothing but shorts and sweatpants for the past month and had no idea if any of my clothes even fit me.

"Melanie, don't waste everybody's time with inane questions," snapped my mother.

"Stan, are you still planning to discharge Melanie after the arraignment?" Richie asked.

"I'll assess her when she returns from court. If she's okay, I'll give her weekend passes and discharge her on Monday." Dr. Lancet squinted at me. "That is, assuming all goes well."

My anxiety over the prospect of being discharged superseded my excitement over the fact that as a voluntary patient, I'd be able to go outside. I was furious at myself for feeling this way.

I tried to picture life outside the hospital, but all I could conjure up was the inside of my mother's house, her being angry at me, long empty days stretching into even longer emptier nights, and the absence of Dr. Lancet and Susan. I began to feel lonely and afraid, as though I was being thrown into a huge void where there was nothing to stop me from shriveling up and dying like a leaf falling from a tree.

I'd never been without a job, school, or friends before. I was terrified I'd have another breakdown. I started to feel as though I were disintegrating. I was afraid if I expressed my thoughts to Dr. Lancet, he would make me stay in the hospital longer. Despite my terror, I didn't want to do that. Beneath my panic, I was aware that what I was feeling was a normal response to losing the security of the hospital. I tried to rein myself in and focus on the meeting.

Dr. Lancet must have picked up on my discomfort. "I feel pressured to discharge you because your insurance ran out and I'm going on vacation for two weeks the day after you're discharged."

"Who'll take care of me while you're gone?" My heart sank at the thought of him being away.

"I've arranged for you to see Dr. Bernstein, the head of the adolescent unit, while I am away." He gave my mother a reassuring smile.

I didn't want him to assign someone else to take care of me. I wanted him to change his plans. I knew this was irrational, but in my fantasies he would have stayed for me. I pleaded with myself to stay present and be reasonable. "Isn't Dr. Bernstein the guy who walks like a duck, has hair like Albert Einstein and wears the same blue polyester suit every day? I see him walking around the hospital when I look out my window."

Dr. Lancet smiled. "Yes, that's him. He's a brilliant practitioner and a lovely man. I'm sure you'll like him."

"That's all I had to say. Does anyone have any questions?" asked Tom as he closed his briefcase and looked at each of us for a moment.

"After the arraignment, will I be allowed to leave the country, or even the state?" I asked.

"As of now, you can go wherever you want. Once you're sentenced, that may change."

My mother turned to me. "Are you planning to go somewhere?"

"Not really, but Scott mentioned going to his father's house in Mexico." I was going to ask Tom about this in private, but it sort of slipped out. Or maybe I *let* it slip to show my mother that I wasn't totally dependent on her. Scott was the one who'd been pushing for the vacation. I didn't care one way or the other. I think it was his way of trying to ensure we'd have time together when I got out of the hospital. I'd felt pressured by him to make the plans, probably the way Luke felt when I kept insisting we go away together.

"Are you out of your mind? Do you have any idea what's going on here?" My mother sprang to her feet.

"Jean, we can talk about this later," Richie said earnestly.

She slowly sat back down. "Last night she was crying with regret over what she'd done. Now she's planning a trip with her *next victim!* She makes my head spin," she said through clenched teeth.

"I didn't say I was going. I just asked if I was allowed to go." I felt defensive, even though I knew I had deliberately riled her.

Richie responded in a soothing voice. "Jean, let's talk about it after this meeting."

Tom said nonchalantly, "Are we all set for Friday?"

"I guess so," my mother said reluctantly.

"Is there anything else?" Tom asked. "Okay. Feel free to call me if you have any questions."

Richie and Dr. Lancet flanked my mother, and Tom walked a foot or so behind them as though to run interference in case I tried to tackle her. *Why is it that I always say the wrong thing at the wrong time?* So often the questions that arose in my mind made sense to me and seemed relevant and important. After I said them, I was confronted with how inappropriate they seemed to other people. Over time, I came to realize that part of my difficulty determining what was appropriate had to do with my illness. Part of it had to do with having grown up in a family where the reactions were so subjective and unpredictable that I never developed the instinct to gauge what was suitable.

As I watched the four of them walk off the unit, I was overcome by a burning desire to talk to my father. It suddenly seemed as if he were the only person who could alleviate my profound sense of despair. Despite how much he'd hurt me, he was still the person to whom I'd felt closest. I'd always believed that he was the only person in the world who could truly understand me and fulfill my need to be taken care of and loved unconditionally. It was precisely because I knew the comfort and reassurance he was capable of offering, that his negligence and erratic behavior had been so painful.

Whenever Luke hurt or neglected me, I'd wished my father was still alive. I knew he would have made me feel better. I would have been less desperate over the breakup if I'd been able to retreat to the sanctuary of my father's love. Even though it had been so fleeting and elusive, I still found comfort in it, even as an adult. I was now seeking this same comfort from Scott. He was probably only capable of providing it in tiny doses and not without reciprocity. Fully cognizant that I didn't have the emotional energy to give much of anything back, I felt that our relationship was doomed to fail. But to fend off my current anguish, I called him. Trying to sound nonchalant, I said, "My mom isn't coming tonight. Do you want to stop by around seven?" I hated myself for using him but didn't want to be alone.

"I'd love to," Scott said enthusiastically.

I felt so relieved that he wanted to see me. I called Dani to tell her what was going on.

As I hung up the phone, Dr. Lancet knocked on the door of the phone booth. "Come with me," he mouthed as he pointed to his watch.

I followed him to the therapy room. "What did you think about the meeting?"

"I shouldn't have asked about Mexico. I knew it would piss my mother off." As much as I wanted to pacify my mother, part of me resisted. I resented her rules and that I needed her so much. My comment may also have been an expression of the hurt and fear I felt at Dr. Lancet's mention of his upcoming vacation. It was more natural for me to express defiance and indifference. *It works both ways, buddy,* I was telling him indirectly. *You leave me and I leave you, no big deal.*

"You should discuss this with Richie." Dr. Lancet's demeanor changed slightly. "I converted you to voluntary status."

"Meaning . . ." My hands started tingling, which made me aware that I was anxious. Would I be worthy of the trust implicit in him giving me more freedom, or would I blow it? I felt unsure of my ability to control my self-destructive impulses without a tight rein around me. I almost felt like pleading with him not to do it. At the same time, I couldn't wait to sign myself off the unit to go for a run.

"Technically, you can sign yourself out of the hospital," he said as he stood. "More practically, it means you can go outside."

I felt light-headed with anxiety as I got to my feet.

" "But Melanie," he said as he opened the door, "please don't do anything foolish."

I visualized myself going for a run on the hospital grounds and visiting all the places I'd seen out the windows: the tennis courts, the gazebos, and the woods beyond the field. I hoped I wouldn't be too tempted to leave the grounds but knew the pull would be very strong.

Of course, I broke the rules. I went running through the adjacent neighborhoods, and one time, I even went to a Chinese restaurant with Bruce to pick up some food. Nothing became of any of these transgressions, but my guilt over having betrayed Dr. Lancet's trust was so great that I ended up confessing to him months later. He was neither surprised nor angry. He said testing the limits was part of my illness and that hopefully, at some point in the future, it's a behavior I'd be able to rid myself of.

CHAPTER 40

"Congratulations," said Susan as she handed me the sign-out sheet. "You have family therapy this morning at 9:30, so just go for a short jog, then go straight to Richie's office."

I located my name on the sign-out sheet, jotted 9 A.M. in the box marked "Time out," signed my initials, and wrote "social worker's office" in the area marked "destination." Then I handed her the clipboard and waited for her to add her initials to mine.

Once outside, I inhaled deeply to savor the smell of freshly cut grass. It felt so liberating to be out in the fresh air, even with the August sun beating down on my head. Since I only had about twenty minutes, I ran as fast as I could around the field, past the tennis courts and then once around the hospital until I saw my mother coming down the driveway. I waved furiously to get her attention. *She probably thinks I'm some lunatic patient.*

As I ran to greet her, my heart sank, remembering how angry she'd been at me the day before.

Mom chose her usual spot on the couch near the door.

Feeling torn between wanting to sit on her lap and wanting to be in a separate room from her, I sat in a chair across the room from both of them. She and I stared at one another impassively.

Richie wheeled his chair directly across from my mother. "Melanie's going to be discharged to your house in less than a week. It's vital that we address what happened in yesterday's meeting."

"I'll say!" my mother flashed me "the Geller look." Then she looked at Richie and spoke about me as though I wasn't in the room. "The night before the meeting, I felt relieved, because she was finally reacting appropriately to the situation. Then, less than twelve hours later, she was talking about going on vacation with

Scott." She clenched and unclenched her fists as she spoke. "She nearly killed Luke, is on the verge of going to jail and losing her medical license, and she's thinking about going on vacation?" I expected foam to come out of her quivering mouth, like some rabid animal. "Where's the remorse? Where's the distress? Where's the concern about her future? She's just like her father!" I flinched at this last declaration.

Richie shook his head to convey to my mother that he sympathized with her. Then he turned his head slightly toward me. "Melanie, what do you think about what your mother just said?"

I finished biting off the fingernail I'd been chewing throughout her tirade and spit it into my hand. "I understand why she's pissed, but what does she think I should do, sit in my room and cry all day? Even in the best of circumstances she looks down on people having fun." I glowered at her for a second and then put my feet up on the coffee table, which I knew would piss her off even more. "If it were up to her, everybody would work twenty hours a day seven days a week. Then she wouldn't resent having to work to earn a living or the fact that she doesn't know how to have fun herself." I tied my shoes together and admired my handiwork.

"Nonetheless, I can't explain why one moment I feel depressed and suicidal, and the next minute I feel on top of the world." My words came quickly. My thoughts started racing and I started feeling very agitated. "Maybe I'm a rapid-cycling manic-depressive, or maybe I'm just manifesting the unstable emotions and wide mood swings that characterize borderlines. How should I know? I'm not the one who married a lunatic and then allowed him to pass on his genes to my children." I felt like a bulldozer blindly razing everything in its path.

I immediately wished I could take back my words. Then I noticed with a start that I was picking at the cuticles of my thumb. *This was my father's habit, not mine.*

Richie cleared his throat. "Jean, you're angry at Melanie for being so much like her father. Melanie, you're angry at your mother for giving you such a difficult father. Realistically, both of you are furious at Melanie's father, not each other. I think you love and care about one another very deeply, but you don't know how to express that. Therefore, I think it makes sense to continue working together after Melanie's discharge. What do you think about still seeing me?"

"I think it would be very helpful," said Mom.

"I think it's a great idea."

Richie nodded. "Good. You're being discharged next Monday. Why don't we meet in my outpatient office a week from Friday?" He glanced at my mother. "Is three o'clock okay?"

"That should work."

"Melanie?"

"Sounds good to me," I said without looking up. *Who's going to pay for this? Since I'm the bad guy, I'm sure I'll have to pay, just like I had to pay for the hospitalization as though my illness was my fault. We should split the costs as a way of symbolizing that we share equal responsibility for the problems in our relationship.*

Richie handed Mom his business card and then shook my hand as I walked toward the door. "Good luck in court and with your discharge."

"Do you want to go for a walk?" I asked my mother as we passed the hospital entrance.

"Not especially."

I felt so disheartened and alone. Instead of going outside I headed back to the unit to look for Susan. It surprised me that after waiting for so long to be allowed to go outside, not only did I lack the energy and drive to do so, but seeking the security and support of people on the unit seemed more pressing.

CHAPTER 41

I looked at the dress my mother brought for me to wear to court. It was uglier than I possibly could have imagined. *Where'd she get this, from my grandmother's closet?* Knowing the dress would make me look fat and frumpy, I slipped it over my head to try it on. I laughed out loud, realizing I didn't even have access to a full-length mirror. While I was busy amusing myself, Dr. Lancet cracked my door open.

I pointed at the dress. "I think my mother's trying to get back at me by bringing the most hideous dress she could find."

He half-smiled but became somber as we walked to the lounge. "How are you?" he asked, assuming his usual spot on the edge of the piano bench.

I slumped into the corner of the couch a few feet away. "My brain feels sluggish. I don't have any energy and I feel really sad. Otherwise, I'm doing great."

"Do you think it has to do with the arraignment?"

"No, I feel surprisingly indifferent about it." I felt so lethargic.

"You're doing your classic compartmentalization act." He sounded bored. "That's okay, as long as you don't act cavalier once you get there."

I knew I had to monitor myself constantly. "If my mother flashes me the Geller look, I'll know I've blown it."

"Your mantra should be, think before you act." He repeated the phrase two more times.

"Dr. Lancet," I said meekly, "Why'd you decide to treat me as an outpatient?" I stared at a stain on the carpet because I was too ashamed to look at him.

"You deserve a second chance and I think I can help you."

"Is it also that you think I'd hurt myself if you refused to treat me?" I raised my eyes surreptitiously to glance at his expression.

He paused, choosing his words carefully. "I think the likelihood of your doing something extremely self-destructive will increase dramatically if I don't treat you. What do you think?"

"I agree." I bit my knee hard enough to leave teeth-marks. "I've only come close to suicide twice. Once, of course, was after Luke broke up with me. That doesn't include the two times I nearly killed myself in a car accident. Both times were after my dad left me. In October of my senior year of high school, I returned home after school one day and found a note from my dad on the kitchen table. "I've gone away for a while; don't know when I'll be back."

The following day, I totaled my car on the way home from school. A neighbor found me lying unconscious in a pool of blood in the street. When I came to, I informed the EMT that she couldn't call my father because he'd left the previous day and I didn't know where he was.

"But you never actually tried to kill yourself?" I was sure we'd already talked about this, but it was probably during the admission interview, and maybe he didn't remember the details.

"When I was a junior in college, I had a plan." I closed my eyes and pressed my palm against my forehead. "I used to do a lot of things that could have been interpreted as suicidal, like riding my bike through really dangerous neighborhoods and along highways."

In college, I lay awake night after night soaked in a cold sweat, plotting my suicide. After hours of tossing and turning, I'd jump out of bed and write poems about dying. I stared out the window during my classes, preoccupied with wanting to die. I stopped doing my homework because all I saw in every line of every book I read were the words, "I want to die."

Finally, I called my mother and told her I was failing all my classes because I was so depressed. She told me to try harder and "get over it." My roommate introduced me to speed. On speed, I could read and concentrate and had the energy to get out of bed. That's when I realized I had a "chemical imbalance" just like my father, and that perhaps drugs like the ones he took, Dexedrine and anti-depressants, could help me as well.

Even though I hadn't spoken to my father for two years, I called him. He flew to my college a few hours later and didn't leave until I made an appointment with a psychiatrist in the college mental health center. The psychiatrist diagnosed me with clinical depression and started me on an antidepressant. Within two weeks, I was able to function without thinking about wanting to die. If my father hadn't come through, I would have killed myself.

I stared directly into Dr. Lancet's pupils. "Won't you be held responsible if I mess up?"

"Yes, if you hurt yourself or somebody else, I'll be liable," he said matter-of-factly.

"So why are you taking a chance with me?" I felt vulnerable like a little girl.

"Because I know I can help you if you'll let me. I'm only reluctant because I can't contend with your overwhelming need to destroy yourself unless you wholeheartedly capitulate to me."

"What if I sign a contract or something? I know borderlines sign contracts saying that if they decide to kill themselves they will call their therapist and then go to the emergency room of the local hospital. Isn't that a prerequisite of accepting a borderline as an outpatient?" I thought how lucky I was in a way not to have to worry about treating borderlines on an outpatient basis.

"I don't believe in contracts. If someone's determined to kill herself, she's not going to call anyone to discuss her plans regardless of any piece of paper she signed. Besides, if the therapist trusts his patient enough to adhere to a written contract, he should trust her word as well."

"Realizing that if I self-destruct I'll bring you down too, makes me feel responsible for you. That's a good way for me to justify not destroying myself. It's as if I can allow myself to be okay because I'm doing it to protect you, not for myself." I wondered why he was frowning.

"Are you thinking she talks a good game, but is this just another of her brilliant borderline manipulations?"

"No. I'm thinking the fact that you have so little concern for your own well-being is very sad."

I was not used to seeing Dr. Lancet express any emotion except sternness, consternation, and warmth through teasing. Seeing him so down on my account, I felt bad; I didn't think I was worthy of feeling sad over.

He drummed his fingers on the lid of the piano, deep in thought. "I'm wondering if I should wait to discharge you until after I return from vacation."

"Please don't make me stay here two extra weeks! I promise I won't do anything stupid while you're away." I wanted to throw myself at him and grab his legs.

"Let's see how tomorrow goes. We'll talk when you return from court."

"Okay." I felt exhausted.

"I'll be here in the morning to write your pass for court. Then I'll see you when you return." He put his hand on the doorknob. "If things go well, I'll write your passes for the weekend."

CHAPTER 42

D r. Lancet strolled onto the unit shortly after my mother arrived. "Hi, Jean!" He looked me up and down and nodded his approval.

"I know, I need stockings. Otherwise, I look beautiful." I gave him a sardonic grin.

He looked at Mom and shrugged his shoulders as if to say, *you can take the girl out of Bronx, but you can't take the Bronx out of the girl.* "I wrote the pass, so you're all set. Have someone page me when you return."

"Where'd you find this dress; it's disgusting," I whined as Mom and I waited for the elevator.

"Don't start," she said icily.

She was either unable or unwilling to respond to my masked plea for compassion. I felt embarrassed for wanting this from her. This scenario triggered an early memory:

My father tells me a story as we walk down the corridor of our apartment building. Or, maybe he was telling me a joke. I am barely listening to him because I'm studying my tiny three-year-old hand clasped in his large callused one. My thumb, the one that I do not suck, caresses the place where his hand joins his wrist. His palm obscures mine, giving the illusion that my arm is growing out of his hand. I squirm with delight at the thought of being an extension of him. I wish we were physically linked; then he could never leave me.

At the elevator, I gasp as he reaches for the down button because I want to press it. He quickly realizes his mistake and lifts me up. "Sorry Mel-Mel, you've become such a big girl that I thought you could reach the button yourself." I stand on my tip-toes and stretch to my full height like a peacock showing off my feathers, as if to confirm my father's perception of my being a big girl.

When we enter the elevator, he swoops down and lifts me up to the button. I giggle in relief. I don't ask where we were going because I am so delighted to be with him, that nothing else matters. When we arrive at the fair, I ask him to give me a piggyback ride. He crouches down. As I scamper up his back, he says, "Okay sweet pea, hold on tight." I nestle my face into the crook of his neck, sling one arm across his chest and rub the top of his head with my free hand. When he asks me if I see anything that interests me, I do not respond right away. I am content savoring the smell of his skin and the feel of his crew cut. I am as reluctant to unbury my head from the sweat-drenched nape of his neck, as I would have been to extricate myself from my toasty warm bed on a cold winter morning.

"The court is in the police station. Make a right and get on the highway going north," I said as we pulled out of the parking lot.

As we drove through the town where Luke and I had lived together, (the same town as the police station), I was filled with nostalgia and an acute sense of loss. "Oh, my God, Luke just drove by!" I felt a tidal wave of sorrow and longing pass through me. Little did I know he was a week away from moving out of town to an undisclosed location.

The police station was an unremarkable yellow brick building sandwiched between an apartment complex and a public storage facility. As we climbed the five stairs to the entrance, I felt nauseated by the reality of what was happening and by the fact that I had just seen Luke.

A police officer directed us to the booking room, a long narrow room with a walkway down the middle surrounded by metal desks on either side. Coffee cups and stacks of paper littered every surface. Scuffmarks marred the gray linoleum floor.

A heavyset officer told me to go to the wall at the far end of the room to have a mug shot taken. I realized that when you've poisoned someone, having a mug shot taken is part of the protocol, but it seemed bizarre to me to be treated like a criminal. I still thought of my crime as being about Luke and me and my mental illness rather than rules and laws.

Next, a swarthy looking officer with an enormous neck instructed me to dab my fingers into an inkpad. He pressed my hand in a rolling motion over the fingerprint card. I became so disoriented that I felt as though I was watching the scene from the ceiling. The disorientation was a fear response to my suddenly realizing the gravity of the situation.

A short officer with kind eyes directed my mother and me to follow him down a dimly lit stairwell. "I'm taking you to a room in the basement where you'll wait until court commences."

As I descended the stairs, I felt woozy. When I saw Tom sitting at a table in the center of the otherwise stark room, I wanted to collapse into his arms.

He stood and smiled at us. "Congratulations! You officially have a police file."

I noticed Mom didn't flash *him* the Geller look. I'm sure if I had said something similar, everyone would have gasped and reprimanded me. Was it that Tom had established his credibility and use of good judgment enough to have earned the license to a bit of sarcasm here and there? Or was it that my mother was so hypercritical of me in all arenas, that her reacting to my comments as inappropriate was just part of the bigger picture? Since I wasn't able to differentiate between appropriate and inappropriate as far as my comments were concerned, I had to assume she knew better than I did.

Once we were seated, Tom said, "We'll go into the courtroom and wait for the clerk to call your name. You and I will stand in front of the judge while he formally charges you. The assistant district attorney, Eloise Lansky, will be there as well."

"Luke's lawyer is a woman? Women intimidate me." I was feeling more and more self-conscious about my looks by the second.

"As a matter of fact, she is quite intimidating," he chuckled. "Don't worry about her though, she can't directly address you. After the judge reads the charges he'll set bail, which is just a formality in this case. Once you pay the bail, you'll be released."

Soon, the officer reappeared. "Court's in session."

The three of us followed him back upstairs to the courtroom. We waited through three traffic violation cases before the judge called my name.

As Tom and I approached the judge's bench, I noticed a tall, lean, woman dressed in a meticulously tailored suit approaching the bench as well. I whispered to Tom, "That's Eloise? She'll eat me alive!"

I was so preoccupied with feelings of inadequacy that I barely heard the judge read the charges. I redirected my gaze from Eloise, the chic professional, to the judge.

I thought about the time my father and I went to small claim's court because we were suing my landlord to get my security deposit back. It was one of those scenarios that I now longed for when my father stepped up to the plate and helped me. We joked around while we waited for the judge to hear us, and my father comforted me because I was frightened to face my landlord. The situation at hand, although critical in terms of my future, seemed miniscule and uneventful to me.

"Do you understand that you are being charged with first degree assault, a felony?"

"Yes, Your Honor," I whispered. *I'm a felon*, I said to myself over and over.

He set bail at five hundred dollars. A female officer escorted us back to the basement.

"Jean, you will have to get a bank check for the bail. Then you'll be on your way," said Tom. "I need to catch a train, so Melanie will have to wait here alone while you go to the bank."

"I'm going to have to lock you in a jail cell while you wait," said the officer, dangling a large key ring in front of me.

Mortified, I looked wide-eyed at my mother. "Please hurry," I mouthed. Her expression mirrored my own.

The officer unlocked the first cell in a row of three. "I guess it will only be for a little while," she said as she re-locked the door and walked away.

I stared at the cement wall across from me and, growing weary, sat on the narrow steel bench attached to the far wall. As I ran my hands along the cold steel, I realized I felt nothing. I wondered apathetically if this was a portent of things to come. I realized later that I couldn't bear to think about the horror of being locked in a jail cell. To think that I may end up spending many years behind bars was beyond horrible. As often happened when I couldn't stand to face the situation head on, I nodded off.

Dr. Lancet greeted me when I returned to the unit. I told him court was pretty uneventful and that the worst part was passing Luke on the way to the court. I also explained about having all my insecurities about my appearance stirred up by his lawyer. "She looks like she came off the cover of *Vogue*."

"You do understand that under no circumstances are you allowed to contact Luke, right?" His voice carried a hint of alarm.

"Yes! I get it," I said petulantly.

"Okay then, are you ready for your pass?"

"I guess so. It's not like I have any big plans or anything." I wasn't looking forward to my pass. I would have preferred to stay at the hospital to wind down after my big day out. If it had not been a weekend when neither Susan nor Dr. Lancet would be at work, I might have reneged on the pass.

"Tomorrow, your mother can pick you up at nine and bring you back at two. If that goes well, you can go home from nine till five on Sunday. Just do me a favor; stay out of trouble." He wagged his finger at me. "Barring any unforeseen incidents, I'll discharge you on Monday."

"Then what? You're going to the Hamptons with the rest of the shrinks?" I started to panic when it suddenly sank in that he'd be inaccessible to me during his two-week vacation. That was only a few days away. "What if I have an emergency and need to get in touch with you?"

"You'll meet with Dr. Bernstein every day. If something happens between your sessions you can call him."

"I feel as though you're handing me off to a foster parent," I whined.

He took a deep breath and blew it out with an hmmph. "Melanie, if you don't think you can handle being discharged while I am away, I'll keep you in the hospital. If I weren't going away, I would have waited until you'd gone on a few more passes. If you weren't going to live with your mom, I definitely would not discharge you until I returned."

"No, I'll be okay." Sweat saturated my entire body.

CHAPTER 43

N ancy wished me luck as I left the unit to go on my first pass. "How pathetic is that?" I asked Mom. "She's wishing me, a thirty-one-year-old medical doctor who's taken care of patients in life and death situations, luck on a five-hour pass from a psychiatric hospital?"

"Very," said mom.

Driving home, Mom focused on the road. I stared out the window contemplating the irony of returning to live in the town I swore I'd never live in again. Many of my peers wanted to raise their children there, but I wanted to leave it behind. I was never happy living in an ultra-competitive affluent suburb. Because my family never had any money and because my father was "crazy," we didn't fit in and I often felt inadequate. I didn't mind bumping into people from this town when I was a doctor, but in my present situation, I dreaded it.

We exited the highway and drove the familiar mile to my mother's house. I knew the exact distance because, as a runner, I had clocked the mileage to every landmark near her house. The highway was 1.3 miles, and the town pool was one mile due west. Haley, my best friend growing up, lived one mile due east of my mother's house. The high school was one and a half miles with lots of hills. Stopped at a red light around the corner from Mom's house, I knew we were thinking about the same thing.

In front of the grand white Tudor at the end of our block, my mother and I place bets as to whether my father's car will be in the driveway. The betting is our way of acknowledging the onset of our dread. We both pray he won't be home.

When he's home, we brace ourselves before entering the house. We exist in a state of high alert, as though expecting the boogey man to jump out of a closet. We open the door quietly, scanning for clues of his location. If he's downstairs, we've essentially walked into the line of fire. If he's upstairs, we have time to prepare for the onslaught. But there's no way we can prepare for the anger and hatred that will destroy the mood like a swarm of bees at a picnic.

I felt a warm rush when I spotted my little black sports car in the driveway and the blooming roses and azaleas in front of my mother's house. As we entered the kitchen through the garage, my mood plummeted. I felt ill at ease, as I always did inside her home. I grew up in this house, but felt like a guest there.

Mom hammers home this feeling by making it clear that everything in the house is hers. I have to clean up after myself immediately (putting any glasses or plates in the dishwasher, sweeping up crumbs, putting pens or telephone books back in their proper place). If I don't, she scolds me. It's as though she objects to my leaving any trace of my existence there.

Mindful of her sensitivities, I walk through the family room, calmly pat Brin and Ashley (Dani's dog) and carry my bag upstairs to my childhood room. Placing my suitcase in the closet, I regard the running shoes dangling like old friends from the hook inside the door.

I wanted to go for a long run, but knew my mother would feel used if I didn't spend time with her. I strolled downstairs to the kitchen where she was doing a crossword puzzle. "Do you want to walk the dogs?"

"Sure," she said, without looking up. "Do you know a ten-letter word for huge? The second letter's "r" and the last letter's 's'?"

I looked over her shoulder. "Prodigious," I said. "Fourteen across is renounce." I smiled to myself, thinking that she still valued me for *something*. My knack for word puzzles never ceased to amaze her. We always joked about what a terrible speller she was. Even though she was a teacher and a stickler for grammar, she couldn't spell to save her life. Sometimes she'd even call me on the phone when she got stuck.

As we walked by the neighbors' houses, shame coursed through my body. "We'd better come up with a plan in case we bump into anyone we know," I said, trying to conceal my face as cars passed us in both directions "What have you been telling people?"

"What do I say when people ask me about my daughter the doctor?" she asked derisively as we meandered into a field near my elementary school. "I say you're fine and then change the subject. Mostly, I try to avoid people."

I started to feel faint from the stress and the heat. "Let's go home," I said. I wished I were back at the hospital.

"Good idea. I'll turn on the air conditioning and we can give the dogs some water."

On our way home, we passed the farm stand around the corner from our house. "Do you want some fruit or tomatoes?" she asked in a hopeful tone of voice. She felt better when I ate.

The last thing on my mind was food, but I didn't want to disappoint her. "Sure, I'd love a tomato."

She bought some tomatoes and handed me one. When I sank my teeth into it, the juice soaked my chin and dripped down my forearm onto my sleeve, conjuring up a childhood memory.

When I was four years old, my parents had a dinner party. My mother was busy in the kitchen and the smell of unfamiliar foods wafted through our apartment. She wasn't much of a cook, so when she deviated from quick standbys like pasta or TV dinners, I knew it was a special occasion.

My father was sitting in the living room, smoking cigarettes and watching television. My mother said, in a nasty tone of voice, "Len, why don't you get off your throne and do something useful?" I threw a furtive glance at him as a chill went down my spine. I prayed that he wouldn't respond in kind to her sarcasm. Luckily, he just snubbed out his cigarette and started walking around, aimlessly straightening pictures on the wall, picking things up off the floor and looking out of windows.

My father and I went out on the terrace "to get some air." I asked if I could stay up past my bedtime to spend time with the grownups. Even at that young age, I knew he was much more likely to say yes than was my mother. He looked at me with a twinkle in his eye and said, "Of course you may, Mel-Mel. I'm sure everybody wants to see you." I was so excited that I went running inside to tell my mother. "Daddy said I could stay up with the company." She just grunted her disapproval.

My mother made up my bath and let me choose my pajamas before the guests arrived. She told me that I could stay with them while they had drinks and appetizers, but that I had to go to bed before they ate dinner. I said okay, but my heart sank as I pictured myself alone in my room while my parents talked and laughed with their friends. I started to worry that they wouldn't hear me calling if I needed them. What if I had to go the bathroom after I went to bed and I wasn't allowed to come out of my room? I turned my face away from my mother so that she wouldn't see my distress.

By the time the guests arrived, I had forced back my fear. There were four couples besides my parents. Everybody was sitting around the coffee table drinking, eating and talking while I flitted from person to person, giggling at the occasional tickle and answering questions in my most mature voice. I whispered in my father's ear that I wanted to walk on his feet. He rose and extended his arms. I put my hands into his and stood on his feet. I concentrated on balancing as he whisked me around the room. I avoided looking at my mother because I knew that she would be annoyed with our folly.

When we finished "dancing," I settled on my father's lap, feeling safe and special. Then, I bit into a cherry tomato and accidentally sprayed the seeds from it into my mother's face. As the seeds struck her, her expression changed from animation to fury. Even though this happened in a split second, to me, it felt like slow motion. I was mortified, but my father broke into hysterical laughter. I was paralyzed by fear as my mother's face reddened. I quickly became overwhelmed by confusion when I felt another cherry tomato being pushed into my mouth. Reflexively, my teeth closed around the tomato and the seeds squirted into my mother's face.

By the time I understood that my father was feeding a continuous stream of tomatoes into my mouth like a tennis ball machine, I had already lost bladder sphincter control. When I felt warm pee sliding down my legs, I jumped off his lap and ran to the bathroom. Slamming the bathroom door behind me, I tore at my soaked pajamas and underpants. I sat on the toilet staring at the wet clothes in a pile at my feet in horrified disbelief. How could I have done this?

Panic-stricken, I tried to figure out how to hide my sopping clothes, clean myself off, change my pajamas and climb into bed without anybody noticing. As footsteps approached the bathroom door, my mind went blank. Somebody knocked on the door and I whispered in the steadiest voice I could muster that I'd be done in a minute. I quickly rolled my wet clothes into a ball and opened the door a crack to make sure the coast was clear. I tiptoed into my room, threw my clothes in the closet, climbed half-naked into bed and buried my face in my pillow, sobbing as quietly as I could.

Mom's answering machine was blinking. When she heard Scott's voice, she gritted her teeth. "It's for you," she said coldly. "Go ahead and call him. Then you can start on the cartons in my playroom." She had the same hostile tone she used with my father.

I didn't call Scott. Instead, I took a deep breath and walked up the back stairs to the playroom. In the sweltering heat inside the room, combined with the devastating sight of ten or so cartons containing the remnants of my life with Luke, I dropped to my knees. Realizing that Luke and I were over, as was my life as a doctor, I closed my eyes to fight back the tears.

I wanted to run downstairs, but I was frightened of my mother's wrath. The first carton I opened contained my favorite jacket, a short, black leather one, the first present Luke ever gave me. With it were some of the clothes Luke had taken me shopping for. I hated shopping but my father, and later Luke, insisted that I have high-quality, flattering clothes to wear to work.

"Let's go buy you some new clothes," Luke would say.

"Okay, but then can we can go to a movie or do something I'll actually enjoy?"

He liked picking out clothes and watching me try them on. He was much more fashion-minded than I was. He always made a fuss over me. He'd tell me how beautiful I looked in certain outfits and sit expectantly outside the fitting rooms waiting for me to come out. "You look awesome, hon," he'd say. "You're some kind of knock out!"

I liked that he doted on me, and that he insisted on paying for my clothes. I could have bought them, but his buying them for me felt like love.

After twenty minutes, I still hadn't gotten past the first carton. I was so upset.

"What happened? It's almost time to go back to the hospital," my mother asked, shaking me awake.

My head was killing me. "Sorry, Mom, but I couldn't do it."

"You should have told me you couldn't handle it. I would have understood," she said sympathetically.

I mumbled. "I was scared you'd be mad at me."

"What's the difference if the boxes stay here a little while longer? I should have known better than to ask you to tackle this project in the first place. I was just reacting to Scott calling within five minutes of your being home."

As we drove back to the hospital, I studied her side profile, with her perfectly straight nose. I felt so grateful to her for sticking by me. I told her what I was thinking.

"Unfortunately, I have a feeling it's only the beginning," she said.

CHAPTER 44

August 17, 1992
On my last morning in the hospital, I met with Dr. Lancet. "I see your passes went smoothly. Are you ready to go home?"

"Yes and no. Actually, I'm terrified." I felt so sad that I wouldn't see him for a while. I studied his face trying once again to memorize it.

He leafed through my chart. "Hopefully you'll talk about this with Dr. Bernstein."

His abdicating responsibility for me reminded me of how my father relied on other people to pick up his slack. He expected my mother's father to take care of us financially, and family friends like Saul to accompany me to father/daughter functions.

"Does he know who I am?" That I was going to be depending on a total stranger frightened me.

"I told him you're a resident in psychiatry, the reason you were admitted, your diagnosis, your hospital course and about your pending legal situation. He's going to review your chart before he meets with you. He'd already heard about you through the rumor mill," Dr. Lancet said somewhat apologetically.

"Guess I'd better get used to that." I wondered just how far reaching the rumor mill was. I feared it was pretty far.

"We'll meet in my office in the hospital at 11:30 the day after Labor Day. I'm sending you home on the same medications you're on now."

I looked at him with tears in my eyes. "Is that it?"

"Yes. I wrote your discharge orders, so you're all set." He shook my hand. "I'll see you in about two weeks."

I felt dizzy with anxiety and the despair of loss as I watched him leave the room.

"Your mom's on her way up," said Susan. "Let's get your stuff."

I plodded down the hall after her. I must have looked very sad because she asked me if I was sure I was ready to be discharged.

"Ready as I'll ever be, I guess."

When my mother arrived, Susan turned to her and was suddenly all business. "You have to go to the finance office, pay the bill and return to the unit with the receipt. Then you can take her."

"I'm paying," I interjected.

"Oh." Susan sounded surprised, although I was sure I had mentioned that to her before. "Then I guess the two of you should go to the office together."

I handed the clerk a check for fifteen thousand dollars. "Isn't it ironic Daddy ended up paying for my first and hopefully last psychiatric hospitalization?" Although Pam had cut Dani and me out of Dad's estate, she did not exclude me from the life insurance policy. I used that money to pay for everything.

"Very," she said wryly.

As we left the hospital, I felt a sense of pride, as though I'd just achieved something important. Then it hit me. I'd been reduced to thinking my discharge from the loony bin was a big accomplishment.

"What are you doing today?" I asked my mother on the car ride home. I tried to conceal my anxiety about having nothing to do by asking the question dispassionately.

"Meeting Doris for lunch and going food shopping; why?"

"Just curious." I calculated in my head how many hours I had left until my appointment with Dr. Bernstein. "What time are you meeting Doris?" I hoped it wasn't right away.

"What is this, the Grand Inquisition?"

It's already starting. She's going to make me feel like shit every time I feel needy or ask her too many questions. Why can't she understand how frightened I am? I'd wait until we met with Richie to bring it up. For now, I figured I'd have to be sensitive to her needs and put mine aside, as usual.

When mom left to go shopping, I slumped into a leather chair in the family room, clicked on the television and stared at the muted screen. *What am I going to do today?* I started to hyperventilate, feel lightheaded and have chest pain as I thought about the blank screen my life had become.

In my life before the "confession," I was accustomed to running from one appointment to the next, frantically trying to meet deadlines and never having enough time to return all the phone messages I received. Now, I had nothing. I felt as if I was vaporizing into thin air, like smoke from a cigarette. I looked at the clock on the kitchen wall: 10.00. *Okay, I'll see Dr. Bernstein in twenty-four hours.* Knowing I had to be somewhere, and someone was expecting me was the fragile thread by which I reeled myself in. Still, I could hardly think straight. My sense of hopelessness was becoming overwhelming. *I have no purpose; therefore, I'm nothing. I need a job.*

The idea of perusing the classifieds energized me enough to rummage through the recycling bin. I spread Sunday's paper out on the kitchen table and started reading. Animal caretaker, automobile mechanic, bus driver.... By the time I got to the Ns, my head was pounding. I lay my head on the paper and closed my eyes.

"What are you doing?" asked my mother. She came into the kitchen carrying two bags of groceries.

I thought she'd be pleased that I was looking for a job.

"How are you going to work when you have daily therapy appointments and pending court dates?" She placed the bags on the counter next to the refrigerator and started unloading them. "Besides, you don't have any skills, and you can't work as a doctor."

She's right. I don't have any skills. I felt even worse. I thought she'd be happy and even insist that I look for a job, yet, here she was telling me I had more important things to take care of.

"I could always bag groceries. Aren't you the one who always says any job is better than no job?"

"Yes, but you just got out of the hospital. Why don't you give yourself time to get your legal situation squared away before you go running off to do some menial work?"

"I thought you'd be mad if I just hung around all day, especially when you go back to work."

"No, Mel," she said, while folding the empty bags. "I'll be mad if all you do is run, hang out with Scott and leave your crap all over my house; not if you're actively trying to get your life in order."

I closed the paper and put it neatly on the corner of the table. "Maybe I should go back to school since I probably won't be allowed to practice medicine."

"Can we talk about this later?" She poured herself a glass of water from the pitcher in the fridge. "I have to get ready for my lunch date."

I wished she had set aside some time for me that day.

"Sure." I watched her leave the room. "Would you mind if I go for a run while you're out?"

"Whatever," she replied from the top of the stairs.

At least she won't be timing me and force me to make excuses for why I was gone so long. She hated when I ran for more than an hour. It was though an hour was her threshold before my running pissed her off to the point where she couldn't hold her tongue.

When I returned from my run, I felt a lot calmer. I decided to call Scott while my mother was still out.

"You're home, but I can't see you?" His voice cracked. "I can't even call you?"

"Just for a little while. I don't want to alienate my mother. I'm already pushing my luck with the running." I was proud of myself for acting so maturely.

"It was better when you were in the hospital." I pictured his pupils constricting with anger the way they did when he spoke of his ex-wife. "At least I could visit you there."

"Please don't make this harder for me than it already is. I'm just trying to do the right thing." I felt really annoyed. "You signed on for this despite my warnings, so don't lay a guilt trip on me now."

"Okay, but do you still want to go away with me?" He sounded desperate.

I heard the garage door opening. "She's home, I have to go."

CHAPTER 45

Driving myself to the hospital for the first time felt strange. As I walked from the parking lot to the hospital entrance, the building that previously seemed like a prison now felt like a refuge. As always, patients were milling around the entranceway, smoking cigarettes and fidgeting. The previous day I'd been one of them. I felt a sense of accomplishment, like a high school graduate returning to the school for a visit.

Smiling at the security guard, I signed the visitors' book on the page dated 8/18/92. Standing in the lobby I watched people come and go, hoping to see a familiar face, especially Susan. I already missed her. Seeing her would help me feel better. Besides, if she saw me, she might be less apt to forget me so soon.

After a few minutes, Dr. Bernstein emerged from the cafeteria carrying a cup with a straw sticking out of it. He was wearing the same dark blue polyester suit he always wore.

"Melanie?"

"Yes," I replied, flashing him a nervous smile.

"I'm Dr. Bernstein; nice to meet you." When he shook my hand, I noticed his nails were chewed to the quick and his cheeks were pockmarked. "Let's go to the administration area and look for somewhere we can talk."

We went to a vacant room containing a long table surrounded by about ten chairs. He sat at the far end. I sat across from him, putting my feet on the seat next to mine.

"I know Dr. Lancet asked you to meet with me every day while he's away. Does that include weekends?"

"No, just weekdays."

Panic pulsed through me. How would I survive a full seventy-two hours without anything to do? "What if I need to talk to you on Saturday or Sunday?" I felt ashamed as I realized how quickly I'd transitioned from needing Dr. Lancet to feeling dependent on Dr. Bernstein.

"You can call the hospital switchboard and the operator will page me. Are you afraid you'll have an emergency?"

I was thankful that he addressed my anxiety directly and didn't give me a line like, "I can always readmit you if you don't think you can handle life on the outside."

I shrugged, trying to make light of it. "It's just that I'm feeling apprehensive and alone, so I'm scouting out my safety nets."

"Do you have a support system?"

I thought about all the friends I'd lost, including Mark, and Luke's clan. "It's small, but yes. There's my mother, sister, and sort-of boyfriend. I'm not in touch with any of my friends from my residency program or before. There's Marion, my best friend from college, who lives on the Cape. I talk to her on the phone occasionally. That helps, especially because she knew Luke. She's a psychologist."

"Well, you can always reach me by calling the hospital switchboard. Is there anything else you'd like to discuss today?"

I told him about how awful I had felt running and walking around mom's neighborhood. "I wish I could move to a place where nobody knows me."

Jiggling the ice cubes in his cup, he said, "Most people are so caught up with their own lives that they barely think about anyone else."

"But people love to gossip about other people's dirty laundry."

"So what if Kim bumps into Linda in the grocery store and says, 'Have you heard about Melanie?' Is that any different than Kim asking Linda if she heard about so and so getting into Harvard? Either way, they may talk about it for a few minutes and then continue shopping. The fact that this conversation occurred is completely irrelevant to your life. Even if Linda tells two friends and they tell two friends, and so on and so on. It wouldn't matter if she told ten thousand people. It still doesn't affect you."

I considered all this, and suddenly a light bulb went off in my head. I'd never really thought about it that way. I'd been so sure that I would be the talk of the town, but he helped me realize that, even if people did talk about me, it would have no bearing on me. The most important part of what he said was that people are so self-absorbed that they don't spend much time thinking about other people. When I applied this to my own life, it rang true.

I met with Dr. Bernstein the next three days in a row. These thirty-minute sessions were the highlight and focal point of my days. Each day, he imparted some words of wisdom. It's not that he said anything so extraordinary. It's more that he had a knack for stating things in a way that shifted my perspective, or was the right thing for me to hear in the moment. During Friday's session, I told him I felt anxious about the impending weekend.

"Try to stay busy and keep a journal of your feelings," he advised. "I'm on call this weekend, so have me paged if you need to."

Saturday afternoon I broke down and called Scott. We got together that evening and practically every night thereafter. My mother wasn't pleased about my spending so much time with him, but other than making snide comments, she didn't try to stop me. Gradually, I came to see him as my flimsy life raft in the shark-infested waters of desolation. I was hanging on to him for dear life.

Adding Scott to my list of activities made the days pass much faster. Before I knew it, Dr. Lancet was due to return in three days. I spent my last session with Dr. Bernstein discussing Dr. Lancet's imminent return and my regrets that I couldn't see both of them.

As I walked down the corridor towards Dr. Lancet's office, I noticed doors with physicians' nameplates on either side of the hall. The only name I recognized was that of the doctor who'd come to see me when I was in the quiet room.

As I waited outside Dr. Lancet's office, I started to worry that he had forgotten about me. Finally, he cracked open the door. "I'm in the middle of taking care of an emergency. Do you mind waiting another ten minutes or so?"

I felt crushed. I couldn't believe that seeing me was such a non-event to him, when it meant so much to me. Then I smiled to myself, thinking how lucky I was *not* to be the emergency.

Finally, he motioned me to come inside his office. I strolled in unceremoniously as though the half-hour delay hadn't fazed me in the least. "This sure is an improvement over the therapy room on the unit," I remarked as I scanned the bookshelves full of books.

"Sit!" He pointed to the brown leather chair on the far side of the huge mahogany desk before sinking into a high-back leather chair with gold studs around the edges. I eyed the back of three photographs, exercising incredible self-control by not picking them up to look at them. If I hadn't had a history of being intrusive, it would have been perfectly natural to look at and ask about the pictures. I was dying to see a picture of his wife. "Your family," I asked, trying to sound blasé.

He turned the photos face down. "I see Dr. Bernstein didn't cure you of your boundary issues," he said lightheartedly.

I studied his face, trying to form a mental snapshot of it. I'd forgotten some of its details while he was away. I didn't tell him how close I had come to calling Luke's office when I knew he wouldn't be there just to hear his voice.

"How are things between you and your mother?"

"Stressful at times, but basically okay. The biggest issue between us is my seeing Scott, but I make sure to come home early so she doesn't have too much to get on my case about. We have our second meeting with Richie this coming Friday."

"Good, and the legal stuff?"

"The pre-sentencing hearing is in twelve days, but I'm trying not to think about it." I assured him I hadn't had any thoughts of hurting myself or anyone else.

"What about Luke?" His voice was grave.

I cast my eyes downward. "I miss him like crazy and I'm dying to call him, but I haven't, and I promise I won't."

He stared at me intensely. "You know what will happen if you contact him?"

"I know," I felt so anxious thinking about how close I had come to actually calling.

He leaned back in his chair and put his feet against the edge of the desk. "We will meet three times a week for forty-five minutes. Your appointments will be on Monday, Wednesday, and Friday, at eleven."

I visualized a calendar inside my head and mentally marked the days with Dr. Lancet with a big check, and the other days with a giant X. What I saw frightened me. How could I endure four days a week without therapy, my grounding force?

"What if I need to talk to you between sessions?" I pinched my thighs to stop myself from crying.

"You can call the hospital switchboard and have me paged anytime."

My stomach twisted in knots as I realized our session was about to end.

"But if you can't handle life as an outpatient, I can always readmit you."

CHAPTER 46

Following my meeting with Dr. Lancet, I arrived home to an empty house. Mom had returned to work after the summer break. She wouldn't be home for four hours. Knowing I'd be alone for that long, I felt antsy.

There was a message on the answering machine for me from Tom. I found his card in Mom's Rolodex and was struck by the fact that his office was on Fifth Avenue. It never occurred to me he worked for a prestigious law firm. Confronted with the reality of the disparity in our present circumstances, I suddenly felt inadequate and inferior to him.

Tom and I exchanged pleasantries and then he got down to business. "I talked to Bill Walsh, the lawyer whose card I gave to you in the hospital, and he said he hasn't heard from you yet. I suggest you call him today."

I'd been carrying his card around for nearly a month, but hadn't worked up the nerve to call him. I was hoping that something miraculous would happen to allow me to keep my license.

"Oh, and one other thing…"

I hoped whatever he was going to say would be benign because I was getting really upset about the license. I didn't think I could handle another emotional challenge.

"You'd be wise to start looking into doing some sort of community service."

I liked the idea of doing volunteer work.

I arranged to meet Mr. Walsh the following day. This was the first time I had to do something on my own and I felt flustered. I had to take the initiative, go meet a total stranger and act like an adult. I wasn't sure I could do it.

I walked around the house telling myself not to be such a baby, but I became more and more upset. The issues of surrendering my license and having to go to the city to interact with a total stranger fed off one another until I felt absolutely petrified.

I called Dani, but she wasn't home, so I decided to drop in on Scott at work. I hesitated before entering the electronics store. He told me weeks earlier that a few of his co-workers had warned him about getting involved with a mental patient. My need to see him superseded my desire to avoid his buddies. When I spotted him, warmth spread throughout my body. I snuck up behind him and tapped him on the shoulder.

His eyes lit up at the sight of me.

"I'm a little shaken up. I really need someone to talk to."

He slipped his arm around my waist. I could easily let him take care of me, I thought, but that would just lead down the path to self-destruction. It would inhibit my growth and independence. I'd eventually turn on him. Not only that, but if I let him take care of me now, he'd expect me to do the same for him someday. I doubted I'd be able or willing to.

"I'll get one of the guys to cover for me."

I watched self-consciously as he talked to his co-worker and pointed in my direction. "Isn't he one of the guys who think I'm psycho?" I asked as we crossed the street.

Scott shrugged. "He knows how much I care about you."

I felt a burning sensation in my chest. I needed so much to know someone cared about me. I also knew my fragility and neediness would prevent me from being an equal partner in this or any other relationship. While I had a strong physical attraction to him, I wasn't sure what feelings I had for him beyond lust and the need for a caring, attentive man in my life.

We walked to the corner café and sat in a booth at the back. He listened intently as I explained the latest legal development.

"Do you want me to go with you?"

I glanced at his bear-like, dark-skinned hand blanketing mine. I studied the Red Indian patterned fabric of his sleeve up to his broad shoulder. Beyond his shoulder, nests of dark hair peeked out from his collar. I followed the line of his collar to his thick neck and beyond. His piercing dark eyes grabbed hold of mine. I felt myself falling in love with him, which was the last thing I wanted to do. I was vulnerable and needy, but I knew if I let myself love him, it could only turn out badly. Still, looking into his eyes, I had a fleeting image of a future with him. I felt hopeful.

I was tempted to accept his offer, but I knew I needed to navigate my way through the next few months on my own.

The following morning I took a train into the city. Feeling anxious and disoriented, I had to remind myself that I did, in fact, know my way around. Walking to Mr. Walsh's office, it was hard for me to believe that a year earlier I'd run through these neighborhoods regularly when I'd worked in a nearby hospital. Everything seemed so foreign to me now.

As I passed the restaurant where Luke and I went on our third date, I had to lean against a wall until the queasiness passed. We had already sensed that the other had great potential to be the missing piece in our lives, which were on track career-wise and in every other way. Walking to the restaurant, I had felt so euphoric to be with him. I acted happy, silly, and childish. I walked on a low wall pretending to be on a tightrope, and skipped beside him for a while. That's when it hit me that I wanted him to be my life partner and the father of my children. Children that, until then, I hadn't even known I wanted.

Mr. Walsh was a thirty-something, sporty-looking man, who struck me as a strange combination of casual and serious. His corduroy jacket was open and he wasn't wearing a tie, but he did not seem warm. I assumed he lacked a sense of humor.

He led me into his office and motioned for me to sit on a frayed, brown suede chair in front of a teak desk piled high with folders.

Sitting across from me, he pushed a manila envelope toward me and pulled a document from an identical envelope. "As per Mr. Aiello's instructions, I put together this document to surrender your medical license. I have the original and you have a copy. If you'll look at your copy, we can go over it line by line."

As I scanned the document, my throat started to constrict as though I were going into anaphylactic shock. My facial expression must have belied my distress. He said, "This must be very difficult for you."

"I've only had my medical license since February. I guess it's just a case of easy come, easy go." I recognized my glibness as a defense against the pain I was feeling.

"The gist of it is that you're surrendering your license to practice medicine because you pled guilty to a felony."

"Right." I scanned the fifteen pages that rehashed the details and dates of my crime. "Everything looks correct," I reported, fighting back tears.

"Good, let's go down the hall to have your signature notarized. I'll mail it certified to the State Board for Professional Medical Conduct.

"How long will it take until the surrender is official?"

"Given all the red tape, it may take a few months. However, receipt of your petition is considered unofficially official. You can tell the judge that you're in the process of surrendering it and have filed the necessary paperwork."

"I wish it had been as easy to get my license as it is to surrender it," I said glumly.

"The fact that you're surrendering it rather than waiting for it to be revoked may work in your favor if you ever decide to petition for reinstatement." He offered a brief sympathetic smile.

I couldn't imagine why the medical board would think better of me because I beat them to the punch. It didn't seem to me to be so magnanimous to give them what they would have taken from me anyway.

Once the documents were notarized, I could hardly wait to get out of there. The sidewalk was crowded with people dressed in business suits. I stood still and felt the air whirling around me as waves of people passed in both directions. I felt despondent. I had lost my professional identity…perhaps forever.

CHAPTER 47

September 14, 1992

The pre-sentencing hearing took place nearly a month after my discharge from the hospital. To my great relief, by some miracle, my case eluded publicity. So far there had only been a tiny paragraph about me in the police blotter of my hometown paper. They spelled my name wrong, referred to me as a "he" and gave the wrong address.

Still, as Mom and I drove down the narrow one-way street to the courthouse, I stared at the gray stone building looming ominously in front of us looking for any signs of a media frenzy. There was none. Nevertheless, I felt sick to my stomach as the reality of what was about to happen broke through the denial I had been in since the issue of court first arose.

Mom and I took the escalator from the parking garage to a huge lobby that resembled an airport terminal. "There's Tom!" Mom pointed toward a sunken area in the center of the room with mauve velveteen couches positioned around the perimeter. I wanted to run to him. Instead, I matched my mother's determined pace.

"Good to see you," Tom said as he shook my mother's hand.

I suddenly felt the urge to escape the building.

"It's time." He touched his fingertips to my back and directed me toward the metal detector across the room.

I waited in line between the two of them as we moved with the steady stream of briefcase-toting professionals through the security check. We crammed into a crowded elevator that let us out into a dingy hallway. Tom paused in front of the third double-door to our left and put an arm around each of us. "Follow me to the front of the court. I want Melanie to sit to my right, and Jean, you sit next to Mel. When the judge calls us, we'll approach from the left. I'll go first. Got it?"

We both nodded. *Go Team!*

I desperately wanted to know if Luke was in the room, but I didn't look around. I stared straight ahead at the judge's bench, a large wooden structure atop a two-foot-high platform.

A graying woman entered from the door to the judges' chambers. "All rise for the Honorable Judge Lory," she announced. A tall, lean, gray-haired man wearing a black robe appeared behind her. He panned the room and nodded to someone across the aisle from us before climbing the three steps to the bench. "This is the pre-sentencing hearing for the State of New York versus Melanie Chase," said the woman.

The entire state is against me. I started to feel unreal.

Tom and I approached the judge's bench, stopping a few feet in front of it. I willed my knees not to buckle when I noticed Luke's lawyer whispering to the judge and pointing to a document she held. Wearing a beige designer suit with matching heels, she towered above Tom and me like a tree casting a shadow over a couple of saplings.

Judge Lory pushed his tortoiseshell glasses up the bridge of his nose as Eloise took a few steps backward.

I stared at the judge as Eloise recited the details of my crime of passion like items on a grocery list. I winced every time she spoke Luke's name. It annoyed me to hear her going on about everything I'd done without accounting for the *emotions* or *reasons*. Then again, I had committed a felony. My feelings were irrelevant.

When she finished speaking, Judge Lory removed his glasses and placed them beside his nameplate. "How does the defendant plead?" He looked directly into my eyes for the first time.

"Guilty," I whispered tremulously.

"Speak up!" he growled.

My tongue felt thick and pasty. "Guilty."

"Ms. Chase, your crime is especially heinous because you are a doctor and should have known better." He curled his lip at me contemptuously as he exclaimed, "First, do no harm!"

As his lecture proceeded, I felt myself leave my body. I had the sense of watching the entire scene from behind. I perceived the judge's mouth opening and closing like a fish out of water.

The judge looked like he wanted to pounce on me. "Are you aware of any other doctors who abused their position to harm people?"

I had no idea what he was alluding to.

"Have you ever heard of Mengele?"

"Excuse me?" *I must have misheard him. Was he really comparing me to the Nazi doctor who did surgical experiments on prisoners without anesthesia and tortured them for the fun of it?* At first I was outraged at his implication. I became frightened. If this is what he believed, he'd punish me severely.

"Young Lady, I want you to read *The Nazi Doctors* and write a paper describing anything you learn that pertains to your own case. I don't care how many pages it is, as long as it's finished by the next hearing, which will be on December 14th." He twirled his glasses between his thumb and index finger. "When court is adjourned, go down to the fifth floor and make an appointment to meet with Mrs. Fallow, the woman in charge of probation. I will design your sentence based on that meeting and the victim impact statement."

"Okay," I said softly, still reeling in disbelief that he'd compared me to Mengele. *Did he think I derived pleasure from hurting people? What could I do to change his mind? I hated people's suffering!* My tendency was to try to make everyone and everything better. I had fantasies of rescuing people, not torturing them. Maybe the judge was projecting his own fantasies onto me. If that were true, then he had just told me in so many words that he was sadistic. If I was on the receiving end of his sadism, I was in big trouble.

"Do you think he knows I'm Jewish?" I asked as Tom, my mother and I entered the stairwell. I wondered if he was anti-Semitic. I couldn't wait to tell Dr. Lancet, who was also Jewish. I trusted Dr. Lancet's opinions more than anyone else's.

"Ssshhh!" hissed my mother. "We'll talk about it later."

The hallway on the fifth floor was narrow and dark. To my right was a bench attached to the wall with chains and a receptionist's area with a dusty, scratched and, I assumed, bulletproof sliding window. A heavyset woman sat behind it. She opened the partition barely wide enough to slip a piece of paper through.

"I need to make an appointment with Mrs. Fallow," I said, telling her my name. She turned the pages of a large appointment book, scribbled something on one of the pages, and passed me a card through the slit in the window. "A week from tomorrow at ten," she said and closed the partition.

I thanked the back of her head as she rolled her chair across the room. I hated being treated like I was invisible. Feeling irate, I whipped open the door to the stairwell and flew down the stairs.

"Can you believe he compared me to Mengele?" I asked indignantly when Tom and my mother caught up with me in the lobby. "And that bitch didn't even look at me!"

"Let's take a little walk," said Tom. "The walls have ears." He jerked his head in the direction of the coffee shop where Eloise stood talking to one of her cronies.

We strolled through the lobby to a cement courtyard outside and stood near the fountain.

"Lory's pissed at you. That's not good," said Tom, loosening his tie. "He can sentence you at his discretion."

Moving closer to the fountain, I watched the droplets dampen my hand. "Is there anything I can do between now and the hearing to make him less angry?"

"Write a thoughtful and provocative paper, do some community service and practice looking remorseful." He frowned. "You don't really come across as being remorseful. That could be your downfall."

I *wasn't* remorseful. I did, however, regret ruining *my* life and scaring Luke. I was still caught up in those feelings too much to empathize with Luke's experience of being sick and close to death.

On our way home, my mother and I stopped to buy the book.

"It's a good thing you're seeing Dr. Lancet tomorrow morning," said my mother as we read the blurb on the back of the book: *A chilling account of the atrocities perpetrated by the Nazi Doctors on the concentration camp victims.*

"What?" cried Dr. Lancet indignantly. "The judge compared you to Mengele, aka *The Angel of Death*?" He shook his head back and forth. "Boy, are you in trouble!"

"Have you read *The Nazi Doctors,* subtitled *Medical Killing and the Psychology of Genocide*? It's a six-hundred-page description of torture. You know, like tossing infants in the air to see how many times they could shoot them." He was shaking his head from side to side in disbelief. "It's so ironic; I don't even kill bugs. I'd spend ten minutes catching a fly to take it outside rather than swat it."

He chuckled and a shadow crossed his face as his mirth turned to consternation.

"What's wrong?" I asked.

"I was just thinking about how much the book may upset you." His expression remained grave. "No matter what, you must maintain perspective. You are not a sadistic brute. You are a compassionate, perhaps overly empathetic person who did something horrible as a consequence of your mental illness."

I slouched in my chair. "Maybe I *do* deserve to spend the rest of my life in prison."

"Melanie," he said softly and sternly. "A fluctuating and distorted sense of self is central to the borderline pathology." He startled me by pounding the desk with his fist. "Do not be taken in by the judge's moronic and ignorant allegations!"

His spontaneous and impassioned outburst reassured me. I was thankful that he was attacking the person who hurt me. Not only was he validating my feelings, he was angry on my behalf. It suddenly occurred to me that he loved me -- not in a perverse, unethical or sexual way, but rather in the way that we all want to be loved. I mattered to him; he believed in me and was willing to risk a lot to protect me.

CHAPTER 48

In the three months between the pre-sentencing hearing and the actual hearing, I saw Dr. Lancet three mornings a week and spent almost every evening with Scott. During the day, I worked on the judge's assignment and volunteered tutoring homeless children. I also met with Tom Aiello a few times, saw Richie once a week with my mother and applied to graduate school for the spring semester.

I tried not to let my relationship with Scott interfere with my relationship with my mother, which, although better, was still tense at times. Nor did I allow it to get in the way of doing what I had to do to start putting my life back together. I could have easily glommed on to him, but I knew it was important for me to keep the relationship in perspective. In the past, I abandoned most things in my life that preceded the relationship and made my boyfriend the center of my universe. I was tempted to do that. It would have made a lot of things much less painful, but I learned from my relationship with Luke how dangerous that was for me.

Dr. Lancet and I spent a lot of time talking about my relationship with Scott and, while he didn't exactly approve of the relationship, he thought it was okay since I was not becoming obsessed with him. We also talked about my relationship with my mother, my meetings with Tom, and what I should be doing to put my life back together.

Dr. Lancet teased me mercilessly, calling the judge "Maximum Lory," because shortly after the first hearing, we found out that Lory had presided over the Caroline Warmus case, a high-profile "crime of passion" trial and had sentenced her to the maximum time in prison, twenty-five years to life.

The typical prison sentence for assault in the first degree for a first-time offender is one to two years. I knew the judge could sentence me at his discretion, but what I didn't know until the actual hearing was that, according to the law, if he sentenced me to prison time, I could not be charged more than $10,000 restitution.

My biggest dilemma was what to do after the hearing if I wasn't sentenced to prison. Dr. Lancet and I agreed that I should go back to school to prepare for an alternate career in case I was not able to get my license reinstated. I wanted to pursue a degree in counseling, but Dr. Lancet pointed out that it may be difficult for me to find employment as a counselor considering my criminal status and what had happened when I was a psychiatrist. We decided the best thing would be to go for a master's in public health. With this degree, I would be in a position to do research, work in a public health clinic or teach. Also, it would complement my medical education.

This phase of therapy was called "supportive" as opposed to "analytic" because he encouraged me rather than challenged me. His goal was to keep my ego and emotions on an even keel. Patients undergoing severe stresses require this kind of therapy in order to weather their crises. More thought-provoking analytic therapy is used when patients are stronger in order to help them understand why they keep repeating self-destructive patterns, or whatever got them into the crisis in the first place.

In addition to trying to keep me stable and help me to better cope with difficult situations, his main objectives were to teach me: right from wrong, impulse control, and how to be a truly good person. He frequently told me anecdotes about people he knew who were truly good people; the kind of person everyone wants to be around and to know. This is a person everyone trusts and knows they can count on. Such a person is humble, honest, generous, and calm. Dr. Lancet was a wonderful role model, for this description fit him very well.

I'd often hear Dr. Lancet's voice in my head when I was trying to figure out how to handle certain situations. Depending on the circumstances, his voice took on the characteristics of a policeman, advocate, or father figure, dissuading me from doing something bad. This is the goal of therapy, for the therapist to essentially "re-parent" the patient to try to heal the wounds inflicted by the patient's real parents. The ultimate objective is for the patient to internalize the therapist (called an introject) so that he is influenced by a healthier parental figure than the one(s) who damaged him. Eventually, hearing the therapist's voice inside your head dissipates and you incorporate him into who you are. You no longer have to consciously summon him, as he is woven into the fabric of your very being.

The way the therapist treats you and acts around you is just as important in shaping you as what he says to you. The patient picks up on and imitates him. It is the therapist's responsibility to provide a positive role model for the patient. The therapeutic process is about "do as I say *and* as I do."

Right before the hearing, Dr. Lancet coached me to be on my best behavior. He surprised me by saying, "Melanie, you've come a long way."

Contemplating his words, I concluded that I had made some progress, although I still had a ways to go. I had less mood lability and better impulse control. I attributed this change partly to the Stelazine and partly to internalizing Dr. Lancet. Even though I still felt the same emotionally in most situations, I was more in control of my behavior. The inside hadn't changed much, but the outside had. I knew that, with time, the inside would follow.

The first month I was home, I often dialed Luke's number and hung up before the phone started ringing, I gradually stopped doing that, then rarely even thought about doing it. Another thing that changed was that when Scott hurt my feelings, instead of fantasizing about ways to retaliate or act out, I sat with my anger for a day or so. Then I discussed with him rationally how he had hurt me and what it felt like. I was acting the same way with my mother. When I was angry with my mother or something she said or did hurt my feelings, I either waited until we were in Richie's office or a stress-free situation to bring it up to her directly. It's not that I didn't want to react, but I was more able to control my reactions and sit with them long enough to reflect upon them.

"

CHAPTER 49

It's deja vu all over again," I said as Mom and I drove down the ramp to the courthouse parking garage.

"That's a quote from Yogi Berra. Your father used to say that all the time."

"Speaking of Daddy, can you imagine the letters he'd be writing to the judge, the medical board, and probably the president of the United States trying to get me off the hook if he were still alive?"

"He'd make a million excuses for your behavior and use every connection he could think of to try and avenge you. In the end, he'd find some way to blame my father."

"Then he'd find somebody to sue." We both chuckled and shook our heads in dismay over the veracity of these statements.

My father would have tried to convince me that it was not my fault and gone to any lengths to get me exonerated. I would have been mortified by his actions as well as totally stressed out trying to stop him. He probably would have harassed Dr. Lancet, too, which would have threatened my status as his patient.

At the top of the escalator, I spotted Tom heading toward us.

"Holy shit!" I exclaimed, grabbing my mother's arm and thrusting my chin in the direction of the elevators where Jack and Steve were standing about five yards away from us. My knees went weak and I started to hyperventilate. Seeing Jack and Steve was like coming face-to-face with my assassins. I wouldn't have been nearly as terrified if Luke had been there. He didn't want revenge. In fact, I thought he felt almost as badly for me as he did for himself. On the other hand, Jack and Steve wanted to see me hang.

My mother turned her body to block me from their view.

"What is it?" Tom asked looking around.

"Luke's bodyguards are here," I whispered into his ear. I felt like I was going to puke.

"It's okay, Mel," Mom she said in a soothing tone. "They're gone."

I took a deep breath. "Okay. I'm ready," I said as we walked into the courtroom.

Jack and Steve were sitting in the back row. We made fleeting eye contact and nodded slightly in acknowledgment of one another. I felt so frightened and nauseous I wanted to run out of the building. Willing myself to think about Dr. Lancet gave me the courage to keep walking.

"Ignore them," my mother whispered into my neck.

As we slid into the front row, Tom said, "Don't let them intimidate you. Their presence won't change anything."

My head bobbed forward like a chicken being prepared for slaughter and the room seemed to grow dim.

"All rise in the matter of The People of the State of New York against Melanie Chase," ordered the court clerk.

Even though Jack and Steve were twenty rows behind us, I imagined they were breathing down my neck. Trance-like, I followed Tom to the judge's platform. Eloise stood a few feet to our right.

As hard as I tried to focus on what people were saying, their words seemed to float and bob around me like debris in the ocean. I watched Eloise's mouth move. After what seemed like a ten-second delay -- I kept fading in and out due to my intense anxiety headache -- I heard "The People move for sentencing . . . the defendant knew what she was doing . . . we can only imagine the pain that Luke felt, . . . " Jack handed Eloise a note.

Black spots danced in front of my eyes. I felt myself about to pass out. I squeezed Tom's arm until the feeling subsided.

Luckily, we got to sit down because the judge was talking to Ms. Cloud, the probation officer who took the victim impact statement. He was trying to clarify what she meant when she *promised* Luke she wouldn't divulge some of the things he said about me in his statement. Lory said that legally I had a right to know what Luke had said. The accused has a right to face his accuser, as well as the right to know of what he's being accused.

After Ms. Cloud left, Judge Lory spent the next hour discussing the distinction between *promise* and *confidentiality*, and whether the promise made to Luke regarding the privacy of his testimony should be offset by the accused's right to know. We had several sidebars with the judge, in which Eloise argued that Luke wouldn't have volunteered certain information if he knew I'd be given access to the report.

Tom said he'd seen the information and was comfortable with not putting it on the public record, but that I should be allowed to read it. Finally, the judge determined that the information should be made available to Tom and me, but not the public. He gave us ten minutes to review the document.

We sat in the front row scanning the five-page report. The report had to do with the fact that Luke had prescribed a controlled substance for me despite the fact that I wasn't his patient. He speculated that I started to become enraged with him months before he broke up with me because he withheld sex. He acknowledged that we possessed videotapes of our joint therapy sessions. Luke said I was an extremely talented psychiatrist and should be allowed to practice medicine again in three years, and that he didn't care whether I went to jail or not. Why he disclosed any of this in a victim impact statement when all he was required to do was describe how the crime affected him made no sense to me.

When time was up, Lory addressed Eloise. "Do the people have any additional recommendations concerning sentencing?"

I studied Eloise, wondering what she thought of me in light of the victim impact statement, and in general. She was an attractive and bright woman; I couldn't help wondering if Luke might be interested in her, or vice versa. I wondered why a stylish, seemingly wealthy and together woman, who could probably do any kind of work, was working for peanuts as an A.D.A. in the domestic violence department. Did she have a personal vendetta against perpetrators of domestic violence? She appeared to be cold and confident. I wondered if that was her professional persona, or if that was really the way she was. She was probably too sophisticated for Luke but, given her confidence and independence, she would have been a better match for him than I was.

"No, Judge." She left the word "judge" hanging as though she was going to say something else, but she didn't speak again.

Lory turned to Tom. "Does defense counsel wish to address the court?"

"Yes. Thank you, Your Honor." Tom took a step forward. "I need to place Dr. Chase's actions in a psychiatric context. Please understand I'm not making excuses, Your Honor. She understands full well that what she did was a horrible thing, something she wouldn't have conceived of doing even two months before she did it."

His voice soothed me.

Tom told him I had been severely depressed, over-medicated, and still reeling from my father's death when Luke told me he was going ahead with our joint plans for the future alone, even though he had strung me along for months after he broke up with me. "This shattered any remaining hope she was clinging to, and sent her into despair. She lost touch with reality, which is common in people with borderline personality disorder."

I doubted the judge cared about any of this, but I was confident Tom knew what he was doing.

"She decided early on not to contest the criminal charges, even though that meant giving up an awful lot—including the medical career she worked so hard for." He paused, letting his words sink in. "She also knew it would be personally devastating to her family. But what I'm here to tell you is that she's a very different person now than when I first met her. After seven weeks of institutionalization and intensive psychotherapy, she's come to grips with some serious problems in her life." His voice grew more ardent as he continued. "She's taking steps to rehabilitate herself and has gone through these proceedings in a manner that would not cause Luke any further anguish. For all these reasons, Your Honor, we ask you not to sentence her to a period of incarceration."

I started to panic at the mention of incarceration. With all the sidebars and distractions, I'd forgotten that the judge might sentence me to jail time.

When Tom finished, the judge slowly raised the glass of water on his desk to his mouth and took a sip. He set his glass back on the desk and closed his eyes. Waiting for his response was excruciating.

Suddenly, he emerged from his hypnotic state. "I'm ready to pronounce sentence."

I discreetly glanced at my mother, who looked as terrified as I felt.

"The defendant is sentenced to five years probation with a fine of five thousand dollars and the following conditions. She shall not engage in the practice of medicine or psychiatry, nor work in any capacity whatsoever, paid or voluntary, in any health-related field for the duration of probation. She shall surrender her medical license for a period of five years. She shall remain in psychiatric treatment, abide by the court's order of protection and pay restitution in the amount of sixty-five thousand dollars to Dr. Luke Shay. The restitution is based on lost wages and medical expenses."

Eloise nodded and I thought I heard my mother gasp.

"Now we come to the issue of incarceration. I'm taking an approach based on Section 1.05 of the Penal Law, which describes the four criteria to be used in sentencing: deterrence, rehabilitation, protection of the public, and retribution. Retribution means that people who cause harm to other people should be punished in the rawest sense of the word, simply to be made to suffer." I expected to hear Jack and Steve say "Amen," but the courtroom was silent.

"When adding up all these factors, it seems that some amount of incarceration is indicated. If I thought the defendant would be seriously damaged by a brief incarceration, I wouldn't impose it, but I have not been persuaded by any of the material presented to me thus far that incarceration would be detrimental to her mental health."

I wanted to put my hands over my ears so I couldn't hear him. Instead, I concentrated on forcing back my tears and thought about my dog and how much I wanted to hold her and see her adorable face.

"I'm going to sentence the defendant to two weekends in the County Penitentiary, from six P.M. on Friday until six P.M. on Sunday. Those two weekends will be January 29 through 31 and February 12 through 14. That will give the defense a little over a month to try to change my mind."

I supposed it was fitting for a crime of passion to be punished on Valentine's Day, the most passion-centric holiday.

"I have the power, under the law, to diminish the conditions of probation at any time and will do so, if persuaded by Dr. Lancet that this is a mistake."

Sirens blared in the distance.

"The question of community service is of great importance in this case. Unfortunately, I cannot allow Ms. Chase to use her hard-won medical knowledge. Anything that would put her in contact with medication is prohibited. She's already started volunteering in constructive ways, which I appreciate. As far as tutoring homeless children, though, how do I know she won't try to intervene with these children by doing therapy, which isn't allowed? I'd prefer she do something even further removed from psychiatry. I'm imposing a total of one thousand hours of community service over the course of five years. I hope the reasoning process employed in reaching this sentence has been clear to all concerned."

"Thank you, Your Honor," said Tom.

"Ms. Chase, good luck to you," said the judge amicably.

I was pleasantly surprised by his seemingly changed attitude toward me. Maybe he came to realize that I wasn't a Mengele avatar as he initially presumed, or maybe it had to do with Luke's Victim Impact Statement, but he no longer seemed angry with me. I thought his sentence was more than fair. Now, I just had to find a "Get-out-of-jail-free card."

Having been in the courtroom for over six hours, I couldn't wait to get out of there when Eloise piped up. "Judge, are we going to discuss the time schedule for the restitution payments?"

I was having trouble remaining still. I felt agitated, but tried not to show it. I grabbed onto my dress and twisted it between my thumb and fist. I clenched my teeth. Tom, Eloise, and the judge spent the next ten minutes discussing my finances. They ultimately agreed on payments of 1,734 dollars per month for a period of three years.

I let out a long sigh of relief when I surreptitiously peeked at the back row in time to see Jack and Steve slipping out the back door. Then it hit me. *I was going to jail.*

CHAPTER 50

I started graduate school a few weeks after the hearing. The graduate school was part of my medical school. The school's sprawling suburban campus was located about thirty miles from New York City and ten miles from my mother's house.

I felt anxious and bemused returning to the same school where I had once been part of "the class of 1990." In medical school, I had clear goals, structure, and a degree of pride. I suffered bouts of depression then, and often questioned whether I had any right to be there. But the structure and rigor of medical school swept me forward like an ocean current. Even though I often felt inadequate and inferior to my peers, I never really had anything to hide. Now I had everything to hide, but nothing to hide behind. I felt very alone pursuing a degree in which I had so much less interest and which, in my mind, was a step backward. I dreaded encounters with my former professors and worried I might not be able to do the work. The specter of failure and humiliation loomed large as I headed toward my first class.

The county penitentiary was at the beginning of the long road to the campus of the medical school. Although I'd passed it hundreds of times, I had never paid much attention to the dilapidated brick buildings segregated by barbed wire fences from the medical school. On the first day of graduate school, a few weeks before my first weekend of incarceration, I pulled over to the side of the road to study the four-story rectangular buildings and contemplate the drastic turn my life had taken.

Staring at the jail, I suddenly recalled being there a few times as a medical student. I'd interviewed prisoners for my forensic psychiatry elective and treated sick prisoners when I was on call.

A chill ran down my spine as I remembered the sound of the six-inch-thick steel security doors clang shut behind me. Even as an authorized visitor who could leave whenever I wanted, the sound was formidable.

If only Dr. Lancet could convince the judge that even a short stay in jail would damage my mental health. He'd written a letter to the judge before the hearing, stating that serving time in jail might send me spiraling into a depression, to no avail. After I was sentenced, Dr. Lancet kidded me about going to "the can."

"Big Bertha's gonna get you," he teased.

Dr. Lancet's banter helped allay my anxiety. I think it was because his teasing and my ability to take it reminded me of my toughness. I wasn't scared of bugs, like most girls. I wasn't scared of physical pain, like my mother was. Because I could go for days without eating I thought I was stronger than most people. Of course I could stand spending a few days in jail, I told myself. Still, I hoped that by some miracle I wouldn't have to go.

At five o'clock on January 29, Scott drove me to the jail. I was terrified. Nothing he said made me feel better. We had been talking about this for weeks. I was all talked out. Now I had to grin and bear it.

As I approached the guard booth, I noticed thirty or so women and children standing in line there. The women wore makeup, tight jeans, and short jackets that couldn't possibly be warm enough to protect them from the cold, damp, night air. The children seemed giddy as they chased one another in a game of tag. Stunned by this glimpse into a culture so foreign to me, I almost forgot to be nervous. As I watched the women go through the gate in the chain-link, barbed-wire fence and walk toward the jail, a rush of fear and dread overtook me.

I was the last person to reach the guard booth. It looked like one of the tiny run-down shacks that line the back roads south of the border; that other world my family used to drive though on our way to vacation in Florida. That's where my father told us cops were hiding like sharks waiting to nail unsuspecting speeders. "Lock your door," he'd warn. "You never know who's out here."

A frail black man in his mid-sixties, with a security badge on the pocket of his uniform, asked me my name. I told him and he leafed through a few stapled pages. "How do you spell that?"

By then, I was shivering from a combination of the cold and sheer terror. *Maybe my name's not on the guest list*, I prayed.

"I found it." He pushed a button to open the gate. "Go ahead."

Spotlights on the roof cut through the darkness, illuminating the area I had to traverse. The haze hanging in the crisscrossing beams left me feeling like a lost ship trying to navigate through fog. I had no idea what was to come. I felt utterly helpless.

Entering what could have been the lobby of any generic building, I saw two guards pat down the last of the visitors—a provocatively dressed, twenty-something black woman. The woman emptied her pockets, removed her huge hoop earrings and several rings and necklaces, and placed them in a tray in such a blasé manner, it seemed as though she'd done this a million times before.

One of the guards instructed me to wait on the bench in the entryway while my information was processed. As I watched this woman, it occurred to me she'd probably had experiences too horrible for me to even imagine. These ruminations put my situation into perspective. I had to laugh at myself for thinking I was so tough. In reality, I was a white kid from an affluent neighborhood who, I'm sure, in this woman's eyes, never had a problem worth talking about. *Things could be a lot worse,* I told myself.

After about half an hour, a female guard with a brown frizzy ponytail dangling out of her hat appeared from the other end of the hallway. "Chase, come with me."

I followed her to a drab, windowless room. She frisked me, then handed me an orange jumpsuit and instructed me to strip down to my underwear, and put the suit on. While I changed, she dumped the contents of my backpack onto a plastic tarp on the floor.

"You can't have these." She dropped my pen, cigarette lighter, and hard candy into a lunchbox size carton. She took my books one at a time, held them upside down by the binding and shook them up and down. "You can keep the books and the cigarettes." She tossed the box and my clothes into a large, clear, plastic bag and labeled the bag with a piece of masking tape. "You'll get these back when you're released. Come on," she said without looking at me.

She led me through a motorized metal door into a dark hallway with five holding pens where prisoners were brought before they went to their cellblocks. The pens were windowless cement rooms with bars on the wall facing the hall. As we walked down the hall, there was a bit of an uproar in a pen on the right, where ten or so black males banged on the bars, whistled at me and yelled things like, "A juicy little white pussy."

"Cut it out," bellowed the guard, which egged them on further. She unlocked the second pen on the left, which was no bigger than a bathroom stall, and nodded to me.

A thin bedraggled woman leaned against the far wall. I took a few steps inside and as the door clanged shut behind me, the catcalls escalated. A splintered wooden bench was suspended from one wall by two chains. The wraithlike, toothless, fifty-something woman hovered in the corner. The room stunk so badly of urine, I felt as though I was inside a litter box.

Keeping my back to my harassers, I moved to sit on the bench. Before I landed, my pen-mate piped up. "Watch out honey, it's wet over there."

I thought how strange and kind it was that this woman, whom I presumed was an addict and perhaps schizophrenic, warned me, rather than letting me sit in her urine. A man in an adjacent pen knocked on our wall and told me to ignore the taunting. I felt comforted by these strangers' gestures. I realized how often such small kindnesses made me feel cared for while the actions of people who *should* have been watching out for me, like my father, often left me feeling hurt.

Locked inside this filthy pen, unable to sit and, even worse, having to endure this cruel, disturbing onslaught, I truly began to understand my plight for the first time. Even though things had been bad before, I always felt physically comfortable and safe. Now I felt neither.

The jeers continued until the guard returned to take me to the infirmary for a physical exam. When I returned from the infirmary, a male guard took me into a small office to interview me. He talked, joked, and flirted with me for over an hour. I enjoyed the attention and found his flirtations flattering, even though Dr. Lancet would have told me they were sexist, if not abusive.

By the time we were done, it was after ten. The other prisoners were gone. He put me into a large clean pen with a pay telephone attached to the wall. I called Scott collect, but he wasn't home, so I talked to his brother Aaron. Scott and Aaron shared an apartment and since I spent so much time there, we had become good friends. Soon a large, red-faced female guard rudely informed me it was time to go my cellblock. She ordered me to remove my shoelaces and then handcuffed my hands behind my back.

"I don't need handcuffs," I said.

She grunted and tightened the cuffs. Back in the lobby, three similar looking guards joined us. They looked me up and down contemptuously before motioning me to follow them. As we walked through a network of tunnels, two in front of me and two behind, they smoked cigarettes and talked about how pissed they were that my transport came at the end of their shift.

My wrists were throbbing from the handcuffs, my eyes burned from the smoke, and I kept nearly tripping because my shoes were loose without shoelaces. Besides the physical discomfort, I felt incredibly vulnerable and irate. I was at the mercy of these rude ignorant assholes.

I tried to imagine what Dr. Lancet would say about this situation. Teasing me, he would say it would show my strength of character to just go along with them and not do or say anything.

They took me to C block, where everyone on psychiatric medication was housed. According to my paperwork, I was considered a high suicide risk. That's why they took my shoelaces away and that's why a prisoner from another block who'd been in jail long enough to earn privileges was assigned to sit outside my room to watch me all night. Some of her friends were sitting outside nearby cells on watch as well. Although I didn't feel suicidal, having them there was comforting. They told me the teacher who'd killed her lover's wife had been in my cell until earlier that day when she was transferred to a nearby women's prison.

The cell was the same size and shape as my hospital room, but it had gray concrete walls, a metal framed twin bed with overly starched sheets and a moth-eaten brown blanket, a steel toilet and sink. The small barred window was sealed shut. From the window, I could see the medical school. Instead of a door, the cell had bars, which only the guards could unlock.

We were locked in our cells a few hours during the day and eight hours at night. I paced back and forth, staring out the window at the barbed wire fence that separated my two lives: jail and medical school, past and present.

When we weren't in lockdown, we were free to roam around the block, which consisted of fifteen cells and a TV room. Most of the women hung out in the TV room, a long, narrow, messy area with a TV suspended from the ceiling, a few folding tables, and plastic chairs. Playing cards, magazines, and ashtrays lay scattered on the tabletops. The best thing about this room was the long window that overlooked the gym a few floors below. A guard sat at an institutional-style desk watching us.

I hung out there with the other women on my block, playing cards and talking. The women ranged in age from early twenties to fifty. There was only one other white woman whom I quickly befriended. She had been sentenced to six months for writing bad checks. Most of the other women had been charged with shoplifting or some drug-related crime. The one that affected me most was a thin, sad-looking woman in her late twenties who had four children. She had stabbed her husband to death in self-defense. Since she couldn't afford bail, she had to await sentencing in jail.

I was interested in hearing their stories and appreciated how easily they accepted me. I learned a lot about the social interactions and politics of jail. It disturbed me that these shoplifters, drug abusers, and forgers were serving far longer sentences than mine. The only reason I could see for that was the color of my skin and the fact that I could afford a topnotch lawyer.

I only had a problem with a woman in the cell across from mine. She made passes at me and slipped notes into my pockets in the game room. She even approached me directly, telling me what she wanted to do to me in the shower. She didn't frighten me, but she became so annoying and persistent that I finally told a guard who put a stop to it by threatening to put her in lockdown.

Time passed quickly, especially because I spent two hours each day playing basketball. By the end of the weekend, I wasn't desperate to leave. I would have preferred staying four consecutive days rather than splitting it into two weekends. I felt as though my life would be on hold until I got the second weekend over with.

The point of this weekend incarceration, called "shock incarceration," was to deter and punish me. It succeeded in doing both. I knew that after my next weekend of incarceration, I would never return to jail again.

CHAPTER 51

On February 12, Scott drove me to the jail in a severe blizzard. The only person standing near the guard booth was a man wearing a long tan parka with the hood tied over his head. A small circular opening exposed his eyes, nose, and mouth. I didn't pay him much attention until he tapped me on the shoulder and said my name. Startled, I spun around to look at him.

"I'm Jimmy Breslin, a journalist from *New York Newsday*." I could see his breath in the cold with each word he spoke.

"I've heard of you. What are you doing here?" It did not occur to me to wonder how he knew who I was.

He untied his hood. As it slid up his face, his bushy salt-and-pepper eyebrows emerged like the tails of two squirrels. "I wanted to forewarn you that an article I wrote about you will be published on the front page of this Sunday's paper. I heard about your story when I was in a bar near the hospital where Luke was." He reached a gloved hand into his jacket pocket and pulled out a white envelope. "I also wanted to give you this letter explaining that I have a potential movie deal for you. I've included my home phone number. Please call me collect from jail."

I took a step away from him. "Thanks for your interest in me, but I don't want any publicity."

That my story might receive any hype this many months later had never occurred to me. I was shocked and upset and felt especially vulnerable and helpless. Having been approached when I was alone with nowhere to turn, I also felt violated. Surely he could have called me or even sent me a telegram at home where the people in my support system were accessible and nearby. Scott and his brother sometimes teased me, saying they were going to call one of the television magazine shows and tell my story for money, but a movie deal? This guy *wasn't* kidding. I wanted to move on with my life and try to put the pieces back together, not sensationalize my story to make a quick buck.

He leaned toward me dangling the envelope in his outstretched hand. "Please take it in case you change your mind."

I took the envelope and shoved it into my pocket. Luke had been in the hospital eight months ago, so why were people talking about it now? I realized it must have been after the hearing, and the nurses and doctors were talking about the sentence. I wasn't embarrassed about going to jail or of having been in a mental hospital. I was ashamed of losing my medical license. If I had never entered what so many considered a prestigious profession, I'm sure my sense of shame would have been much less. Having "fallen so far," made it harder for me to face people. Expectations of me had been so high, and therefore, the potential for public ridicule and delight at my failure felt enormous. That was probably what made Jimmy Breslin and his editors think my story was front page newsworthy.

It would have been more fitting and commensurate with my self-image if I *had* been a nobody and my story barely worthy of a footnote in some obscure paper. As it was, my present status, or lack thereof, felt more appropriate to me in terms of my self-image than being a doctor had. I had no sense of being special. I sort of envied the woman I'd seen going through the metal detector that first weekend; nobody expected anything of her. She could be who she really was. That's what I wanted, to be who I really was. But I still had to figure out who that was.

In a therapy session, shortly after Luke broke up with me, I cried hysterically about losing the "Luke and Mel" identity. Josh asked me what was wrong with only being "Mel." I sobbed, saying that I didn't know who that was. I still didn't.

In college, I used to fantasize about making some obscure discovery about the brain, perhaps being a pioneer in my field.

Those hopes were buried by my severe depression when my greatest desire was to die. The closest I came to being "famous," was during my freshman year of college when I ran the Boston Marathon. My college was the halfway point of the marathon, so I achieved instant celebrity on campus. Total strangers congratulated me and asked for running and training tips. A story about me was in the school paper. That attention felt good. My father found out about the marathon through the grapevine and started bragging to anyone who would listen. I resented his using my accomplishment to bolster himself -- especially when he knew nothing about me, or my experience. The same thing happened when I co-authored an article in a prestigious psychiatric journal about a year after graduating college. He bragged about me without even reading the article. This pissed me off to no end. I did not want people to think I was special in any way; that would only set me up for exploitation by my father and, I assumed, raise peoples' expectations of me. Maybe that's why my actual accomplishments meant so little to me. Maybe that dynamic played some part in why I threw away my medical career.

The thought of being the subject of a movie, which would bring infamy to me and therefore destroy any chance of creating a meaningful and productive life, was abhorrent. I was horrified about the article, too. I hoped it would blow over quickly and people would forget they ever heard my name.

I suddenly missed my father acutely. I felt childlike in my vulnerability. I practically trotted the hundred or so feet to the jail and ran to the lobby payphone to call Tom. I needed to get his take on the whole thing, but his secretary told me he was in Hawaii.

Lost in thought, I was unfazed when the guard knocked on the door of the payphone and directed me to the holding area. Locked in a large pen where I had my choice of three benches and enough light to read by, I read the letter over and over. As I read about how he found out about me and about the potential movie deal, what I wondered most was why he had urged me to call him immediately instead of waiting until I went home. I knew I would never get the answer to that question, though. I had no intention of contacting him.

The rest of the weekend was similar to the first one until Sunday morning, when a guard came to tell me I had a visitor.

It was Tom. I was so relieved to see him

"The strangest thing happened when I arrived at the airport on my way home from Hawaii," he said, sounding perturbed. "There was an article about you on the front page of the newspaper."

It hadn't occurred to me he'd find out this way. I felt sort of cheated by the fact that I had not been able to tell him about the article myself. I told him about my encounter with Jimmy Breslin and asked if he had read the article and if he had it with him.

"Yes, I read it, and no, I don't have it with me. It went into excruciating detail. I hope you didn't call him. Did you?"

I wondered if he really thought I was stupid or impulsive enough to do such a thing.

"If there's a movie made, I want Tom Cruise to play me," he said, winking. "Seriously, though, do not call him under any circumstances." He assured me that "few people, if any," read that newspaper. He was sure it would blow over.

"Time's up," shouted a guard. She took me to a tiny room at the end of the hall. "Take off your clothes, pile them in the corner, and put on the robe hanging on the door."

Stunned, I unzipped the jumpsuit and let it fall to a heap around my feet. I slipped my arms through the sleeves of the robe and wrapped it around my waist. Leaning against the cold cement wall, I removed my bra and underpants and shook off my work boots, which landed with a thud. I saved my socks for last. The floor was freezing.

"Bend over," she ordered as she donned a pair of latex gloves.

I couldn't believe this bitch was going to stick her fingers inside me.

She frisked me, smeared Vaseline on one index finger and thrust her finger into my vagina and then my anus. Then she put on a new pair of gloves and examined my clothes.

"Get dressed," she demanded before marching out of the room.

The rest of the day raced by and, before I knew it, a guard came to walk me to the lobby.

"Hey, Chase, you made the front page of the paper," hooted the officers outside the holding pen. "Congratulations!"

I couldn't believe they thought making the paper in this context was an accomplishment. Perhaps if they were in my shoes, they'd understand that this was nothing to be proud of or to make light of.

In the car, Scott dropped a copy of the paper on my lap.

The headline, "HER LOVE WAS POISON," spanned the entire front page. I was horrified.

"Don't worry," he said again, "Nobody reads this paper."

I had no idea how I could face anyone. Everyone in town, school, and the soup kitchen where I'd been volunteering for a couple of months, would discover the truth about me. They would reject me, or worse, laugh about me behind my back. I wished I could move some place where nobody knew me and start with a clean slate. I already felt self-conscious wondering who knew and who didn't, which was the same way I'd felt after I was fired.

I was struggling so hard to make retribution and put my life back together. Yet every time I was finally progressing and getting a handle on things, another challenge arose. I felt like the battle was impossible and would never end.

CHAPTER 52

So much for keeping a low profile," Dr. Lancet teased when I arrived at his office the following day.

"You know about it?" I said incredulously.

"I was at the Penn Station yesterday picking up my son. When I glanced at a stack of papers in the newsstand, I nearly fainted."

When I told him about Jimmy Breslin coming to see me at jail, he said, "A movie deal? I want Robert Redford to play me."

As far as I could tell, the fallout from the article was minimal. Unlike when I was hospitalized, my mother didn't receive phone calls from long-lost relatives or ambulance-chasing acquaintances. *Maybe Tom was right. This whole thing could just blow over.* Still, my exuberance over having completed the jail time was tempered by my horror at having made the front page of a newspaper. I tried not to let it get the better of me, but I felt more self-conscious than ever.

During the following weeks my shame and paranoia over the article lingered like a virus. I felt this acutely at school. In most of my classes, we had to introduce ourselves and give a brief biography. I was careful not to say my last name. Instead of revealing that I'd been a psychiatric resident, I said I was pursuing a residency in public health.

Despite my discomfort at being found out, I wanted to leave myself with real options. I wasn't going to compromise my academic performance for anything. So although I shied away from close relationships with classmates, when it came to participating in class discussions or talking to professors, I didn't hold back

Try as I might to feel normal, weekly meetings with my probation officer, Joanne, made the reality of my situation impossible to deny.

Each time I went to see her, she was at least fifteen minutes late. The first few times she kept me waiting, I sat among five or so black men also waiting for their probation officers. As the minutes ticked away, I became more and more irate and felt on the verge of losing control of my anger. But as I looked around at the other probationers, it struck me that they were all taking the whole thing in stride, listening to a Walkman, looking through their wallets or just sitting calmly. I realized how out of line I was.

I took Joanne's lateness as a personal affront and felt incensed and indignant. It took every ounce of self-control for me not to curse her out or to leave before she got there. I got so angry it felt physically painful. The only way I stopped myself from acting out was to think about the consequences and summon Dr. Lancet's voice saying, "Think before you act." I felt helpless having to meet on her terms. I was sick of being at the mercy of people in authority. The degree of my anger drove home the fact that I was still potentially a loose cannon and had a lot of work left to do on myself.

Apart from her tardiness, I really liked Joanne. She was an attractive woman, many years my junior, who dressed on the sexy side and projected a rock-and-roll-star image, not like a government employee. In every other way, she was warm and down-to-earth.

For the first few months of probation, she treated me formally, keeping the sessions to fifteen minutes or so, calling me Ms. Chase and sticking to the protocol. She processed my restitution checks, asked about my activities and kept the focus on me. After a few months, she became more casual, calling me Melanie and telling me about herself.

Once the formalities were out of the way, we'd talked like old friends. She told me about her boyfriend and their future plans. I told her about my latest accomplishment at school or what was going on with Scott. If the setting hadn't been an overcrowded government agency room, we could have been two friends, just shooting the breeze. She told me, "Everybody's done at least one terrible thing in their life. Your problem is you got caught."

I could be myself with Joanne, but I continued to hide who I really was with everyone at school. However, as the semester progressed, I became involved in my classes more than ever before. In medical school, I usually sat in the back of the room and had mediocre exam scores. Now in graduate school, I sat in the front row, asked lots of questions, and aced all the papers and exams. At the end of the first semester, I decided to look for a job in the field of maternal and child health, my declared major. I wanted to do something I found interesting enough to use for my thesis, but I needed to avoid anything medically related in accordance with the conditions of my probation.

Ultimately, I chose to become involved with an upstart program designed to teach parenting skills to HIV-infected and drug-addicted women. I went on the interview with trepidation. I had no idea how much of my situation to disclose. I ended up telling the interviewers I was a doctor with a severe illness (implying cancer, not depression) that required me to take an indefinite leave of absence and that, in the meantime, I was pursuing a master's in public health.

The two women in charge of the program interviewed me and hired me on the spot. I was ecstatic. Having had no patient contact for almost a year, the idea that I would actually be allowed to help these women, using skills and knowledge I'd acquired throughout my medical training, excited me. I felt validated. I was also happy because I'd get a jump on my thesis.

My interview was at the beginning of June, 1993, one year after Luke was hospitalized. I was supposed to start working two weeks later. Two days before the start date, an article titled "Bad Apples" appeared on the front page of the local newspaper. It gave an overview of the misconduct charges and their consequences for all the medical doctors in the county who'd been disciplined by the Board of Professions in the past year. It said I had been convicted of assault in the first degree and had surrendered my medical license.

Shortly after I read the article, one of the women who'd hired me called. She said she was very sorry, but that she couldn't allow me to work for her because I had a felony conviction. I collapsed to the floor, distraught.

I called my mother at work to tell her what happened. She emitted an "Oh, Mel!" filled with such compassion I felt as though she were hugging me to her chest and stroking my hair. That spontaneous response comforted me and I longed for more of the same from her.

"That must have been why someone from the paper kept calling the house to talk to you."

She was right. But the reporter was so vague about her reason for calling that I thought refusing to speak to her would preclude any such article being written. Whenever the reporter called, my mother, very uncharacteristically, lied, saying I wasn't home. Since Mom hated lying more than anything, the fact that she did this without complaining was evidence that her feelings toward me were changing. She was becoming more protective, appreciative, and accepting of me. That she was responding to me differently had a lot to do with the work we were doing together with Richie, and my changed behavior.

"I should have spoken with her. I would have known about the article ahead of time and this whole disaster could have been avoided. The way it stands now, I feel so bad about losing the job and so humiliated by the article, I'm not sure I'll be able to recover."

"You're not thinking about hurting yourself, are you? I'll call Dr. Lancet right now," she said, sounding alarmed.

Hurting myself was the furthest thing from my mind. I regretted having called her when my feelings were so raw. I should have called Scott instead and taken time to distance myself from the pain before telling her. I didn't mean to frighten or worry her; I just wanted some TLC.

"No, but maybe I'm running out of energy to keep fighting what seems like an uphill battle. The 'rah' has gone out of the 'rah rah.'"

"Don't be silly," she said. "You're the most resilient person I know. I bet you'll turn this into something positive."

Seeing myself through her eyes, I felt a bit stronger. Anyway, I knew my only real options were to continue to fight the fight or take to bed in defeat like my father had. The thought of giving up like he had was so abhorrent that I didn't consider it a real option.

I re-read the article and thought about what had happened and what she had said. The article listed about twenty-five doctors with infractions and punishments ranging from failure to keep accurate records and license suspension to Medicare fraud and license revocation. Despite my horror that I was one of those listed, I found it a fascinating read. When I realized I could not remember the names of any of the other doctors, I had to laugh. If I, who had a vested interest in the information, couldn't recall the names, then surely the average person reading it wouldn't either. I thought it ironic that this little article in a local paper, which listed me with twenty-five other doctors, had already had more of an effect on me than the front page article in February.

Slumping into the soft leather seat in the family room, I reflected on the past year. Having made the worst decision ever, to poison Luke, everything that happened after that was a consequence of that tragic mistake. In my struggle to recover, I had fallen into the depths of despair, but had always pulled myself up by the bootstraps and came out on the side of hope. Sometimes the minutest of triumphs was enough to motivate me to continue marching toward recovery. Yet each obstacle had the potential to make me lose belief in my progress and potential, and discourage or throw me from my path. At every turn, I questioned whether the challenge, along with the accumulated stress of the previous challenges, would override the hard-won confidence and momentum of having prevailed. I knew how easy it would be to slip into defeat mode because what I was doing was so damned hard. Still, I'd fought hard for my sanity and

I was not about to allow this new setback to undo everything I had gained. I was chipping away at the mountain of shame and humiliation that buried me, but the mountain kept getting higher.

CHAPTER 53

A few days after the "Bad Apples" article appeared, Tom called to tell me he'd received a call from a lawyer representing Luke in a civil suit against me. "They want to settle out of court."

"Settle what?" I was already paying him sixty-five thousand dollars and couldn't for the life of me figure out why he was demanding more.

"For a relatively small amount of money and several reasonable promises from you, he's willing to commit to never suing you in the future." Pausing, he added, "The statute of limitations for assault in the first degree is ten years, so realistically he's doing you a favor."

I was incredulous. "No, leaving me the fuck alone would be doing me a favor. Having never been born would be doing me a favor. This, my friend, is no favor. This is out-and-out extortion!" I felt like a teapot that wouldn't stop steaming until I exploded. Not only would this nightmare never end, I was blindsided again before I'd had a chance to recover from the most recent blow.

I slowly reigned myself in. "So what does he want from me?" I knew I should be writing down everything Tom said, but I felt so defeated I didn't have the energy to reach behind me for paper and a pen.

"Fifteen thousand dollars and promises that you won't harass him or anyone in his family. You'll continue to make restitution payments on time, you won't interfere with his personal or professional life in any way, and you'll make full financial disclosure."

I was fuming! "I've made all the restitution payments on time and haven't done anything to bother him or the gang. What's his problem?" Maybe he met someone and he wanted to make sure I wouldn't discover that, and then freak out. Even though I no longer pined for him, I would have been devastated if I knew he was in love with someone else or, worse, getting married. In my heart of hearts, I still held onto a tiny sliver of hope that he'd either be too devastated over losing me to get involved with someone else, or that what his friends had told me was true, that he was incapable of love and would always be alone. If he were in love with somebody else, it would mean I was in fact unlovable. Also, it wouldn't seem fair that he moved on so quickly, while my life was still in shambles.

"Why now?"

"Who knows, but regardless of the reason, I suggest you settle this quickly."

"I still owe Luke over fifty thousand dollars; I'm paying Dr. Lancet a thousand a month; I'm paying for school and my legal fees. I'm living off the inheritance, but if I pay fifteen thousand now, eventually I won't be able to make the restitution payments." I lay down on the kitchen floor, overwhelmed and exhausted.

"I'll offer him ten and see what happens." He started talking to someone in the background. "But Melanie, you'd be wise to settle this as soon as possible, even if it means borrowing the other money later." His voice became emphatic. "Don't take this lightly, and don't give him time to change his mind. He could come after you anytime in the next nine years for millions of dollars. God forbid he starts having seizures, memory loss, or something else that he can relate to what you did to him. You may not realize it now, but he's doing you a huge favor."

"With favors like that. . . , Okay, I'll do whatever it takes." I hung up the phone, and rested my head on the kitchen table. Looking around my mother's kitchen, I considered my situation. I was living in a comfortable house with a mother who loved me as best she could; I was thriving in school and had a good relationship with Scott. None of this had changed. The only thing that had happened was I lost a job I never really had, and was going to have less money than I thought I had. Neither one of these things worried me much.

So what really had happened was that things hadn't worked out the way I had hoped they would. *Big deal*, I'm *the most resilient person I know!*

I decided right then and there to throw myself into community service and complete the thousand hours sooner rather than later. Since my classes were mostly in the evening, the soup kitchen was on Sundays and the three appointments per week with Dr. Lancet were early in the day, I had afternoons to do community service. I'd just have to adjust my studying schedule and see less of Scott.

Half an hour later, I was in the local social services office perusing literature on volunteer opportunities. I wanted to work with people diagnosed with HIV and AIDS, but knew it had to be peripherally because of the terms of my probation.

There was an abundance of not-for-profit organizations in the county whose mission was to help HIV-infected individuals. I called the head of each organization, briefly explained my situation and asked if they'd be interested in having me as a volunteer.

Most of the women with whom I spoke asked for my phone number and said they'd get back to me. But Anne, a seventy-year-old divorced mother of ten grown children, enthusiastically asked me to meet with her the following day. She was president and founder of The Pantry, a non-profit organization dedicated to preparing and delivering meals to homebound people with HIV/AIDS. Shortly after her son died of AIDS, this former housewife and wife of a doctor started the organization out of her kitchen with small donations from local restaurants. In the beginning she served four clients. By the time I met her, she had eighty clients, four employees, a hundred volunteers, and rental space in a local church.

Anne was warm, humble, nonjudgmental, and spiritual. Even though she didn't ask me to recount the details of my story, I felt compelled to tell her everything. She welcomed me with open arms. Joanne gave me permission to work there on the condition she could call Anne to check up on me, and perhaps even make surprise visits while I was there. That was fine with me.

I started working for Anne the following day and initially committed to two hours per day, five days a week. At first I worked with the other volunteers, making sandwiches and helping prepare the hot meals that were delivered to the clients around the county. Before long, I was helping in the office and implementing more efficient systems for getting all the work done in the few hours allotted to us by the church. Since I was there every day and most other volunteers only came once or twice a week, I was able to see the big picture. I figured out better ways to organize and delegate the work. I was also aware of the behind-the-scenes workings since I was in the office. Within a few months, I was promoted to volunteer coordinator, working fifteen hours a week. The Pantry became my home away from home.

Gradually, I began to confide in the people I felt closest to there, especially a retired male volunteer and the chef. Rather than being horrified or rejecting me, they shared some of their own past shames and secrets. It was a great relief and surprise to find the fears that led me to guard my secrets so vigilantly were unfounded.

By September, a month before my sister's wedding, I was working at The Pantry, attending school at night, working in the soup kitchen on Sundays, performing data entry work on a volunteer basis to supplement my community service and seeing Dr. Lancet three times a week. I lived half of the time with Scott, the rest of the time at my mother's house.

I had achieved one of my most important short-term goals, which was to be comfortable enough with my situation to participate in Dani's wedding. To me, this meant I could meet and talk to her in-laws and their friends, many of whom were doctors, without hanging my head in shame.

Dani and Arty were third-year law students with demanding schedules. I was not nearly as busy as they were, so I volunteered to help with the pre-wedding logistics. I met Dani in the city to shop for a bridesmaid dress, and I managed to remain cheerful when she chose a long, pink, chiffon dress that, under any other circumstance except maybe Halloween, I would not be caught dead in. I organized tuxedo rentals for the ushers, all of whom would arrive from out of town. I delivered their tuxes to the hotel, and collected and returned them to the store afterward. I wrote and delivered a beautiful wedding tribute to the bride and groom.

Anyone who didn't know me would never have suspected I was shame-filled, sorrowful over my losses and struggling to create meaning in my life. *If only things had turned out differently, this could have been mine and Luke's wedding, or at least I would have been sharing this day with him.*

It wasn't so much that I wished I was married to Luke or even involved with him. It was more about the fact that I'd lost everything of which Luke was a part. If I was still living that life, I would have been proud of what I was doing and who I was. Had I been a doctor with a doctor mate, my mother would have been proud of me, too. I would have felt on a par, at least, with my sister and her new in-laws. Instead, I was doing "unskilled" community service, and my boyfriend worked in an electronics store. I spent most of the evening diverting questions about myself and avoiding conversations or situations where the truth might be revealed. Despite all this, I managed to make a good showing.

Dr. Lancet was proud of me. He declared, "You could have been resentful of your sister for having all the things you lost and so much want: a committed relationship with the love of her life, a fulfilling career, and the respect and admiration of society and your mother. But rather than act like sour grapes and sabotage her wedding, you rose to the occasion. You're becoming a really good person!"

I knew that I'd done right by my sister and did it with grace and style. But it never would have occurred to me to do otherwise, no matter how difficult it might have been. She was my sister. I loved her, rooted for her and wanted to see her happy. Sure it would have been easier for me if I had what I wanted in my life. But my sadness over my own life did not make me want her life to be bad. My behavior was a reflection of who I had always been, but I still felt like a fuck-up.

After a long, thoughtful pause, he added, "Being a good person is about writing thank you notes, taking pleasure in other people's achievements, having integrity and helping others. It has nothing to do with degrees or status. You're the best you've ever been."

I knew I had become a better person since I'd been in therapy with him. But the fact remained that I had poisoned someone. While I was working hard to understand why that happened, I feared I would never live up to anyone's expectations or realize my potential.

CHAPTER 54

M y struggles with depression started in sixth grade, around the same time I got my period. This was also when I began having trouble paying attention in class. I was unable to concentrate. The slightest distraction made me lose track of what I was doing. When I studied, I jumped from book to book to book, inevitably misplacing the one I was sure held the key to the entire subject. These struggles plagued me for most of my life. Because nobody understood this was ADD (it wasn't diagnosed until I was in my twenties) and could be easily addressed, I felt stupid, ashamed, and inadequate.

That changed in graduate school. I was surprised and thrilled to find I could pay attention in class and while doing homework. The material was interesting and in some cases familiar to me from my medical education. The lack of pressure in the form of expectations from my father, and competitiveness from classmates, contributed to my newfound lucidity. While Mom, Scott, and Dr. Lancet supported my going back to school, they never pressured me to do well. They focused on what I could handle emotionally. Could I dedicate, commit and apply myself to something that was such an unknown? Was I strong enough to make this endeavor meaningful? Would I slip into depression and despair returning to my medical school for a lesser degree? Their concerns were not about my grades.

Most of the other students were adults returning to school to advance their careers. They had families, jobs, and lives. They cared about learning and balancing everything in their lives. All this was helpful to me. The more I learned, the more I wanted to learn. By the second semester, I started to believe I could be satisfied with a career in public health. I wanted to learn more, especially as my interest in HIV and AIDS crystallized.

The most important factor in my academic improvement was that I was finally working through my psychological issues. The lack of emotional intrusion allowed me to be clearheaded, in and out of school. Also, I sat in the front row and used the professors' body language and inflection as cues to discern what information was important. Focusing on the teacher helped me become less aware of my classmates. I usually felt as though I had a scarlet "F" for felony emblazoned on my forehead. With my back facing the other students I could forget about this while in class.

Fueled by a newly discovered confidence and an engagement with the lecture material, I devised a method to study and learn effectively. I separated significant information from insignificant information by photocopying the pages, cutting out important words and concepts and taping them to a blank page. Using this strategy, I excelled in my classes. For the first time since elementary school, I enjoyed school.

I was sitting front and center the night Mr. Good guest-lectured in my Law and Health class in the spring of 1994. Ms. Leeds, the host professor, introduced him as one of the top authorities on medical misconduct in the state. For fifteen years, he had been the prosecuting attorney for the Committee of the Professions. He'd been in private practice for the past ten years, handling defense for medical misconduct cases.

Mr. Good was an imposing, impeccably dressed black man with a booming voice. He stood in front of the room a foot or so away from me. His size, combined with his powerful and articulate speech, made him seem incredibly intimidating.

He spent two hours detailing cases involving doctors charged with various offenses, such as sexual misconduct, Medicare fraud, and writing illegal prescriptions. He recounted actual cases, but used made-up names. He walked us through cases from start to finish: the charges, the revocation or suspension, the application for reinstatement and, in some cases, the appeal.

He was such a charismatic speaker. I was fully drawn into the lecture. I'd known nothing about misconduct hearings (those didn't apply to me as I was convicted of a felony, which was grounds for immediate revocation) or the process of applying for reinstatement.

As the evening progressed, I started thinking I might just have a chance at getting my license back. Even though I knew when I surrendered my license that there was a slim possibility of getting it back, it had seemed more like an abstraction than something that could actually happen. I decided early on not to think about it. But sitting there visualizing the possibilities, my desire to be a therapist was reactivated. I would have gladly been a psychotherapist without the doctoring part. But I didn't think anyone would allow me to be any type of therapist unless the medical community showed enough faith in me to restore my medical license.

I started fantasizing about being back in the role of a therapist. I liked how it felt. I decided I was meant to be in that lecture on that particular evening and that Mr. Good held the key to my future.

I asked Dr. Lancet during our next session, "Don't you think it's an omen?" I knew he was much too grounded in reality to believe in omens.

"Omen or not, are you ready to return to a career in medicine?" he asked.

It was only June 1994. My sentence prohibited me from doing anything medically related for another three-and-a-half years, so it didn't matter that I wasn't ready.

We decided it couldn't hurt to meet with Mr. Good to feel him out.

On the morning of my appointment, I was extremely nervous. I wanted to come across as articulate and bright, but I knew my tendency to be at a loss for words when feeling intimidated or self-conscious. I had no idea what to expect. I wasn't even sure what I wanted him to tell me. If he said it was a lost cause, I would have been disappointed, but at least I would be clearer about my future. If he said go ahead and try, I wasn't even sure I would.

Mr. Good's office was in a landmark building in the center of the town where I grew up. I stood in front of the frosted-glass doors to his office and took a deep breath before knocking. Within seconds, the secretary, a congenial forty-something woman buzzed me into an enormous, plant-filled anteroom. "Dr. Chase," she said, flashing me an ingratiating smile.

It felt so strange to be called *doctor*. *Loser* felt more appropriate.

A few moments later, Mr. Good approached me with an outstretched hand. "Dr. Chase?

Please come with me." He strode back in the direction he'd come from, opened an oak door and waited for me to enter the massive office. Inside, he waved me toward a chair in front of a mahogany desk. I sat up straight, crossing and uncrossing my legs self-consciously.

"So, what can I do for you?" He leaned back in his chair.

"I'm hoping you can tell me." I smiled awkwardly. "I surrendered my medical license, and until I heard your lecture in Mrs. Leeds' health and law class – do you remember me? I was sitting in the front row?" *I'm such an idiot.*

"I'm afraid not. I don't focus on faces when I'm lecturing."

"Oh, my God!" I began speaking quickly, too quickly. "I agonized through that entire class. I thought you knew who I was and you'd use me as a case study any minute." I started to chuckle, but his expression didn't change. "I guess when you've been through what I've been through, you get pretty paranoid."

He asked what I'd been through and how he could help me. I

recounted my story and then asked him timidly if he thought I had any chance of getting my license back.

"I won't sugarcoat it by saying it will be easy, but I don't think it's a long shot. Everybody deserves a second chance. If you meet the three criteria for reinstatement — remorse, rehabilitation, and re-education — you have a decent chance of being reinstated."

"Would you be willing to represent me?" Even though this was his job, and even though I'd be paying him, I felt embarrassed as though I was asking him for a favor.

"I charge two hundred dollars an hour. Your case will require at least two hundred hours." I did the math in my head. "Also, I'll require a five-thousand-dollar retainer up front."

"That's no problem," I said too eagerly. I mentally went through the list of people who might be willing to lend me money. "How long do you think it will take?"

"The process has become longer recently due to the downsizing of staff and the increase in applicants. It could take as long as three years from the time you submit the petition to the date of the hearing. Are you prepared to start now?"

"Yes," I said, without thinking.

"You'll need to get ten to fifteen letters from character witnesses who support your application for reinstatement. Ideally, these will be prestigious people with clout, say doctors, lawyers, political figures …"

"I know a few Nobel prize winners," I said in an effort to get him to smile. He didn't.

"You'll have to write an essay explaining why you surrendered your medical license, what you learned from what happened, and include your future plans, hopes, and dreams." He wrote all this down for me as he spoke. "As I see it now, although I'll reevaluate as we proceed, the centerpiece of your case will be the abusive relationship you had with your father." He looked at me then. I thought I glimpsed a tinge of sympathy in his eyes. "I'd like to talk to your psychiatrist."

"Sure, no problem." I started feeling very tired.

"I'll send you a bill for the retainer. Once I receive the check, I'll get started on your case."

CHAPTER 55

I told Dr. Lancet about the meeting with Mr. Good. We were in his private office, which was on the third floor of a converted house. After meeting in his hospital office for a year and a half, we switched to this location. It had become clear that I was his patient for the long haul. Another hospitalization was no longer a probability or even a possibility. Moving to his private office was like graduating from being an ex-inpatient to being an official outpatient.

The informal atmosphere reflected how far our relationship had progressed. I had proven myself over and over by weathering a variety of storms, including an unwanted pregnancy and abortion with Scott a few months earlier, and Dani's move to Atlanta after her graduation from law school.

He no longer worried that I would harm Luke or any of the other gang members. I had stayed away from them completely. We spent a lot of time discussing what had happened with Luke. Although we continued rehashing it, we had a pretty good handle on it. Most importantly, we were sure I would never put myself in a position to become desperate enough to do anything like that again. Even my weight was less of an issue.

I was doing well in school. I had tolerated Scott going away for two weeks with his family, something I could have never endured when I was with Luke. I dealt extremely well with several more of Dr. Lancet's vacations without even needing to see a back-up therapist.

Dr. Lancet had the additional reassurance of my probation officer who called him periodically to check-in. Mom, Richie, and Scott never called him, but each had been given permission by me to do so if they ever felt worried about me. This, combined with his personal experience of me (he said I was calmer, more focused, and more self-reflective) allowed him to trust me and let down his guard with me.

It's not that everything about my life was smooth sailing; it's just that I was now able to see difficult and painful things from a more rational perspective. I could think or talk instead of acting out. There would always be things that were difficult for me. Some wounds never heal completely. The goal is to be aware of these, to make the pain less and less and manage the pain in healthy, self-contained ways.

Your issues will always be your issues. It's just a matter of figuring out a way to cope so that you can tolerate the inevitable pain associated with your triggers without acting out or falling apart. The severity of the associated pain can be dissipated by facing that pain head on in a safe (therapeutic) environment with someone you trust.

I told Dr. Lancet, "He thinks it's worth a shot. The worst thing that can happen is I'll waste a lot of people's time, spend a ton of money and end up pretty much where I am now."

I never wanted to be a medical doctor, and I still didn't. I wanted to help people who were emotionally, not physically, ill. My greatest thrills came from working with adolescents and their families or making breakthroughs with difficult patients. I loved being a therapist and helping my patients. If I could create my fantasy job, it would combine my work with abused and neglected children and unwanted pets in a therapeutic setting. Still, trying to get my medical license back seemed like the path of least resistance.

"What if I get my license back and then nobody hires me? What if I can't even find enough character witnesses to write letters for my petition in the first place?"

Thoughts about my inability to get anyone to rally behind me escalated into thoughts about being unworthy of anyone's support. They settled at the place where I felt like I was worse than worthless and didn't deserve to be alive. This spiral of thoughts was familiar. It was as though a path had been carved from my feeling hopeful and feeling like I had value, all the way down to feeling worthless and afraid. The predominant emotion was anxiety, which was often so intense that I had a physical experience of disintegrating.

Dr. Lancet pressed a fingertip to his lip. "Regardless of what happens, you can't return to medicine for another three years. True?"

"Three and a half."

"Well, look how far you've come since I met you. You're more than halfway through a master's program in which you're doing incredibly well. You're on the verge of completing a thousand hours of community service and being hired by your supervisors. You're getting along much better with your mother. And most importantly, you're learning to control your emotions instead of acting out." He smiled. "We still have a lot of work to do on your self-image and your inability to feel true remorse over what you did, but so far you're proof that it's possible to rehabilitate a borderline!"

While I knew that I was doing better than anyone could have hoped for, I still berated myself for having screwed up to begin with. It was as though I was a marathon runner and had been in a terrible car accident where I was paralyzed and nobody thought I'd be able to use my legs again, but I was already starting to walk without a walker. It was an accomplishment, but given where I'd started out it still seemed horrible to me.

"Yeah, but this isn't the way my life was supposed to turn out." I started to cry.

He leaned toward me and became animated. "Don't you see? You're actually a success story."

Knowing we'd never see eye to eye on this, I changed the subject. "The hardest part of the application is going to be asking people to write letters on my behalf. I hate asking people to go out of their way for me."

"A lot of people are rooting for you. I bet they'll be thrilled to help."

It suddenly occurred to me, that maybe, just maybe, he would write one. I asked him shyly, as though I barely knew him.

"I have to put my money where my mouth is, do I not? Of course I'll write one."

"So you think I should do it?"

"I think you should not let fear get in your way. By the time you'd actually be allowed to go back to medicine, you'll be in a much better position to do so. It would be a shame for you not to be a psychiatrist; you'd make a great one. You're not ready to practice now. You're still too fragile and lack enough ego strength to be truly objective about your patients. I don't think you could handle the pressure of a residency with all the rules and paperwork. But with your progress and how hard you've been working, I think you should seriously consider it. It couldn't hurt to help feeling out people sooner rather than later."

I ran down the three flights of stairs and around the back of the house to my car, resisting the urge to peek inside his car, which was parked next to mine. *Boundaries*, I thought, as I looked away from his car window. The driving compulsion to know, to violate boundaries at all costs is a borderline compulsion. Previously, I looked in my therapist's car windows and even studied his cassettes to figure out what music he liked. The fact that I looked away from Dr. Lancet's car felt huge.

CHAPTER 56

Scott was upset that I didn't ask him to write a letter for me. He told me this at the kitchen table in the apartment we'd rented together at the beginning of the month. His brother had moved to Canada to join their father's business, so Scott and I decided to move in together. Dr. Lancet and I discussed the move ad nauseum. We decided it would be okay, and that it was the most practical thing to do from a financial point of view. Scott and I were getting along really well. He knew I needed time to figure out where my life was going before I made any long-term commitment to him or anyone else. If it were up to him, we would have been married already.

"Why would the medical board care what my boyfriend thinks?"

He reached across the table for my hand. "The reasons I love you are the same reasons I think you should be allowed to take care of patients."

The way he said he loved me was so pure and genuine, it awakened that thing inside me that says, "You can't love me, because nobody can. I'm unlovable and if you really think you love me, you must be defective or kidding yourself. If you really do love me, watch out, because one day I'll have to hurt you for that very reason."

I wanted him to stop touching me; I started to feel myself recoil.

"You've become like a mom away from home to my boys. Not only that, but your tenacity and resolve inspire me and everyone who knows you. Instead of sinking into despair over everything you lost, you've used it as an opportunity to better yourself and the people around you."

I tried to let his words sink in. True, I was great with the boys and I had made their lives better. They were from a broken home and all their parents did was fight even from 200 miles away. I had inserted myself as an intermediary between their mother and Scott, which did make the boys' lives easier. They no longer had to experience their parents' acrimony toward one another and lines of communication were much more open. I spent time with the boys when they stayed with us, especially when Scott hurt his back or had to work. If Scott was impatient with them, I'd intervene and take them somewhere. I had made their lives better and they had done the same for me. And yes, I could have given up in despair, but I didn't.

So what? I thought. *So what, my ass! He said I was an inspiration.* I wanted to inspire people. That was akin to helping them. I wanted people to know they could lose everything and still be okay. I wanted to give them hope for their own lives. I didn't think anything I was doing was so remarkable, but if it could help other people get out of bed when it felt like the hardest thing in the world to do then, by golly, I'd do it. That's why I went into psychiatry in the first place. I wanted to help people like I wished I could have helped my father… or myself?

I grabbed a pen and pad and started making a list. "My mother, my sister, my aunt …"

"Michael," he added. Michael was a magazine writer friend of Scott's who often stayed with us on weekends and whom we visited a lot, too.

"My mother's friends, Jan and Barbara, who've known me forever," I said, writing as fast as I could think. "My community service supervisors…"

"Your professors," he said, keeping up with my momentum.

I dropped the pen and stared at the page. "Then I'd have to tell them." I suddenly felt disconsolate. "I was hoping I wouldn't have to."

"Don't you get it? What you did was an aberration, a tragic

mistake. Now, you're trying to put your life back together. People respect you for that. We've all done things we regret; the only difference is most of us didn't get caught."

I knew he meant well, but he was getting on my nerves. He was right, what I had done was an aberration and a tragic mistake, but I still didn't think I was as great or deserving of a second chance as he did. Besides, he had screwed up his life pretty badly with a failed marriage, becoming violent toward his ex-wife and having financial difficulties. Who was he to judge me? He had stuck with me when I was at my lowest point, so I was skeptical about his ability to see me for who I was, as opposed to who he wanted to see.

He sat in the chair next to mine. "You've gotten straight A's, showed up to every class prepared, and proven you care about school. That's what your professors know about you. Telling them what happened isn't going to make them think less of you. In fact, it may make them think more of you, because they know how hard you work."

"I'll think about it," I mumbled as I added my advisor's name to the list.

I needed to stop interacting with Scott. His presence and his praise were annoying me. I would discuss my irritation at him with Dr. Lancet another time. Now I needed to get going on my project. I always felt better when I had a project, and short-tempered when anyone was in the way. I became compulsive and driven and couldn't tolerate having my attention drawn away from what I was doing. I went into the bedroom to type the list on the computer.

"What are you doing?" he asked as he clicked on the television and started channel surfing. The sound of the TV and even his very presence infuriated me. I hated when he watched TV while I was trying to work. The sound of the changing channels and even the shows he chose got on my nerves. We needed more space, but this is all we could afford, a one-bedroom apartment where they allowed dogs. I had two dogs, since I had adopted Dani's dog. "Would you mind letting me have the apartment to myself for an hour or so while I make these calls? I think having you here, especially with the TV on, is too distracting."

He shut off the TV and grabbed his keys. "I'll see you in a bit."

I immediately started calling people. Four affirmative conversations later, I was getting so energized, bordering on manic, that I went back to the computer to start writing my essay.

I cannot even begin to express how sorry I am for causing Luke and his loved ones so much suffering, I wrote. As I stared at this sentence, I became too sleepy to continue. It may have been the stress of thinking about Luke, or a sign that I was not psychologically prepared to pursue this application, or even that I did not fully believe what I had written. In retrospect it was probably a combination of all these things.

I didn't hear Scott come in until he sat on the edge of the bed. "How'd it go?" he asked. His breath smelled like coffee and cigarettes, so I assumed he went to meet his friend who worked at a local café.

"Great," I replied still half asleep. "Everyone I called said yes."

He slipped in next to me under the covers. I stiffened as he caressed my face. I was not in the mood to be touched or to pay attention to him. I felt guilty though because he had been so good to me. I felt I owed it to him to show him some affection. But his demanding my attention when I was still involved with my project pissed me off. *Didn't he have enough sense to know when to leave me alone? Did he think that just because he was being kind and supportive, I'd want to make love to him?* If Scott were Luke, I would have gladly dropped everything to be with him, even if I were involved in the project of a lifetime. Now I understood how Luke must have felt when I demanded his attention when he preferred to be doing something else. I felt guilty that I did not want him, then livid that my emotional attention had been shifted from focusing on my project, to reconciling my anger and guilt about Scott. He reminded me so much of my former self that I could barely stand to be in the same apartment with him. The more I knew he wanted me, the more I wanted to get away. It was kind of funny. *I had become exactly what Luke must have wanted from me. I was just like HIM!*

I left messages for a couple of people and set up an appointment for the following day with my professor, Dr. Mahoney, the head of the maternal and child health department. She taught three of the twelve classes I'd already taken toward my master's degree. She knew me better than any of the other professors did.

As I drove to the appointment, my dread about telling my story escalated. I feared that telling her was going to destroy the image I worked so hard to develop and preserve. The more I thought about how on the ball she was, the more I started to think of myself as a loser, fraud, and failure.

Standing at her door, hot and sticky from a combination of anxiety and the June heat, I wiped the sweat from my face and knocked.

"Excuse the mess!" she said as she moved a pile of mail off a yellow director's chair in front of her desk and put it on a shelf. "That's better!" She settled into a purple office chair on the other side of the desk. "Now, what can I do for you?" Her voice was soft as she smiled, looking directly at me.

I focused on the Lucite framed photographs of her family displayed on the shelf behind her. As I recounted my story, she listened intently. "The reason I'm telling you all this," I concluded, "is that I'm in the process of applying for reinstatement and I wonder if you'd be willing to write a letter on my behalf." I contracted every muscle in my body while I waited for her answer.

"I'd be glad to."

I couldn't believe how amenable she was.

"Come, it's time for class. On the way over, you can tell me what to include in the letter, to whom I should address it, and where I should send it."

I explained that she had to include a paragraph with her credentials as well as a paragraph about how she knows me and why she thinks I should be reinstated. I also told her she had to have the letter notarized and that I would be allowed to read it.

CHAPTER 57

After receiving affirmative responses from everyone, I met with Mr. Good for the second time. It was two months after our first meeting. "Three relatives, two family friends, my criminal lawyer, three of my community service supervisors, three friends, one professor, and my psychiatrist," I told Mr. Good when he asked about the letters, adding, "an author, town mayor, three attorneys, a priest, a journalist, and three doctors."

"Excellent," he said. He informed me we needed my school transcript, a resume, letters of recommendation from medical school professors and residency advisors, as well as the transcript from the court hearing, and my essay.

"That essay's a bitch." I'd made several attempts at writing it, but each time, I became too sleepy to continue. It was hard for me to write about my feelings about Luke because I hadn't totally sorted through them yet. Another problem was that I kept drawing a blank trying to discuss what I would do if not reinstated. Was public health really something I would pursue? Would I change gears totally and work with animals? Would I spend the rest of my life as a volunteer coordinator? Given the external unknowns, it was nearly impossible for me to feel like anything I wrote was totally honest. Mr. Good said my passion for medicine should come through in the essay. But I lacked that passion, and it was hard to fudge.

"Write from your heart and do the best you can," he advised. He asked me for Dr. Lancet's number and the release I had signed giving him permission to speak with him. After the meeting, I hurried home and started writing.

It's easy to hide behind the title of doctor; people automatically respect you. When suddenly you're stripped of that title and your status becomes that of "psychiatric patient" and "convicted felon," the experience is quite the opposite. Accordingly, the past two years have been the most challenging of my life. I have had nothing to hide behind, yet everything to hide.

Once I got those words out, the rest of the essay kind of wrote itself. Before I knew it, I had three pages of solid, honest material. I still wasn't sure I wanted to practice medicine, but I was sure I wanted my license back--partly to help undo what I had done, and partly because I thought it would enable me to pursue a career as a vet, therapist, or anything else I might ultimately choose to do.

Mr. Good filed the petition for restoration of my medical license on October 25, 1994.

Shortly thereafter, I started working on my master's thesis. I chose my topic, "Stress, Coping, and Adjustment in HIV Infected Adolescents," because it allowed me to pursue my interest in child/adolescent psychiatry and HIV/AIDS.

Ever since treating a patient with AIDS who'd tried to commit suicide, I had been thinking about how people deal with having this fatal disease and how to help them better cope.

I viewed my thesis as having potential to open some doors in the future, especially if I was not allowed to return to clinical medicine.

I worked with two thesis advisors: Deborah Addle, a child and adolescent psychologist, and Ruth Falco, a public health physician who directed the graduate program in public health, and who had taught several of my classes.

Deborah co-taught the Adolescent Health class I took in the fall of 1994. She was a large, attractive woman, who always hurried into the classroom at least ten minutes late. Looking harried, she'd sling her purse and a canvas Public Broadcasting book bag over the back of a chair and launch into an apology.

"I had to see a patient at the last minute," or "I received an important phone call on my way out the door," she'd say. She'd sit at the desk in front of the room and rummage through her book bag. Once she finally settled in and focused on teaching, she was fabulously interesting, knowledgeable, and engaging. During her lecture on chronic illness in children, I decided to ask her to be one of my thesis advisors. Directly following the lecture, I set up an appointment with her for the next day. No surprise, she was late. Because she was late, her arrival was a great relief, almost exciting. This was the same dynamic I experienced with my father.

Deborah looked scattered as usual, but was polite to me. There was nowhere to sit in her cramped office that she shared with another physician who treated adolescents, so I had to stand. I told her about my thesis and asked if she'd be willing to be one of my advisors. She immediately said how busy she was and that she'd never been a thesis advisor so she might not be the best person to help me. I began to feel crushed and embarrassed as she made each excuse for not helping me. I practically tuned her out in anticipation of her final rejection. As I tried to figure out how to leave without further humiliation, she unfolded a chair and invited me to sit. "But your topic interests me, tell me more about it."

Regrouping, I explained that I was interested in studying the psychological aspects of HIV/AIDS in children and adolescents and that I had been so turned on by her lectures that I wanted to work with her further. When I started complimenting her, she warmed up and focused on me more fully. She said she thought it was a fascinating topic and that we could use the patients in her adolescent HIV/AIDS clinic. She said I was her best student, so she'd be glad to work with me. I had the sense that if I were *not* her "best" student, she would not have helped me.

Deborah told me that her husband was a psychiatrist who had given some of the lectures in the adolescent class. I suddenly realized that I knew her husband from class and from medical school. *Maybe it wasn't such a good idea for me to work with her.* I didn't think he'd recognized me in class, but I was pretty sure he would know my name and my notoriety.

As I drove away, I felt panicky. Perhaps I shouldn't have committed to working with her so quickly. Was she going to make me jump through hoops and stroke her ego in exchange for her help? I already knew the answer was yes. I hoped the benefits would outweigh the costs.

Ruth Falco taught several of my classes, including an intensive five-hour-a-day summer class called Health Quantitative Sciences 1 & 2. There were only five students in the six-week-long class, so I came to know her quite well. She was a down-to-earth, fifty-something woman who came to class early and greeted each student individually. She was always available during the break or after class. She was warm, approachable, and seemed to genuinely enjoy teaching and interacting with students. Dr. Lancet would agree that she was one of those "really good people."

A few days after I talked to Deborah, I asked Ruth to be my other advisor. She invited me to her office to talk about it. Her office was spacious, bright, neat, and welcoming.

I explained my topic and told her that Deborah agreed to help me as well. She listened attentively and, after asking me a few logistical questions, said, "I don't know much about psychology. As long as you can teach me along the way, I'll be glad to help you any way I can."

I felt so calm after this meeting. I knew I could count on her. She'd follow through on what she said she was going to do without making me jump through hoops. This wasn't about her ego. She did not see my request as an imposition. Each encounter would be friendly and helpful.

What I did not know was how closely my dynamics with Deborah and Ruth would recapitulate those between my father, mother, and me. Given my training in psychiatry and especially the work I'd done to understand what had happened between Luke and me, I should have known I would make such choices. The relationships stimulated the same feelings I had when dealing with my parents. This urge to repeat similar situations to those we grew up with and couldn't manage, or hadn't worked through sufficiently, is called "repetition compulsion." We all do it in an effort to right the wrongs of the past and put ourselves in familiar situations. That's what we're used to and where we feel comfortable, *even* if the situation itself is painful. Hopefully, we enter each "new situation" better equipped to handle it , thereby eliminating the need to keep repeating it. Though I did not consciously choose this situation, I was able to recognize it for what it was, work on it with Dr. Lancet and make the best of it.

Dr. Lancet was delighted with how even-tempered I remained with and about Deborah. Both he and Ruth were much more outraged by Deborah's behavior than I was. Maybe I was used to paying the price to get what I needed from my father, or maybe it was a true sign of progress. My goal was to write a good thesis. I wasn't going to let Deborah or anyone else undermine my success. At times it was incredibly difficult for me to tolerate her lateness, lack of follow through, and seeming indifference to me, but nevertheless, I did. I'd learned the hard way that to confront someone like her, someone who thrived on praise and was ambivalent about putting themselves out for other people, meant asking for trouble.

Since the graduate school and medical school were part of the same institution, Deborah's office was on a hallway with some doctors I'd known in medical school. When Deborah was late, I sat on the floor outside her door. While I waited, doctors I recognized walked by me. Though I doubted they recognized me, I hid my face, just in case. Watching them and fantasizing about their "important" destinations and "successful" lives intensified my feelings of worthlessness and confirmed to me that my life was a farce. On a good day, I cut myself some slack and gave myself credit for the progress I'd made. On a bad day, I berated myself for being such a fuck-up. I usually landed somewhere in the middle -- mad at myself for messing up, but acknowledging how hard I was working toward redemption.

When Deborah finally arrived, she made one of her endless excuses, looked for lost items in the office, told me about her problems at home and took at least one personal phone call. Sometimes she even asked me to photocopy documents for her while she talked on the phone.

That she thought my time was so much less important than hers, and even went so far as to use me as some kind of extra secretary at times, infuriated me. However, I talked myself out of my rage by reminding myself that I entered this situation with my eyes wide open. I needed her more than she needed me. For that very reason, I put up and shut up.

It took me six months to design my research protocol. Then I began patient interviews at the adolescent clinic. After Deborah introduced me to the clinic staff, she left me there. The staff was comprised of ten clinicians, including nurses, social workers, and doctors. Prior to meeting with the patients, the staff convened around a table in a conference room where they ate lunch and reviewed patients' charts. I sat in on the pre-clinic rounds, but the staff virtually ignored me. They passed food across me as though I wasn't there. I felt invisible.

During clinic hours, each patient was seen successively by a physician, a nurse, and a social worker. I constantly had to remind the social worker that I needed to see the patients; she kept telling them they could go home after she saw them.

Deborah and I chose five mental illness symptom questionnaires, some of which I had been given by Dr. O'Riley. These questionnaires were designed to assess the presence and severity of depression, anxiety, mania, and psychosis.

My patient contact was circumscribed and limited. I read the questionnaires aloud and filled in their responses. I did not talk to patients other than to explain a question they didn't understand or clarify an answer I did not understand. Even this minimal interaction overwhelmed me a bit, confirming to me that I was not yet ready to take care of patients. At the same time, the patient contact did stir up my desire be a therapist. Dr. Lancet and I discussed my longings and the fact that I was getting back in touch with that part of myself.

One day, in the fall of 1995, Deborah hurried me into her office.

"We're going to have to reschedule. Jerry's just been arrested for molesting one of his patients." Jerry was the physician who shared her office.

I could hardly believe this happened so close to home. Here I'd been trying to hide from the doctors on the hallway and worrying about being found out. All the while, they had probably been preoccupied with rumors and investigations about Jerry.

I wanted to ask what happened, but knew not to. I did, however, ask the question I most cared about. "Is he going to lose his medical license?"

"It's already been suspended. I'll call you," she said and waved me toward the door as she picked up the phone and started dialing.

I didn't care that my time was superseded by this emergency. I wished she'd let me stay to listen to her conversation though. I was totally fascinated and excited by what was happening. That another doctor was going down made me feel less bad about myself. I could see how some people did not care about the mental illness component of my act and blamed me, thinking I was despicable. I got this now because my immediate reaction to Jerry was that he was the lowest of the low. Realistically, though, he had to be mentally ill to do something like that (assuming he was guilty).

A few weeks later, Jerry's things were cleared out of the office. I never heard another thing about him. *So that's how it works; they love you until you mess up. Then, they kill you off.*

CHAPTER 58

The preliminary interview with the NYS Board of Regents was scheduled for December 28, 1995. The point of this interview was to verify the information in my petition.

On the morning of the interview, Mr. Good and I met in a coffee shop. "There's nothing to be nervous about," he said as we sat down at a table. "This is the tame, non-confrontational interview. The hearing is the thing you'll need to worry about. The people on the panel there will challenge everything you say. It will feel like an interrogation, if not a firing squad. This one is just to verify what you wrote in your petition."

When we finished eating, he said, "Okay, here's what's going to happen. We'll sit in a room with the interviewer. He'll ask you a lot of questions pertaining to the information we provided in the petition. I want you to answer in as few words as possible. I'm going to interrupt you if you start saying too much." He opened the door and a cold blast of air smacked me in the face. "When I talk, do not say anything."

We entered the room we'd been assigned. A man with thinning blond hair and a baby face introduced himself as Don Doyle. Once we were seated, Don asked if we had any objection to being tape-recorded.

"We have no objection," said Mr. Good. His voice echoed off the far wall.

Don pressed the record button, stated the date, listed the people present in the room and outlined the purpose of the interview with exaggerated pronunciation.

"Dr. Chase, would you describe in your own words why you surrendered your medical license?" He flipped through a manila folder on the table to the left of the tape recorder.

I answered, glancing at Mr. Good, who nodded at me.

"And you are currently on probation?" asked Don in a monotone.

"Yes, for five years. I've already served three." I sat up straight and rested my hands on the table.

"A condition of your probation is that you not engage in any practice related to the profession of medicine?"

Mr. Good cleared his throat and leaned toward Don. "All of this information is contained in the petition," he said as though he was fed up. "Nothing has changed since she filed the application except that she's further along in her activities than she was a year ago."

Don leafed through the folder. "So you're still doing community service?"

"I finished my community service a few months ago. I'm working as a paid employee at all the places I was volunteering," I said matter-of-factly.

"And school?"

"I completed the classes toward the master's. Now I'm working on my thesis."

"You're still in therapy with Dr. Lancet?"

"Yes, but only once a week since he moved an hour and a half away a few months ago." I glanced at Mr. Good, who nodded again.

"Have you been in any legal trouble since the assault?" asked Don as he scanned the page in front of him.

"No," I replied. "I haven't even had a parking ticket."

"Is there anything you want to tell me that I haven't asked you about?"

"No," boomed Mr. Good.

"All right then," Don spoke into the tape recorder. "This concludes the interview of Dr. Melanie Chase." He clicked off the tape recorder and offered his outstretched hand to me. "Thank you for coming and good luck with your petition."

"How'd I do?" I asked Mr. Good as we stood at the door watching the snow swirl around the sidewalk.

"Fine," he said. "But this was merely a formality."

I was hoping he would expound a bit more. Having no ability to assess my own performances, I needed feedback. Sometimes I thought I did great only to discover I'd done horribly. Sometimes it was the other way around. I had absolutely no confidence in my self-perceptions. "So what happens now?"

"Mr. Doyle will call your character witnesses to verify that they did indeed provide affidavits and letters of recommendation for the petition. He'll also call your probation officer to confirm that you have complied with the terms of your sentence. Once the phone calls are completed, which could take as long as six months, he'll compile his findings into a progress report and submit it to the Board of Regents. Another person on the Board will review his report. Assuming everything checks out, he'll recommend that your hearing be scheduled."

"How long do you think it will be before the hearing?"

"Anywhere up to two years. If it takes too long, we might have to file a supplemental petition."

"Oh, great," I said sarcastically. "But I don't have to do anything else for a while?

"Nothing specifically for the Board, but you must continue working on your re-education, rehabilitation, and remorse. Attend some medical conferences and have your attendance documented." He wrapped his cashmere scarf around his neck. "I'll call you when I hear something." He opened the door and a gust of arctic air blew in.

CHAPTER 59

Shortly after the preliminary hearing, my relationship with Scott began to deteriorate. As my life became fuller and more satisfying, Scott's headed in the opposite direction. The store where he worked closed; he was unable to keep up with his child support payments and his social life diminished once his brother moved to Canada.

I tried to help him, but he spiraled into a depression. He became more dependent on me, resented my relationship with his ex-wife and started calling me a traitor whenever he heard us talking amiably on the phone. To deal with his money problems, he started selling drugs. I could deal with his angry outbursts, but I drew the line at the drugs. I was on probation for a felony, yet he was doing something illegal in *our* house. I told him to stop, but he said I was crazy to be worried. He told me that if he got caught, nothing would happen to me.

I threatened to move out or flush the drugs down the toilet. That made him irate. I withdrew from him emotionally and tried to figure out how to break up with him without getting him ballistic. Perhaps because he felt me slipping away, Scott asked me to marry him in May 1996. I declined his proposal and, a month later, fearing for my safety, I moved back to my mother's house while he was out.

Scott wanted me back. When I refused, he threatened me. He started stalking me. In July, I had to file a restraining order against him. Shortly after that, he moved to Canada to join the family business. He continued to contact me from Canada in a threatening manner. Once again, I had to get the police involved. After a while, he apologized and we stayed friends.

I began to spend more time with Jay, a man I had met playing tennis the summer before. Jay was a corporate man, eighteen years my senior. When we first met, I told him we could only be tennis buddies because I had a boyfriend. We played tennis together a lot and often spent some time afterwards talking. I told him about my situation shortly after meeting him, but it did not deter him. With Scott gone, Jay now pressured me to date him, but I was not ready for another relationship. Despite my reluctance to become involved with yet another man, we ultimately started dating in September of 1996.

That summer, I had completed the research for my thesis and started analyzing the data and writing up the results. My thesis results were worth presenting to the medical community, and they warranted further studies with a larger number of patients. Deborah asked me to present the findings in a research forum at the medical school. While I was proud of my work and pleased to be a presenter, I was uncomfortable interacting with my former professors.

Deborah asked me to write a grant proposal as a spin-off from my thesis. I was thrilled that she had that much confidence in me and my work but knowing that grants can take up to a year to be approved, I needed to start pursuing something that was more of a sure thing. I thought I should continue to prepare for an alternative career in case I didn't get my license back. After further consideration, I decided to write the grant proposals while putting the final touches on my thesis. As I wrapped up the grant proposals and my thesis in November of '96, I decided to apply for a Ph.D. in public health.

I wasn't passionate about public health, but I thought a Ph.D. made sense for several reasons. The school to which I applied had a program in Psychiatry and AIDS. Also, Dr. Lancet and I had discussed the possibility that, even if I were to be reinstated, I still might be precluded from treating patients directly. If I were relegated to doing research or working behind the scenes in a medical lab, the Ph.D. would make me better prepared. I was far from enamored with the idea of continuing school, but I thought if I earned another degree on a par with the M.D., I might be able to hold my head up high one day and put my past mistakes behind me. CU was the only school in the area that offered a Ph.D. in public health. Since I had to stay in the area, I applied there. I was intimidated by the thought of going to CU. It was a prestigious school with international recognition, and I didn't know anyone there.

Deborah and Ruth both wrote compelling letters of recommendation to support my application. Despite the letters and a 3.9 GPA, I wasn't accepted into the Ph.D. program. I suspected the rejection had to do with my "situation." I hadn't told anyone besides Dr. Maloney about the felony and losing my license. However, I was sure that the higher-ups at CU knew about me. There was a lot of contact between people at the places where Luke and I had worked and the institution to which I applied. It's possible I would have been rejected regardless of my history. At the time though, I was convinced that the big "F" on my forehead was what stood in my way.

Shortly after the rejection from CU, I applied for a job as an HIV/AIDS educator with a local non-profit agency. The job entailed giving talks about HIV/AIDS prevention and treatment throughout the county. I figured I was a shoe-in, but I didn't get the job. I attributed my rejection to the fact that I was so overqualified that it made them suspicious. Maybe they hired someone from inside the organization, or maybe they found out about the big "F." Regardless, I was not fazed by the rejection because I didn't really care about the job. I only applied because I thought it was time to find a full-time job, and this was one that did not violate the terms of my probation.

I submitted my thesis in February of 1997, but I was at a loss as to what to do next. I had outgrown The Pantry, although I was still working there twenty hours/week. I needed a change. Since the licensing hearing wouldn't be scheduled for another year or so, I was in limbo and starting to panic.

After submitting the thesis, I dropped in on Ruth to thank her for her support and say goodbye. She asked if I was planning to return to practicing medicine. Although I hadn't intended to, I ended up telling her my entire story! She listened attentively, interjecting a few sympathetic "Ohs." She asked if there was anything she could do to help me. I was so shocked and grateful for her kind response that I was momentarily rendered speechless.

Mr. Good had recently told me that we had to compile a supplemental petition with more character witnesses, since so much time had passed subsequent to filing the original petition. I asked her if she'd consider writing a letter to the Board of Regents on my behalf.

"Absolutely. Do you need me to testify at the hearing as well?"

I could barely contain my joy. "You wouldn't mind?"

"Of course not," she said. "Everybody deserves a second chance. I think you'd make a wonderful physician; you taught me so much about psychology."

At our bi-weekly meetings, I always had to explain the psychiatric and psychological terms and concepts to her. I taught her about the diagnostic tools and mental illness diagnoses as well as about various psychological theories and family dynamics. It was gratifying to be able to teach her things. I realized that I did have something to offer to her. Perhaps that meant I had something valuable to offer others, too.

But her generosity and praise also made me so self-conscious and anxious that I needed to get away from her. My defenses were constructed to protect me from criticism and abuse. Being appreciated and complimented, things I yearned for, left me feeling vulnerable and embarrassed. They also felt so tenuous. If I allowed myself to take them in or experience how good they felt, they would surely disappear.

"Thank you," I said as I stood to leave. "I'll call you when I need you."

I hurried down the stairs to Deborah's office. To my amazement, she was there.

"I was just thinking about you," she said, clearing the papers off a chair. "One of the counselors in the AIDS clinic just quit and I thought you might want the job."

My heart sank as I realized I'd have to refuse a job I would have died for because it would entail breaking the terms of my probation. I also realized I had to tell her my story.

She kept interrupting me to ask questions, such as: "Where did Luke work?" and "He was what kind of psychiatrist?" Deborah cared about getting the dirt, figuring out if she knew the players, and seeing if any of it affected her. Her apparent interest in the story kept me talking. Before I knew it, I was blathering on about how ashamed I'd always felt coming to her office. I told her how shocked I was when Jerry got into trouble because I had the impression that I would be the only doctor I ever knew who got into trouble.

She laughed at this last remark and assured me she'd known plenty of doctors who lost their licenses. In the ensuing years I, too, found I knew many doctors who had been reprimanded or lost their licenses.

I told her I'd been on probation for four years, so I couldn't do anything medically related for another year. Saying it out loud, I felt a little less discouraged. A year didn't seem that long.

"But you can still do research?" She stared at the phone that had just started ringing.

"Yes," I said, hoping she had something in mind for me to do.

"Well, maybe our grant money will come through, but we won't know for at least six months."

Returning the pile of papers to the chair, I asked, "Would you mind writing another letter for me, this time for the Board of Regents?"

"Most definitely. Just call and let me know where to send it."

I ran out to my car and leaned my head against the steering wheel. The two interactions had totally drained me. I felt so relieved to have finally come clean with these two women. The dishonesty had kept me constantly anxious. Despite my relief, I couldn't help thinking that there would be unwanted consequences at some point.

CHAPTER 60

In March of 1997, I decided to move to Georgia for a few months to help Dani, who was about to have twins. Jay went with me. He had friends there and he could take his work with him.

In order to leave the state, my probation officer and I had to consult with her supervisor. I had to take the formal letter of permission from the Probation Department wherever I went. Obtaining permission was easy, but carrying the letter with me was annoying. It was a constant reminder of my situation.

At the end of April, a week after I arrived in Georgia, Mr. Good called to tell me the hearing had been scheduled for July 23. "You should return to New York in the beginning of July."

I was planning to come back then, anyway. My mother was coming to replace me in Atlanta during her summer break from teaching for six weeks. She'd be in Atlanta during the hearing. I felt stressed out. I knew my mother had to be at the hearing, but that would take her away from Dani. I didn't want her to leave Dani to come back to New York for me.

"She has to be there," Mr. Good said adamantly. "It's okay if you stay in Atlanta, but you'll need to make a lot of phone calls and have access to a fax machine. We're going to have to file a supplemental petition to bring your profile up to date. It needs to include everything you've done since we filed the original petition. Is there anybody influential who didn't submit a letter for the original petition who'd be willing to write one now?"

I told him about Deborah and Ruth and Jay. Jay wanted to help in any way possible, including appearing as a witness.

"Good," he replied. "We also need an updated letter from Dr. Lancet. Tell them all to call me. I'll give them the specifics."

Dani came into the room and pointed to the clock, indicating it was time for me to take her to her doctor's appointment.

"In the meantime, think about who should appear at the hearing as witnesses. I'll do the same and we'll compare notes next time we talk."

"Wouldn't you know it?" I told Dani, "They've had two-and-a-half years to schedule the hearing, but they waited until I was here to do it."

"At least you'll have some closure. Besides, it could be worse. It could have been scheduled for when the girls are born or during the months you're staying down here. Realistically, the timing is perfect. You'll be home anyway and you don't have a job or anything, so you'll have plenty of time to prepare. Then you can relax for the rest of the summer."

She was right, but it didn't seem fair that Mom was going to have to come home just for the hearing. We decided she'd probably prefer that to taking a day off school. She hated to miss school.

Later, we called Mom to update her on the twins' progress and tell her about the hearing. She wasn't upset that she'd have to go home for it. She said she kind of expected it to happen that way.

"It's not your fault," she said warmly. "Have you called Jan and Saul?"

"Not yet. I'll call everyone tomorrow."

A few days later, I called Mr. Good to tell him I had contacted everybody and they would be in touch with him shortly.

"I'll need copies of your transcript, degree, commencement program, the rejection letters, and your thesis. Is the fact that you received highest honors on your thesis documented anywhere?"

"I have no idea. You can ask Dr. Falco when she calls you."

On the morning of May 12, Dani went into labor. I met my mother at the airport about six hours later. We went directly to the hospital. Dani gave birth to healthy twin girls. We were ecstatic!

My mother returned to New York after a few days while I stayed to help Dani for the next month and a half. I left Georgia on July 1, five years to the day since I'd been committed to the psychiatric hospital. On the drive home, I had a lot of time to reflect on all that had happened and how much I had changed in the past five years. When I first met Dr. Lancet, I was suicidal, my judgment was impaired, I was at the beck and call of my emotions, which were intense and volatile, and I hated myself. Thanks to Dr. Lancet, I was much more thoughtful, rational, and calm. I had learned to handle my emotions, think before I act, and to be much more considerate of other people's feelings. I had become a better person.

CHAPTER 61

Dr. Lancet, the most important witness, made the hour-and-a-half drive to Mr. Good's office on the Tuesday after the July Fourth weekend. Throughout the meeting, which lasted nearly two hours, Mr. Good asked him to discuss my father's mental illness as well as mine, to explain how our relationship was re-enacted in my relationship with Luke, and then to take the panel through the process of my recovery, emphasizing that I was rehabilitated and remorseful.

I studied Dr. Lancet, the man who taught me right from wrong, the man whom I had grown to love and trust, the man to whom I owed my life and, of course, my recovery. It was strange to be sitting next to him and watching him interact with someone else. My heart swelled with admiration and gratitude as I listened to him tell my story from his perspective.

As the meeting came to a close, I realized how sad I felt about ending my relationship with Dr. Lancet, a man whose face and mannerisms I had memorized. He had been the voice of reason for those many years. He had been strict and kind at the same time. He set limits for me and taught me to write thank you notes. But I also realized that even though I would miss him tremendously, I was ready to move on, and he was letting me go. I knew I could call him anytime, and even go see him. He was not disappearing from my life. He was only taking a step back. How far I had come from the time when I could barely stand the thought of him being away from the hospital on weekends. I thought about how amazing it was that he was rooting for me and willing to put himself on the line to help me. I not only appreciated it, I almost believed I had earned it.

The following day, Jan and Saul took the morning off from

work to meet with Mr. Good and me. Throughout the meeting, they alternated speaking and finishing one another's sentences.

"How long have you known Melanie?" asked Mr. Good.

"We moved down the street from her family when she started fifth grade. We have two children, one of whom is a year younger than Melanie, and one a year older than Melanie's sister."

Mr. Good wrote furiously on a yellow legal pad.

"Jean and Len were among our closest friends for twenty-five years. Well, at least Jean was. Len died seven years ago. He alienated everyone after the divorce. That was around the time Melanie went to college. Our families spent holidays together. They came to our house for dinner every week or so. Sometimes they dropped in unannounced, and vice versa. That's the kind of relationship we still have with Jean."

"Can you tell me about Melanie's father?"

"He was brilliant with a phenomenal sense of humor, but he was crazy! He'd dream up these elaborate schemes to make his fortune. He'd be so excited and enthusiastic you'd almost forget the ideas were crazy. He convinced us to invest more than once. The problem was, he'd bring everything to a crescendo and then drop it."

I recalled countless examples of times Dad did that with me. That's how it always was with him, a big lead-up to an even bigger letdown.

"He did the same thing in relationships. There was a two-month period when Melanie was about twelve. He was at our house every night working on creating a board game called Eulogy. Every night, we laughed so hard we cried. Then without explanation, he disappeared for months and didn't even return our phone calls. That was typical of him. It was all or nothing." Their accounts of my dad were so vivid I felt like I was reliving the experiences.

"Do you think his behavior had anything to do with what happened to Melanie?" asked Mr. Good.

"Definitely. It was especially hard on Melanie."

Jan said, "We watched her starve herself, and he didn't even notice. Sometimes she'd come to us crying when he let her down. Saul tried to soften his blows by playing the role of father to her, but it just wasn't the same." Saul nodded. I remembered when he took me shopping for a car after my father stood me up. "We think she snapped when Len died."

A part of me wanted to put my hands over my ears, but another part was mesmerized. Hearing them describe those painful times, I felt sad on the one hand and validated on the other.

Jan and Saul were amongst a handful of people who did not shut their door in my face after the poisoning. They reached out to me and continued to invite me to family functions as though nothing had happened. They were there for my mother through every trauma and celebration. Jan went to my mother's house the moment she heard about what happened with me even though my mother surely told her not to. That's how it had always been with the two of them. Jan and Saul were like family to my mother.

Suddenly I remembered it was Jan who always used to tell me, "You're so bright and talented, you'll do whatever you want in life." Right then I felt angry. *Didn't these people know anything about mental illness? Didn't they know that I could end up just as crazy as my father? All the brains and talent in the world wouldn't make any difference. Why didn't they do anything when I was starving myself?*

My anger evaporated as I just as quickly recognized they did the best they could. I felt grateful to them for all they had done for me and my family, especially their friendship toward my mother. They were the type of truly good people that Dr. Lancet always talked about.

Mom came home two days before the hearing to meet with Mr. Good and me.

"I know this is hard on you, especially because you had to leave your other daughter and grandchildren," Mr. Good said to Mom.

"It's difficult for a lot of reasons." She sat next to me.

"As you know, the core of our case is Melanie's relationship with a mentally ill and abusive father. Clearly you're in the best position to describe that relationship. Do you feel up to it?" For the first time since I'd known him, he spoke very softly.

I put a supportive hand on Mom's shoulder. "This should be a joyous time when we're focusing on the twins. But Daddy's back on the scene to ruin it." I felt a diffuse and complicated anger at my father. I was angry at him for all the good times he had ruined, and angry at him for not being here to meet his granddaughters and share in the family joy. He would have been a fantastic grandfather. He was like the Pied Piper. He loved kids. They adored him, too, as long as they weren't his responsibility and they didn't have to count on him. He would have been thrilled that one of the twins even resembled him and had his name for a middle name. I fought back tears.

"He's not ruining it," said Mom. "He's just interrupting."

Mr. Good cleared his throat. "Melanie, it would be very effective if you cried in front of the panel. The more raw emotion you show the better, especially when you talk about what you did to Luke. That's the remorse part of the triad."

"I can't fake it. If the tears come, so be it." I deeply regretted what I had done to Luke, and felt sorry and sad that I had caused him pain, but I had not yet cried over what I put him through per se. I did feel panicked that I had become desperate enough to do such a thing and feared there was something terribly wrong with me beyond the psychiatric diagnoses and the history of emotional abuse. I was sure there were thousands of other women with my same diagnosis who had suffered much worse abuse, who would never have conceived of doing what I did. I suspected there was something defective inside of me that nobody knew about. Many years later, my therapist Tim, called this defective thing inside me, Post Traumatic Stress Disorder.

"Definitely do not fake it. The panel will see right through you."
He wrote something on his pad and then looked at my mother.
"Once we expound on the trauma she suffered from her father, we
have to draw the parallel with Luke. We need to convince the panel
that she's worked through, and come to terms with, all the abuse
and is a healthier and better individual than before. Do you agree?"

Mom looked at me and smiled. "Yes, she's become a much
better person." Although we had stopped seeing Richie together
after a year, our relationship continued to improve. We were even
closer now that we shared the excitement of the twins and the
desire to help Dani.

"Okay, then, I think we're ready."

CHAPTER 62

On the morning of the hearing, I was nervous, but I felt relieved that it was finally happening. I was sick of living in limbo. With probation nearing an end, I had reached a critical juncture. I wouldn't know which way to turn until I knew about my license. If I were reinstated, I would return to medicine in some capacity. If I were not reinstated, I'd still be okay. I had learned to accept myself. Even my mother was learning to appreciate me.

The word ONE was engraved in gold script letters on the ledge above the glass doors of the gray marble building that housed the Office of Professional Discipline. Pushing open the door, I entered a narrow lobby with gold nameplates in a glass case on the wall. I took the elevator to the seventh floor, where the doors opened into a gray-tiled hallway that smelled faintly of perfume. I suddenly felt flush with anxiety.

Straight ahead, a glass door led into an expansive, gray-carpeted area with a freestanding mahogany lectern in the center.

Mom, Jan, Saul, Jay, and Ruth chatted near the three leather couches in the corner of the room. Mr. Good emerged from the direction of the lectern. He looked like a professional quarterback dressed for the office. "We need to talk," he exclaimed ominously.

He flung open the door to a small room where Dr. Lancet was sitting at a long wooden table. He smiled at me as I sat down next to him.

Mr. Good started talking before he sat. "The legal advisor for the Board of Ed just told me one of the panel members has to leave early. We only have until two o'clock."

"But that's not fair; we're supposed to have until five!" My eyes welled with tears as I looked from Mr. Good to Dr. Lancet, then back to Mr. Good. "That won't give us time to present all our witnesses. They all went out of their way to be here." I shook with rage as I thought of my mother flying to be here, and Dr. Falco, Jan, and Saul taking the day off from work.

"I agree," replied Mr. Good. "But the panel members can do whatever they want."

"They suck!" My impulse was to scream and stamp my feet. Instead, I closed my eyes, took a deep breath and repeated *Think before you act* over and over to myself.

"Melanie," Dr. Lancet said in a soothing tone. "This is one of those instances we prepared you for. You have to accept that life is unfair and deal with it."

I blinked back my tears. *Dr. Lancet's right. It's frustrating and infuriating, but it's not the end of the world.* I felt badly for inconveniencing my witnesses in the first place. Now I felt responsible for the fact that they were going to have to be doubly inconvenienced. Maybe my rage was out of proportion to the situation, but it's what was triggered when people in authority, or people I needed, reneged on their promises. That's how I was wired. What really mattered was that I could take a step back and analyze the situation more calmly and act more rationally. "So what happens now?" I asked Mr. Good.

"We'll rearrange our witnesses. The ones who will have the most difficulty returning will go first." He studied his pad. "We'll start with Dr. Lancet as planned, next we'll go to Dr. Falco, and then Jan."

Dr. Lancet and I followed Mr. Good down the hallway to HEARING ROOM ONE, a large carpeted room with about fifteen rows of chairs to our left and a stage to our right. Three people sat next to one another on the far left side of the stage. One woman sat alone in the opposite corner. A woman sat at a steno machine immediately below the stage.

Mr. Good stopped at the table nearest the door and motioned to Dr. Lancet and me to sit. I felt nauseated as I stared at the people on the stage. These panel members would decide my fate. The woman sitting alone was Ms. Lockhart, the panel's legal advisor.

Dr. Zarris, a seventy-something public health and preventative medicine physician, with a stern looking face and thinning gray hair, sat on the far left. Dr. Quornos, a psychiatrist in her late forties, sat next to him. She had a bronze tan and warm features that reminded me of the Flying Nun. Mr. Chimborazo, the layperson on the panel, sat next to her. He looked like the actor Andy Garcia. Ms. Lockhart was a thirty-something woman with dark frizzy hair pulled back with barrettes. *These are the faces of my executioners.*

We had not known the panel members ahead of time, but as Dr. Quornos, the chairperson of the panel, explained, the executive secretary of the State Board for Medicine appointed this particular peer committee to review my case. The peer committee consisted of three members of the State Board for Medicine. Two of the members were licensed professionals, and one member was a public representative. I understood why they chose a psychiatrist and public health/preventative medicine physician, but I had no idea why that particular layperson, a C.P.A., was on my panel.

Mr. Good stood with a flourish. "Good morning," he said to the panel.

The three of them glared at me. At least that's what I thought.

"Since we're pressed for time, I'd like to call my first witness and forego the usual introductions."

Ms. Lockhart addressed the panel members. "Do you have any objections?"

They all shook their heads no.

"Very well." She turned toward a man sitting alone at a table across the aisle from ours. I later found out he was the prosecutor. "Mr. Lapel?"

His light blue polyester suit looked like something a teenager might have worn to a bar mitzvah in the 1960s. "No."

Mr. Good thanked them all. "My first witness is Dr. Lancet, the applicant's treating psychiatrist."

Dr. Lancet strode up to the lectern in front of the stage.

Mr. Good picked up his pad and approached him. "How did Melanie come into your care?"

Angling his body toward Mr. Good, Dr. Lancet leaned an elbow against the lectern. "I was contacted by her outpatient psychiatrist. He said he had an extremely serious case. He told me she was a resident in psychiatry at a prestigious hospital who'd been involved in a failed love affair, and she had progressively deteriorated over the past six months. He said her companion had been ill for some time and then it came out he'd been sick because Melanie administered Prolixin to him." Someone on the stage coughed. "We discussed the case and agreed Dr. Chase should be in the hospital."

"Why did you think this was a case you could work on?"

"Melanie was extremely depressed, suicidal, guilt-ridden, and anxious. She felt she had no future and that her life was over." Dr. Lancet turned toward the panel. "She also had a history of an eating disorder as well as severe emotional abuse. My expertise is in treating women who have serious disorders like these."

Mr. Good furrowed his brow. "Emotional abuse?"

"Her father was a very ill man; he treated her very badly."

"What was your diagnosis when you met her?"

Dr. Lancet answered quickly. "Major Depressive Disorder on Axis 1 and Borderline Personality Disorder on Axis 2."

"Could you say a little more about these diagnoses?" asked Mr. Good.

As though lecturing to a medical school class, Dr. Lancet said, "Major Depressive Disorder is characterized by severely depressed mood, disturbances in basic biological functions such as eating and sleeping, impaired thinking, and a severe breakdown in the person's ability to function – to the point where the person can't perform her normal duties. These people often have disturbances in their self-esteem having to do with their capacity to perceive not only themselves, but the world around them. In severe cases, they suffer from impaired judgment to the point of becoming psychotic or losing touch with reality." The panel members listened intently.

"Can you explain Borderline Personality Disorder?"

Dr. Lancet walked toward the stage and faced the panel members. "Borderline Personality Disorder is characterized by instability of mood, relationships, thinking, and self-perception. Their ability to see themselves accurately and to see other people accurately is distorted. When they believe a relationship is in danger, they frequently react by making frantic efforts to avoid real or imagined abandonment. A feeling of impending separation or rejection, or the loss of an external structure, can lead to drastic changes in self-image, affect, cognition, and behavior."

I could totally relate to the person Dr. Lancet was describing. I remembered walking through Luke's house howling like a wounded animal after he broke up with me. I could summon the emotional pain and irrational thoughts that accompanied the pain, such as *I can't live without him, my life is over, I need to die,* and then the feeling of literally vaporizing and losing touch with my physical self as though I no longer existed.

"So, for Melanie, having her boyfriend break up with her could have triggered this desperate response?" Mr. Good asked.

"The breakup was the last straw. Over the course of two years, ever since her father died, Melanie had deteriorated from a high-functioning, moral person into a severely depressed young woman who had markedly impaired judgment. The break-up, then being fired sent her spiraling downward even faster."

"Did the fact that she was taking several psychiatric medications, including Prozac, contribute to her deterioration?" Mr. Good approached the stage.

"Absolutely, although Dr. Chase has chosen to take full responsibility for her actions and not blame any of it on medication."

"Since you think the drugs contributed to her deterioration, can you say a bit about what drugs she was on and how they could have affected her?"

Dr. Lancet nodded. "When she first came into my care, she was taking 80 milligrams of Prozac, an anti-depressant, five milligrams of Desipramine, an antidepressant from a different class of drugs than Prozac, and ten milligrams of Dexedrine, a psycho-stimulant not unlike Ritalin." He paused briefly. "There is scant literature on the effects of taking these three medications together. Taken alone, Prozac has been putatively implicated in suicidal and homicidal behaviors and Dexedrine can cause hyperactivity, insomnia, anorexia, and severely impaired judgment."

"Were these drugs prescribed to her?' asked Mr. Good.

"Her treating psychiatrist prescribed the Prozac and the Desipramine. Dr. Shay, her ex-boyfriend, prescribed the Dexedrine. Because it was a controlled substance, she could not prescribe it for herself. She said she needed it to treat her Attention Deficit Disorder. He went along with her. But, as we all know," Dr. Lancet glanced up at the panel members, "writing prescriptions for a non-patient, especially for a controlled substance, is a form of misconduct."

Good, let the panel register that bit of information.

Mr. Good glanced at his notes. Is Prozac typically used to treat Borderline Personality Disorder?"

"Not to treat the disorder itself, but to treat the depression and anxiety that sometimes accompanies BPD. Recent literature shows that it may help in the treatment of some eating disorders as well."

"Do we know what causes BPD?"

"Nobody knows for sure. We assume there's a biological as well as an environmental component. At least seventy-five percent of borderlines have a history of physical or sexual abuse. Nearly all of them have a history of emotional abuse."

"Is it curable?" Mr. Good stared at the panel.

"People can recover from borderline personality disorder with a lot of therapy and rehabilitation. If one looks at all the parameters one would measure to distinguish one borderline personality disorder from another, there are long-term studies of borderline personality disorders that indicate certain types get better. She certainly is that type. This is a reputable study that demonstrates a process of recovery, rehabilitation, and going on to become a productive member of society. In this study of more than five hundred patients, the ones who had the best prognoses were those who had excessive compulsive components of their borderline personality disorder, which Melanie fits into. She is incredibly compulsive, a perfectionist, and is terribly hard on herself. She never leaves a stone unturned when it comes to a project or pleasing others, and she also has those skills necessary to follow through. Some people are compulsive, but they don't have very much that would back it up. She does."

Mr. Good looked at me and then back at the panel. "Do you think Melanie has recovered?"

Dr. Lancet turned toward the panel. "Yes, definitely. I've observed enormous differences in her inter-psychically from the person I met on July 1, 1992, and the person I see now. She has improved insight, judgment, emotional regulation, mood regulation, and controls. That is confirmed by what I observed in her capacity to handle herself in stressful situations on the outside.

There has not been one episode in all these years of anything that would make me even slightly anxious about her, and she's had plenty of opportunity. I've even seen her in two relationships, one with Scott, and now with Jay. The quality of these relationships is much less intense and much more stable than any of her previous relationships with men."

I smiled to myself. Hearing him talk about me this way, and go on to give examples of how I handled my sister's graduation and wedding, the birth of the twins, the relationship with Scott, my relationship with my mother, and even how I dealt with Deborah, I felt like he really listened to me, knew me, and cared about me. I mattered. I felt closer to him. I also felt proud -- proud of the way I had in fact handled a lot of difficult situations, and of how far I had come. Regardless of whether the panel took any of this in, or still saw me as high-risk because of the heinous nature of my crime, seemed momentarily irrelevant. What *was* relevant was that this man, who knew me so well, believed in me.

"And how do you understand what happened?" Mr. Good tapped his pen on the pad. "The administering of the drug, I mean?"

Dr. Lancet approached the stage. "Sometimes stresses, both past and present, come together at the wrong time to make someone do something totally out of character – something the person would never do again."

Mr. Good stepped toward the prosecutor. "So you think that event was out of character for Melanie?"

"Oh, gosh ... yes."

"You say now, five years later, that you think she's fit to practice medicine?"

"I feel more confident about Melanie than I do with a lot of people. I know she's spent an enormous amount of time assessing herself, this act, and its impact on other people – including the victim, his family, her family, and society." He winked at me. "Also, I know her very well. She is a compassionate person who truly cares about people."

"Thank you. I have no further questions." Mr. Good slowly and deliberately walked around the table and sat next to me

For the next half-hour, the panel members and the prosecutor grilled Dr. Lancet. They began to sound like broken records asking the same two questions again and again. How could I stand by and watch Luke deteriorate without doing anything to help him, and how could he be sure I wouldn't abuse Prozac again?

Dr. Lancet answered each question calmly and with aplomb, but there were only so many ways to say the same thing. He assured the panel that I had no history of drug abuse and that I had resisted going on the drug in the first place. Furthermore, he pointed out that, although they insisted on using the word "abuse," the word was misleading. While I had increased my prescribed dose from 40 mg to 80 mg based on the reasoning, albeit fallacious, that if 40 mg made me feel less depressed, than 80 would make me feel even better, taking Prozac was a symptom of – and a contributing factor to – my impaired judgment. Besides, he said, "Prozac is not an addictive drug like alcohol or cocaine. One does not develop a physical addiction to it, nor does one suffer symptoms of withdrawal when stopping it." He assured the panel I had been taking the same dose, 20 mg, for the past five years. I had requested a lower dose and taken a break from it all together. As far as he was concerned, I was only taking it because my depressive symptoms recurred when I stopped it. He added that I was not happy about having to stay on it long-term.

To the second question, he admitted he was still somewhat baffled. "My best answer is that Melanie's judgment had become so impaired and she had so perfected the art of compartmentalization in response to her father's abuse that she actually lost sight of the fact that Luke's illness was related to her actions. Denial is a very strong defense mechanism."

CHAPTER 63

Dr. Falco was our second witness. In his direct examination, Mr. Good established that she was the program director of international and public health at the graduate school, that she was board certified in pediatrics and public health/preventative medicine, and that she had known me quite well, and in several different capacities during my four years in graduate school. Once he verified her credentials, Mr. Good questioned her about my academic performance and her observations of me inside and outside of the classroom. He asked her to describe the significance of the highest honors award. The award was only given to one student and was only presented every few years or so. She said my thesis far exceeded the expectations and requirements of a master's thesis and, in her opinion, was of Ph.D. caliber. "Melanie was a stellar student who seemed to grasp material other students did not. She was always willing to help the other students."

The most important aspect of her testimony was that I always appeared calm, stable, and exceedingly tolerant of frustration, especially when it came to working with Deborah. "She put up with a lot more than most people would have," she said.

Dr. Falco and Dr. Zarris had done their residencies at the same institution. Still, he and the rest of the panel were unimpressed with her testimony. They said neither my intellect nor my academic performance was in question. They drilled her about her qualifications to recommend whether I was fit to practice medicine, given her limited insight into my psychological makeup.

In response to their skepticism, she discussed her expertise in domestic violence. "There are situations where women are pushed past their breaking point to do things totally out of character."

She said she didn't know the exact circumstances that led to the poisoning, but she presumed that domestic violence had come into play.

I hadn't known she assumed this, but I suddenly understood why she was neither shocked nor deterred by my actions. It occurred to me, while I did not suffer domestic violence in the true sense of the word, just as I had not been the victim of physical or sexual abuse at the hands of my father, I was the victim in both instances of emotional abuse. Emotional abuse is much more subtle and less recognizable to the untrained eye, but it's just as damaging, if not more so.

I felt grateful to Ruth for making this assumption. Understanding her thought process helped me to feel less defective and crazy.

Our next witness, Jan, looked professional and classy in her off-white linen suit. Mr. Good established that she had a Ph.D. in education and was an innovator in her field at the university level. His line of questioning echoed our discussion in the pre-hearing meeting. There was a noticeable silence in the room as Jan described my father's blatant abuse of me and the rest of my family. She discussed her intimate knowledge of my family dynamics and, specifically, my struggles with depression and anorexia. She wove a tale of emotional anguish and domestic violence. "Melanie loved her father, who had the capacity to be very violent. I witnessed his violence towards her mother; I witnessed their arguments. I remember a terrible experience between her parents in my home. When Jean told me what Melanie had done, I thought to myself, is this Melanie's act of violence? Is this something that she has done to someone that she loved, in the same way that her father was so violent towards the woman he supposedly loved? That's what went through my mind, and how much the dysfunctionality in the family had contributed to it."

She also emphasized that, despite my father's multiple transgressions, I treated him with sympathy and compassion. "I can't even recall how many times Melanie came to our house in tears because Len had gone on a rampage. Never mind the black eyes and bruises Jean claimed were accidents. She added that most people in my situation would have been furious with him, but that I tried to help and understand him.

I remembered huddling in my room with Dani or running to my cousin Eddie's house, when things had gotten really bad. As for the violence towards my mother, as far as I recalled, that didn't come until shortly before I left for college. Hearing this account of what my life had been like frightened me because I didn't remember it like that. It did explain a lot though. Maybe my sense of being inexplicably defective was not so inexplicable, having grown up in this violent, unpredictable environment. Maybe what was really defective was my memory of how bad things had been. Perhaps I minimized the trauma of my childhood so I could still love both my parents, who I needed so desperately to love me back. Maybe I became hyper-vigilant, and a caretaker, because I learned early on that I had to protect my mother by anticipating my father's volatility.

One theory of anorexia is that the patient starves herself in order to gain control over her body because everything around her feels out of control. I understood my starvation as an attempt to control my body and to stop myself from becoming a woman. Being a woman was dangerous in my house. It elicited rage and violence from my father. Also, by obsessing about my weight, I was able to pay less attention to what was going on around me. Turning inward shielded me from experiencing the full extent of the chaos. To some extent, it worked. I was able to function well enough to make it through high school, college, and medical school, even though I never lived up to my academic potential in terms of grades. Despite my clinical depression since junior high, I was able to hide much of my despair from the outside world. That I held it together enough to function for as long as I did without intensive professional intervention bode well, at least in my mind, for how well I'd do in the future now that I was getting the needed help.

My traumatic past, and the fact that I'd grown up around and experienced my own mental illness and successful treatment, put me in an excellent position to treat patients. I'd been there and back, experienced mental illness from all sides and triumphed over it. In my estimation, my ability to recognize, empathize with and treat mental illness in others was much more honed than people who had not experienced any of these things. Still, I knew the panel was wary of me. I didn't blame them. They didn't know me; they only knew what I did. No matter how you slice it, what I did was extreme and frightening. Since they could not get inside my head or my heart, they only had the information in my petition and the testimony of my witnesses, some of whom they might view as biased. They were in an untenable position. Had I been in their shoes, I would be wary and skeptical as well.

Regarding my role as a doctor, Jan said I used to regale her with stories from medical school and residency that indicated an enthusiasm for my experiences, as well as sensitivity and compassion for my patients. Finally, she said that I'd opened her eyes to the plights of the "less-fortunate" by encouraging her and her husband to contribute to and participate in the soup kitchen as well as The Pantry.

I always thought of Jan and Saul as being socially minded and philanthropic. Was she overstating this? I decided that if I *had* done that, it was another positive outcome of my journey.

The panel members challenged her minimally. The prosecutor, however, was a whole other story. He started by asking her if she thought I should be re-licensed as a physician. She replied, "I absolutely think so. I think that was a one-time aberration. She's worked very hard over the last five years to understand why she did it, to rehabilitate herself and assume maturity."

"Is rehabilitation something you've observed, or something you were told by someone else?" he challenged.

"I've observed a person becoming whole again, going to school, volunteering, establishing friendships, supporting her mother and sister and being there for people."

"Yet, she wasn't there for Dr. Shay, was she?"

"No, but that was five years ago."

"I have no more questions," he said with what seemed to me to be a smug look of victory on his face. He wore the same look when he finished questioning Dr. Falco.

By the time Ms. Lockhart excused Jan from the witness stand, it was nearly 2 p.m. A discussion ensued between the panel members, Mr. Good, Mr. Lapel, and Ms. Lockhart regarding future availability for a continuance. After fifteen minutes, Ms. Lockhart announced the day for the continuance. It was October 23, exactly three months later.

CHAPTER 64

In the three months between the two hearings, I terminated my five-year relationship with Dr. Lancet. I saw him two more times after the hearing. In those sessions, we reflected about the past five years, but focused most on what it meant to me to be leaving him. "Bittersweet" was the best word I could come up with. I was glad to be healthy enough to be moving on, but I would definitely miss him. However, that wouldn't be too extreme since I carried him around inside me.

We also talked about the hearing and what I would do if reinstated. He thought I'd make a "great" psychiatrist. "Much better than a lot of the residents I'm training," he said. When I expressed doubts as to whether anyone would hire me, he said, "You never know. Maybe there's someone out there looking for a Jewish woman from an affluent suburb who lost her medical license, then got it back, so they can give her a second chance. Stranger things have happened."

As I drove home, I felt sad, but proud of myself for being able to let him go.

Shortly after terminating with Dr. Lancet, I started treatment with Tim, a social worker who was covered under my health plan. I met Tim a few weeks before the second hearing. When I filled out the paperwork as to why I needed treatment, I wrote, "to figure out what to do with the rest of my life in terms of my career and my significant other." Jay had recently started talking about marriage, but I was not sure whether I wanted to marry him. Tim was certified in psychoanalytic psychotherapy and was psychologically minded, sharp, and involved.

Tim talked to Dr. Lancet for background on my case, so we

began where Dr. Lancet and I left off. Between the two hearings, I started volunteering at an animal shelter, something I'd always wanted to do, but either didn't have the time for or the courage. The animals' lives were so sad. I sent away for applications to veterinary schools.

I barely felt motivated to go to the second hearing. Given the way the initial hearing had gone, and based on the panel's questions and demeanors, I was convinced they were going to deny my petition. It was difficult to summon energy or enthusiasm to face these people I believed had already decided against me.

"Come on, Mel," said my mother in the car on our way to the hearing. "You're in the home stretch."

I smiled at her baseball reference. It sounded like something my father would say. She was right; I was in the homestretch, in more ways than one. I was two months away from the end of my probationary period and three months away from receiving the peer committee's decision about my license.

Being on probation had been a pain in the ass, but at times it had been comforting to know that I was on their radar screen. It had always been reassuring to me to live under a defined set of rules and to know explicitly the consequences of breaking those rules. For the first two years, I welcomed the oversight. By the third year, I began to long for more freedom. Now, five years later, I was practically indifferent because the appointments with Joanne had become monthly and mere formalities. At the same time, it was a graduation of sorts. As a one-time offender, I had never seen myself as a threat to society. Having proven that over the course of five years gave me a small sense of pride.

I still didn't know if I wanted to practice medicine. It was hard to know *what* I wanted. After losing so much I was terrified of finding out my true desires because of the potential for disappointment. "I just don't want to get my hopes up."

When we entered the lobby, Jay and Mr. Good greeted us.

"Your mother will be the first witness, then Jay, and then you. After you're finished, I'll give the closing statement," said Mr. Good. Hearing Room 2 was about the size of an elementary school classroom. The air was stifling. As Mr. Good and I walked to the front of the room, I noticed the panel members, Ms. Lockhart, and Mr. Lapel, had arranged themselves exactly as they had at the first hearing.

Ms. Lockhart stood and faced Mr. Good. "If there are no objections, we can begin immediately. You may call your first witness."

Mr. Good stood, turned toward my mother, and nodded. After introducing her to the panel, he prompted her to tell the story of my father's mental illness beginning with his first psychiatric hospitalization at age seventeen and ending with his death seven years earlier. She described in detail his dramatic mood swings, his frequent and unexplained absences and his constant undermining of my achievements. She set the stage for the ultimate blows, which in her opinion were his marrying a woman close to my age and then dying during my fourth year of medical school.

"When Luke came along," she said, "Melanie thought she'd found her knight in shining armor. When he left her, which in her mind was the same as her father leaving her, she re-experienced the rejection, abandonment, and utter despondency she'd felt with her father. That, plus losing her job, sent her over the edge."

I watched my mother with amazement as she recalled the most painful events of both our lives with poise and sympathy. I felt grateful to be her daughter.

"Since her tragic mistake, Melanie has devoted all her energy to a program of rehabilitation and to establishing responsible and productive patterns of thinking and behaving. She has restructured her relationships with immediate and extended family members on a realistic, sensitive, give-and-take basis." She looked at me and smiled. "It's my deepest conviction that Melanie now has the emotional health to make a significant contribution to society – both as a person and a medical doctor."

Letting Mom's words sink in, I realized that regardless of the outcome, what had happened to me as a consequence of the poisoning had been worth it. In the process of rehabilitating, I had earned my mother's love and respect.

The panel members asked her to clarify a few points, but overall, they were gentle with her.

Ms. Lockhart dismissed my mother and instructed Mr. Good to call his next witness. Jay, my boyfriend for the past year, had a thirty-year career in corporate America and was quite eloquent. I'd questioned having him testify, but Mr. Good thought it would be helpful for the panel to see that I was in a stable relationship with a calm, solid man who clearly loved and trusted me.

Jay's testimony was brief. He described how we met, how our yearlong friendship eventually became romantic, and how he learned about the poisoning — that I'd told him early on in our friendship.

The panel asked a few questions about how I handled anger in the relationship, but they seemed uninterested in hearing more from him.

Finally, it was my turn. I walked up to the lectern, nodded at the panel members and sat in a metal-backed chair with my hands folded in my lap. I tried to block out the glares (real or imagined) from the prosecutor, who sat a few feet to my right.

Mr. Good stood a foot or so away from me and gently prodded me to tell my story. I talked about my relationship with Luke and how much I'd loved him and wanted to marry him. I recounted that toward the end of the relationship I'd lived in a constant state of dread, sensing he would leave me. I described my desperation after he broke up with me, giving a vivid account of my many weeks of suicidal ideation. Then, I said, I discovered Prozac and the despair dissipated, but my judgment wavered. I described my anguish at the thought of living without Luke, and the moment of epiphany when I realized that if somehow I could make him need me, he would take me back. I recounted my thought process about how to make him need me, as well as Mark's participation in choosing the drug and egging me on.

"So you didn't want him to die," asked Mr. Good pointedly.

"Definitely not! I wanted to marry him." Turning my attention back to the panel, I described going to his house and pouring Prolixin into the drinks in his fridge, emphasizing that I never once considered the legal consequences of my actions. I only knew that since I always had to compete with his patients for his attention, I had to make Luke sick enough to stay home from work for a while.

I described how, once the whole thing started spinning out of control, I lost sight of the fact that I'd caused his illness. Along with his family and friends, I became panicked lest he die. I never thought, "I'll be in big trouble if he dies." Rather, I thought, "He has to get better so we can get married."

By the time Mr. Good handed me over to the panel I felt spent.

I know the members of the panel spoke one at a time, but I felt as though I was on the firing line, being assailed by everybody simultaneously.

"How is it you watched Luke deteriorate without doing anything to help him," asked the prosecutor over and over again.

"Did you know right from wrong?" asked the psychiatrist.

"Didn't you know the potential effects of the drug?" asked Dr. Zarris.

"How do we know you won't abuse Prozac again?" asked the layperson repeatedly.

I explained over and over again in different words. "Looking back, it's hard for me to believe I actually thought that way. It's next to impossible for a sane, rational person to get inside the head of someone who's irrational and insane. It's difficult to put myself back into that mindset. Mark didn't come forward until after the brain biopsy, approximately three weeks after Luke was hospitalized.

Maybe you should talk to him."

I became increasingly frustrated at their line of questioning. I understood it was not possible to comprehend how I was able to watch Luke get sicker and sicker without stepping forward to help him. I was running out of words to try to explain it. Clearly they weren't getting it, or maybe they just didn't believe me. I felt backed against a wall. Short of letting them read my mind and examine my heart, I couldn't figure out a way to convince them that what I was saying was true, or how I was sure that nothing like that would ever happen again. I knew it, Dr. Lancet knew it, my mother knew it, and so did Jay and my sister. But there was no way to prove to anybody what would happen in the future. As far as they were concerned, the past was a predictor of the future.

Finally, after a half-hour, the assault ended. When Ms. Lockhart dismissed me, I felt lightheaded. My clothes were sweat-soaked. I wanted to go home.

Mr. Good approached the stage, unbuttoned his blazer and cleared his throat. "Ladies and gentleman," he said, pacing in front of the stage, "you've now heard from six witnesses, including Dr. Chase's treating psychiatrist, her academic advisor, and several friends and relatives. In addition, you've read fifteen letters written by influential people who've known Dr. Chase in many capacities for varying amounts of time. All this testimony describes a compassionate, bright, hardworking, and honest person who, despite growing up in a dysfunctional family with an abusive and mentally ill father, planned to devote her life to helping other people."

"Her life was on track and her goal in sight, when a series of unfortunate and devastating circumstances occurred in rapid succession. These events set the stage for her breakdown and led her, out of total desperation, to make a tragic and irreparable mistake, a mistake she deeply regrets and something that will stay with her forever."

"I ask you, is this reason enough to punish her for the rest of her life? As you've heard and seen for yourself, she has accepted responsibility for her mistake and spent the last five years working assiduously to come to terms with her past and to rehabilitate her self. Dr. Lancet said he would trust her implicitly to pursue a medical career. He said that she, of all people, would be the least likely to harm a patient or anyone else, because she knows firsthand what's at stake. Do you think he would put himself and his career on the line by saying such a thing if he was not a hundred percent confident in her?"

Wiping his brow with a handkerchief, he continued, "As human beings, we've all done things we regret and, if given the chance, would take back. It is, after all, the nature of the beast. However, even the victim in this case hoped Dr. Chase would be allowed to return to her chosen career after three years. He recognized her talents and was able to forgive her." He took a couple of steps toward the two physicians on the panel. "Both our justice system and our medical system are predicated on the belief in rehabilitation. Dr. Chase is living proof of that. So, I ask you, after reviewing all the testimony on her behalf, to give her a second chance. Her future is in your hands." He walked slowly past the stage before returning to his seat beside me.

Ms. Lockhart said, "This concludes the hearing. The panel will reconvene on December 18, 1997, to deliberate. Thank you all for your time."

Mr. Good cupped my elbow in his hand and led me out of the room. Jay and Mom joined us, and the four of us rode down the elevator in silence.

Outside, Mr. Good said, "It went very well, but they were stuck on how you could watch Luke deteriorate. If you'd come clean right away, at least before the biopsy, I think you'd have a better chance. Now all we can do is wait and see." We walked to the corner and crossed the street.

"How long until we receive the decision?" I asked, feeling

downtrodden.

"With this panel, there's no telling. Ordinarily, it would be within three months. I'll call you when I hear something."

CHAPTER 65

In the months following the October hearing, I continued volunteering at the animal shelter, had weekly therapy sessions with Tim and adopted a shelter dog, Jake, a Golden Retriever/yellow lab mix. Brin and Ashley had each died two months before I went to Atlanta.

I started volunteering at the shelter because small animal experience was a criterion for applying to vet school and it's something I'd always wanted to do. It was difficult to see these poor abandoned animals living in cages and kennels, dying for love and attention. In many ways I identified with these helpless, lonely creatures. Being able to give them a bit of what they craved, and having them love me in return, was extremely gratifying. Before long, I was going to the shelter seven days a week for five hours at a time.

Being at the shelter reawakened my original desire to become a veterinarian. When I applied to medical school, I would have applied to vet school instead, but it was even harder to get into than medical school, so I didn't think I had a chance. If reinstated, I could apply to vet school without having a black mark on my record. A black mark would prohibit me from doing anything that required professional licensing or state certification. I imagined that being reinstated would erase some of my shame. What I came to understand many years later was that the shame could only be addressed from within. No amount of praise or external confirmation could affect the way I felt about myself on any type of long-term basis. That change could only be affected by the work I had yet to do on myself.

I was astonished when Mr. Good called me a few days after the scheduled deliberation. Caught off-guard, I realized how much the actual decision meant to me. Even though I'd tried to convince myself that it didn't matter, I would have felt crushed if the peer panel decided against me. It wasn't so much about my desire to practice medicine. It was about my need to undo the loss.

"The panel didn't even start deliberating because one of the panel members went outside the record to obtain information to use in deciding the case."

"What does that mean?" I asked.

"Once the hearing begins, the panel members are prohibited from consulting any outside sources. It's an administrative law, the violation of which is called ex parte. These administrative laws were created to mimic the rules of juries, so that their decisions are based on the facts of the case, the evidence presented, and whatever knowledge, information, and experience the panel members bring to the case. If they feel they need more information on which to base their decision, they're supposed to acquire it during the course of the hearing. He consulted the *Physicians' Desk Reference* to look up Prolixin, but the information obtained was less important than the fact that a panel member, a person who should be an icon of ethics, committed ex parte."

"Was it the same member who had to leave early without explanation on the first day?" I asked. We'd both assumed it had been Dr. Zarris.

"Yes."

"What an asshole! He's judging my behavior when *his* is blatantly unethical?" Rage caught in my throat. "It will serve him right to be thrown off the panel!" I fought back tears of fury, slamming like tiny fists against the back of my eyes. "This is a man who has the power to decide my future and, so far, he's shown nothing but indifference to me, my witnesses, and the other panel members. Clearly, he only cares about himself. Doesn't that run counter to what the board is about? Doesn't that selfishness or narcissism, or call it what you want, undermine everything that doctors are supposed to represent? How could they allow this man to judge me, or anyone else for that matter?"

"Those are all valid points," said Mr. Good. "But for now, let's deal with the matter at hand. Removing him from the panel would appear to be the reasonable course of action for the board to take. However, it won't necessarily happen. If you'd like me to write a letter to Ms. Lockhart stating that as our preference, I will."

"These people are allowed to do whatever they damn well please and get away with it? That's bullshit!" I was irate. I could barely believe this was happening. I wanted to punch a wall or exact some sort of revenge, yet acting on my emotions was not an option. I forced myself to think about this rationally. "Do we have any options besides asking to have him removed from the panel?"

"We can ask to have Dr. Zarris dismissed from the panel, leaving two members, or we can request a substitute who'll review all the transcripts. A third option is to ask for a new hearing." His voice didn't reveal which option he favored.

"What do you think we should do?" I knew I couldn't endure a whole new hearing, but I was sorry he hadn't mentioned beating the shit out of the bastard as an option.

"Let me think about it." His end of the phone became so quiet. I thought he put me on hold. Suddenly, he spoke. "I think we should ask to have him removed from the panel and let the two remaining members make the decision."

I visualized the other two panel members. Dr. Quornos, the psychiatrist, was the least aggressive and the most knowledgeable, rational panel member. Mr. Chimborazo was stuck on the Prozac question, but Dr. Quornos wasn't. I figured she could straighten him out, as she appeared to be the leader. That would essentially leave the decision up to her. As a psychiatrist, she, more than anybody, should believe in rehabilitation and recovery. "I agree. Let's do that."

Mr. Good wrote a letter to Ms. Lockhart expressing our outrage, demanding the member be dismissed and asking that a decision be made regarding this matter as promptly as possible.

In response to our letter, Mr. Lapel, the prosecutor, recommended dismissing the offending member and having him replaced with a totally new member who would read the transcript.

"No way," I said when Mr. Good told me Mr. Lapel's solution. I was adamantly opposed to a virtual stranger having this power over me. While Dr. Zarris was clearly flawed, at least he was a known entity. I knew his concern was how I could sit by and watch Luke deteriorate without speaking up. I would have no way of knowing how this nameless/faceless person thought, which left me feeling very unsettled.

This unexpected drama felt much the same as when my father messed with me. I was familiar with this chess game of sorts and even found it kind of exciting. It allowed me to redirect my focus from what was really at stake, to anticipating the next move. But the board should have been above this kind of crap. I lost all respect for them and the process. I knew I was better than their process would give me credit for being. No matter what they did, they couldn't take that away from me.

Mr. Good replied to Mr. Lapel immediately.

We didn't hear more until three months later, when Ms. Lockhart dropped another bombshell. Eight months after the hearing, Dr. Quornos revealed that she'd known Luke when he was a resident. She denied this was a significant relationship. In the same correspondence, Ms. Lockhart informed us that she'd decided to give the outside information Dr. Zarris had procured in violation of the rules, to the other two members of the panel. Once they had a chance to read the material, she would schedule a second deliberation with all three of the members.

"She just happened to remember knowing Luke *now*?" I said incredulously. "They're going to let all three members do ex parte, to level the playing field? You've got to be kidding! It's like four wrongs make a right." I started to laugh with frustration at the absurdity and seeming hopelessness of the situation. "What a farce!"

As the reality of the situation started to sink in I became increasingly angrier. Just as suddenly, my anger turned into a sense of helplessness, followed by resignation. "What's the difference? They'll probably end up screwing me anyway." I realized that this was a no-win situation. I just had to go along for the ride and accept that the process was unfair, like life in general. It wasn't in my nature, though, to give up without a fight.

"I'll write another letter to Ms. Lockhart if you want me to," offered Mr. Good. I sensed the frustration in his voice.

"You might as well. At least that way, we'll have everything documented." I had started to contemplate exposing the imperfections in the system, partly as a means of retaliating for the unconscionable way they treated me and partly as a sort of public service.

Ms. Lockhart overruled our protestations and scheduled a second deliberation for April 28, 1998.

I submitted an application to vet school in May and was invited to an interview in August, indicating I was a serious candidate for admission.

In September of 1998, Mr. Good called me for the first time since April. "The peer review committee recommended that your petition for re-licensure be denied. I'm very sorry." He sounded truly apologetic.

Even though I'd expected this outcome, I felt worse hearing him say it. I remembered how much I loved working with patients as a therapist and had visualized myself doing so again in the future. I knew I could find satisfaction and fulfillment from being a vet, but I wasn't sure I had the energy to spend another four years going to school not knowing if anyone would hire me when I finished. Because the medical board did not deem me fit to practice medicine I doubted that the veterinary board would view me any differently.

"Did they explain their basis for denial?" I felt disheartened.

"Yes, I'll send you a copy of the written report. But Melanie, we haven't reached the end of the line. I urge you to consider pursuing the final step in the restoration process, which is to meet with members of the Committee on the Professions. COP has the final authority in all re-licensure cases. They can overturn or support the recommendations of the peer committee." He paused. "It's up to you if you want to go through with the final step. It's unlikely, though not unheard of, that COP will rule in your favor."

My head was spinning at the thought of enduring yet another inquisition. However, I thought I'd be remiss if I did not see it through to the end. I said I'd do it.

The peer committee's report was filled with discrepancies, contradictions, and omissions from the hearing transcripts. For example, the committee wrote, "...she was and remains a very disturbed person." Dr. Lancet testified, "...she is an excellent example of what the rehabilitation process is really all about...she is expected to improve with time but has already reached such a high level that there is not much room left for obvious improvement...I highly recommend restoration of her license." Regarding Dr. Falco's testimony, the peer committee wrote, "Dr. Falco did not know the specific details of petitioner's crime...suggests to us a lack of real honest and open communication by petitioner with her. We infer petitioner was never honest in this relationship." Meanwhile, Dr. Falco had testified, "My understanding is that she attempted to murder her boyfriend, at least succeeded in poisoning him sufficiently to have an acute serious medical problem. I was told by Melanie." Another example, "Nothing in the testimony, even from physicians, is compelling to say that she is no longer at risk of harming another person." Dr. Lancet testified, "I feel confident that there would not be a repetition of this behavior.... in some ways, I feel more confident about Melanie than I do about a lot of people...There has not been one episode in all these years that would make me even the slightest bit anxious about her."

I was furious at the blatant misrepresentations of the testimony and seeming disregard for the person I'd become. It seemed to me they hadn't made their decision based on the information in my petitions or during the hearings. Instead, I thought they'd passed judgment before meeting me or my witnesses. I responded by constructing tables illustrating the disparities and contradictions point by point. I sent copies of my findings, along with a three-page cover letter, to the panel members and their superiors in State Board of Regents.

My inclination was to respond with my refutation and leave it at that. But my sense of curiosity combined with my inherent tenacity compelled me to see the process through to the end.

CHAPTER 66

The meeting with COP was on October 14, 1998, four years after I filed my petition. Jay and my mother offered to go with me, but I wanted to use the time to think and to process the encounter alone. I needed to face my emotions without having them distilled by the supportive presence of people who cared about me.

I enjoyed the solitude of the two-hour drive and noticed I was at once nervous, resigned, and excited about the meeting. I felt a sense of maturity and pride for following through with this process when I could have easily given up. I had elected to do it alone, without anybody to lean on if things became painful, and with no one to keep me in line if my rage was ignited. I knew I could handle any pain, anger, or other feelings of distress that might be elicited during this meeting. I had developed the strength, self-control, and self-confidence to trust myself to react and behave appropriately no matter what happened.

I looked forward to telling my story to a new group of people. Perhaps I'd give a fresh perspective, given the further insight, knowledge, and self-awareness I had gained in the year since the last hearing. I had been in a calm, stable relationship with Jay for two years without any incidents that even bordered on the irrational. I had suffered some cruel treatment by my mother, which I was able to discuss with her and work through rather than letting it simmer to the boiling point. I had maintained a wonderful relationship with my sister and nieces despite the distance and continued to work hard and make significant progress in therapy with Tim. In addition, I had become an integral part of the shelter and was learning to train dogs, as well as to facilitate adoptions. I was more confident and optimistic than I had been at the first hearing.

The gray marble lobby of the Cultural Education Center at the State University of Albany was spacious, cold, and void of people. The large columns and ornately framed photographs of founding fathers and benefactors on the walls seemed more like a museum. The sound of my heels clicking on the marble floor echoed through the maze-like corridors.

I studied the posters encased in glass, announcing the names and dates of upcoming lectures, exhibits, and concerts. Standing alone in this modern building steeped in tradition, I felt like an outsider. I didn't belong there. I sensed the founders and benefactors symbolized what had made me: my father, my childhood, and my suffering. The cold marble represented the protective barrier I had erected against my history. The incongruity of the modern architecture represented the new me, who could view my history behind a glass case but could not assimilate it with my exterior. I was suddenly ready to acknowledge, as I had not been until that time, that I would never fit into a traditional, established, culturally accepted way of life. I was not going to have a "normal," professional career and enjoy concerts and lectures with my colleagues. I was not going to conform. I had never fit into this mold, the one my father insisted I squeeze myself into for his satisfaction -- the one he could never fit into, either. I was going to create my own mold. Wasn't that what I had been doing for the past six years? Figuring out who I was, what I wanted and how best to achieve my own goals?

I followed the signs to the reception area of the Division of Professional Licensing Services. The office looked like the waiting room of a doctor's office with a blue vinyl couch against either wall, a coffee table in front of each couch, and a receptionist's area opposite the door. Mr. Good was sitting on the couch to my right, filling out a form on a clipboard. When he stood to greet me, I felt suddenly vulnerable. In this new context, alone and far away from home, I felt like I hardly knew him despite all he'd gone through with me. I sat next to him on the couch.

"Let's review what we talked about in our last meeting," he suggested. "No matter what happens, be nice, not antagonistic, to the committee members."

Just his saying the words, I already felt defensive and concerned that they might be more aggressive than he had indicated.

"Remind them that due to the unusual delays in the peer committee's decision, you've been under the care of a new therapist for over a year and his letter is included in the packet we sent them."

I was developing a mild case of stage fright and worried that I'd forget my lines.

"Tell them your plans if you don't get your license back. You mentioned vet school. Is that still an option?"

"Yes."

"Make sure you tell them you want to practice medicine if you do get your license back."

I wasn't dying to return to a medical career, but I knew that if they overruled the peer panel's decision, I'd go back to medicine in a heartbeat.

"I'm going to talk about the impaired physician program. Just make sure we're on the same page with this."

I thought about my ex-boyfriend, Johnny, who had been put on the impaired physician's program because he was drunk at work several times when he was a psychiatric resident. Finally, he was hospitalized for eight months for depression and alcoholism. When he was discharged from the hospital, he was allowed to return to work if he agreed to enroll in the impaired physician's program. This meant that he had to remain in therapy, have weekly blood and urine tests and be on probation for a period of two years. During the probationary period, he was supervised and closely monitored. The doctor in charge of monitoring him was also in contact with his therapist and his supervisor. He made it through the two years without further incident, so he was taken off probation and allowed to practice as though it had never happened. If there had been a recurrence while he was on probation, he could have been summarily fired, mandated to go into inpatient treatment, and his license would have been suspended or revoked, depending on the nature of the transgression.

When Mr. Good finished speaking, I looked around the room. On the wall to my left were individual cubbies labeled with their licensure information. I extracted a packet of information from the Veterinary Medicine slot and slipped it into my bag.

"My daughter's an architect," he said, scanning the various cubbies.

It had never occurred to me he had a family. I didn't know what to say. Even though he had brought it up, I'd had the impression he coveted his privacy.

"I didn't know you had a daughter." I thought even my mother would approve of this benign response. It wasn't really what I *wanted* to say. I would have preferred to ask if he was married, how many children he had, what his other children did, and so on.

We continued talking about his family in a superficial way until a tall, thin woman with a pageboy hairdo came over to us. "Good morning, Will," she said affably to Mr. Good. "Dr. Chase?" She extended her hand to me. "I'm Juanita Puerto."

"Hello," I said timidly. I knew she was the Deputy Commissioner of COP because I'd seen her name on the letterhead.

She led us to a room at the end of the hallway. Two men sat at the far end of the table. The man to my left, Mr. Mendez, was the executive coordinator of COP. The other man was Mr. Butler, the assistant director of COP. Juanita introduced us. They nodded at me and said, "Hello, Will," to Mr. Good.

Mr. Good pulled the chair closest to me away from the table and prompted me to sit. He sat to my right, placed his briefcase in front of him and clicked open the latches.

Juanita sat midway between Mr. Mendez and me. "Why don't

we get started?"

Mr. Mendez leafed through the packet of papers in front of him and then looked up at me. "Dr. Chase, would you please explain in your own words, what led to the surrender of your license?" His voice was mellifluous.

As I launched into what had by now become a familiar monologue, I gradually found myself becoming more comfortable and improvisational, pausing only to take a breath or to make eye contact with one of the committee members. Perhaps it was a combination of the kind demeanor of the audience and the fact that I'd already been on the stand and knew what questions to anticipate. I felt self-assured and candid. When I finished talking, Mr. Mendez thanked me.

"Dr. Chase," said Mr. Butler, "would you say you knew what you were doing when you put the drug into the drinks?"

I answered as thoughtfully as I could. "Yes...and no."

They took turns asking me questions, such as why I felt I was ready to practice medicine, and if the misconduct was a mistake or intentional.

The question and answer period went on for close to an hour and a half. Mr. Good stood and cleared his throat. "The key to Dr. Chase's behavior was her relationship with a mentally-ill father. Because of this relationship, she was impaired throughout her relationship with Luke, who, she has admitted, repeated many of the same destructive patterns her father did. When her father died in February of 1990, she started spiraling downward. Because of his death, the breakup with Luke in January of 1992 was much more traumatic. It essentially completed her downward spiral. But, that was then. According to Dr. Lancet and everyone else who knows Dr. Chase, she is rehabilitated. Her judgment, ability to tolerate stress, and her self-control are all good."

Mr. Good removed his sports coat and started pacing back and forth. "This brings me to the issue of the Professional Assistance

Program which helps impaired professionals regain entry into their profession." He stopped pacing and stood behind me. "While the majority of these impairments include some type of substance abuse, other categories include major debilitating illnesses, depression, dementia, or other psychopathologies that might interfere with an individual's ability to function at work as normally expected. You take a risk in giving them back their licenses. How is Dr. Chase different?" He let his words hang in the air a moment. "If anything, Dr. Chase is less of a risk than most because she's undergone five years of treatment with Dr. Lancet, a highly respected psychiatrist. He has so much faith in her that he put himself on the line, testifying that he thinks she should be reinstated."

I felt the heat coming off his body. "Dr. Chase and I have discussed this extensively. She would welcome a conditional return of her license with something like two years probation, during which time she would be carefully monitored." Returning to his seat, he said, "Ladies and gentleman, Dr. Chase has done everything humanly possible to assure that nothing like this will ever happen again. She has kept up with her medical knowledge, rehabilitated herself via therapy and exhibited remorse for what she did. As to what happens from here on in, her future is in your hands."

Mr. Good called me five months later to break the news. "I'm very sorry," he said. "COP concurred with the assessment of the peer committee. In short, they wrote that "given the severity of the initial behavior and the lack of full rehabilitation, despite petitioner's significant efforts in this direction, it does not seem appropriate to restore her license at this time."

"What do they mean by 'lack of full rehabilitation?'" I focused on their words rather than the heartbreak that made it hard for me to breathe. Although I wasn't able to identify the exact source of my grief, it felt like a combination of finally mourning the loss of my medical career, combined with grief over having worked so hard to get better, but not having gotten better enough, at least not in the opinion of these judges. The sorrow was enormous, the pain excruciating.

"They don't think you fully comprehend the gravity of your act."

I fought back the tears that had been pounding on the back of my eyes on and off for nearly a year. I had not allowed myself to cry, or even to experience the depth of my sadness, over the loss of my career and everything else I had lost in the past six years. I was not ready to allow myself the full awareness of how much I'd really lost, and what it all meant to me. I wanted to appear strong. I didn't want to elicit anyone's sympathy, especially because I had brought it all upon myself. At the same time, I did not want to be paralyzed by the pain. I needed to keep moving forward and not get bogged down in despair.

Wanting to hide how upset I was, I said, "Well, we did the best we could."

"We can always file an appeal," he said.

"I don't think I could go through this again. If I change my mind, I'll call you." I hung up the phone quickly because I was too upset to talk further. I collapsed onto the couch next to my dog, Jake. I considered calling Dani, but instead, I indulged in a long overdue cry before taking Jake for a nice long run.

Sixteen years later, I realize I concur with COP. They were right. At that time, I did not truly understand the gravity of what I had done. Now, however, I finally get it.

On Memorial Day, 2006, I was covering an event on the Village Green for the local paper. I had contributed photos and occasional articles to the paper for about six months, but this was my first actual assignment. I had lived in this town for five years and was just starting to carve a little niche for myself. A series of speakers gave speeches at the podium -- WWII veterans, members of the American Legion, politicians. By the time it came to honor Dave Lory as Citizen of the Year, I had settled in a seat, front and center. I was startled when Dave Lory told the crowd, "I'd like to introduce my father, the Honorable Judge John Lory, longtime resident and former mayor of our town, and videographer for our cable TV station."

The Honorable Judge John Lory, whom I had not seen in more than thirteen years, ascended to the podium. I'd been a stone's throw away from him for the better part of the morning! I was mortified. I had worked so hard to keep my past separate from my new life, and there he was!

After that day, I covered many more events that Dave Lory officiated and Judge Lory videotaped for the local cable station. By the third event, Dave and I were on a first-name basis, emailing back and forth about various activities and bumping into one another around town. The topic of his father never came up. I wondered, in a sort of paranoid way, if the judge realized who I was. If he made the connection between me and the person he had sentenced nearly fourteen years prior, he did not let on.

I was back on the Village Green a year later covering the July Fourth celebration, which Dave Lory organized. As I walked past the honorable judge, he handed me a schedule of events and addressed me by my first name. Totally floored, I thanked him and walked on. I was now a regular photographer at local events and a known fixture in town.

Two months later we were again both covering some festivity. The judge's daughter and grandchildren were with him. Since the event was in a local park, I had my pit bull dog, Baby Bop, with me.

Throughout the day, I was a foot or so away from the judge. I took still photos as he videotaped. Later, the judge's daughter and grandchildren came over to pet Baby Bop. The judge watched as Baby Bop (who, ironically enough, my friends and I call "the mayor" because she meets and greets everyone who walks by), rolled over on her back, licked the kids and let them climb all over her.

I still don't know if Judge Lory knows who I am, but thinking back on the scene with Baby Bop and the judge's grandchildren, I am reminded of a phrase people say often to me. "Your dog looks ferocious, but she's one of the friendliest animals I've ever encountered. She's the *opposite* of a wolf in sheep's clothing." I thought how this so aptly describes me, if defined by "the act." Perhaps the honorable judge would now agree.

I now have a different perspective on the entire transaction that occurred in the courtroom sixteen years ago. I wonder if the Mengele reference was meant to shock me in a similar manner as the shock of incarceration. Perhaps the judge did view my act as an anomaly and gave me the benefit of the doubt. Maybe he knew I was a sheep who, for one awful period of time under the duress of mental illness and circumstances, donned a wolf's costume.

Rather than locking me up and throwing away the key, which he surely could have done, he laid down enough ground rules and watchdogs to keep society (and me) safe, while providing me with enough freedom to again become a contributing member of the community. Though I doubt he imagined my contribution would be right in *his* community!

Perhaps his sentence, and giving me a second chance, was similar to my rescuing Baby Bop from the shelter. I never in a million years thought I'd own a pit bull. But I was able to see past the reputation of her breed and see her for who she really was and would become: a beautiful, loving animal who, by her constantly wagging tail and gentle demeanor, brings joy to those who encounter her.

I am so grateful to Judge Lory for my second chance.

AFTERWORD

In the summer of 2001 my cousin Eddie and I sat by the side of his mother's pool watching his sons play with my nieces and catching up on each other's lives. He was in from France, where he now lived, for the annual family reunion.

This was the first reunion I'd been to since before "the confession." I'd been too ashamed to face anyone. I only attended that year because Dani asked me to help with my four-year-old nieces and two-year-old nephew. She had recently moved back home from Atlanta and lived a half-hour from me. My aunt lived midway between the two of us.

Eddie said, "Someday I'll tell you why I wasn't there for you when everything happened. That is, to the extent that I understand it myself."

"You don't have to. I'm just glad you're talking to me now." I was afraid I'd be considered the relative who "went mad," the one to avoid for the rest of my life.

I told him about the verdict and about being accepted to vet school. "I decided not to go. I doubted anyone would hire me since I'd lost my medical license." I described my volunteer work at the animal shelter and a pet sitting/dog training business I started. I regaled him with stories about the second shelter dog I'd adopted, a ten-month-old pit bull, named Baby Bop. I told him about Stray Alive, the not-for-profit dog rescue organization I founded.

"Whatever happened to Mark, the guy who egged you on?" Eddie asked.

"Absolutely nothing. As a matter of fact, he won some prestigious awards and is now in private practice."

"That hardly seems fair," he said. "After all, he was an

accomplice."

"Perhaps," I said. "I don't even want to go there."

He nodded and gently touched my shoulder.

"What about Luke?"

"He went ahead with his plans to build his family compound and still works where he used to. I'm glad they're both fine. I have no desire to have anything to do with either one of them. Recently, though, I've felt a need to write a book about my experience to better understand it. I still feel virtually paralyzed." I felt embarrassed at this seemingly grandiose proclamation.

"I'd love to read it," he said enthusiastically.

I was surprised that Eddie, a successful attorney and worldly family man, with whom I had not spoken in such a long time, was interested in anything I had to say. I'd assumed he hadn't wanted to get involved, or was upset with me for not reaching out to him eight years earlier when he and his wife, Isabel, had a stillborn child. It was this tragedy that compelled them to move to France where Isabel's family lived. I'd felt ashamed about not being there for him when that happened. It's hard to know the right thing to do when somebody you care about is suffering. I wanted to help, but I didn't know how. The longer I waited, the more awkward it became. I wished I had said these things to him then, but I didn't.

Shortly after the poisoning, Aunt Jill, Eddie, and my other two cousins had a surprise party for my uncle and didn't invite me. I cried inconsolably when I discovered pictures from the party, years later.

After that reunion, Eddie and I emailed each other on a regular basis. I sent him the beginnings of a manuscript. He told me stories about his sons and asked my advice about treatment for his running injuries. We filled each other in further about the years we'd missed since losing touch.

By the next family reunion in August 2002, I was nearly finished with the first draft of my book. Eddie and Jay were the only ones reading it.

As we lounged around the side of the pool, Eddie said, "You really should come visit us in France. We'd love to have you."

"Maybe when I finish the book," I said, knowing it would be nearly impossible to leave my dogs. My pet-sitting business was hard to leave for *any* length of time.

"What are you going to do with the book when you finish it?"

"Probably nothing." I looked over at him relaxing in a lounge chair. I remembered how proud I always was that we had the same-shaped fingers and toes -- that we were related. I'd grown up with Eddie. We were the same age. In elementary school, we used to pretend we were twins.

"I'm just hoping the writing process will help me move on. I've been at a loss for what to do with my life since the verdict."

"Have you considered publishing it?"

Just then, his middle son, seven-year-old Paulie, climbed onto Eddie's lap. I watched with longing and admiration as he wrapped Paulie in a towel and hugged him to his chest. "No, I'm really just writing it for myself. It's not written that well. And, anyway, who else besides family and friends would want to read it?" Each giggle from Paulie seemed to underscore the emptiness in my life.

Seeing Eddie in his role as a father highlighted to me how much I had missed and how much I'd lost, not only by neglecting my relationship with him, but by making such a mess of my life. I had longed for a family with Luke. I used to imagine what our kids would look like, even how they would smell. I'd suppressed those longings. Now I feared I'd missed the boat. After all, I was already forty-one.

"Would you mind if I showed it to my friend in publishing?" he asked as his youngest son, five-year-old T.T. piled on top of Paulie. "I think it's a story worth telling. It's an excellent read." He tickled both kids who could not stop giggling. "Besides, I think it could help a lot of people."

I watched them play, wishing I could join them "You can show it to whomever you'd like."

"I hope you don't mind, but Isabel has been reading it, too," he added. "She thinks it's great." T.T. stood, tugging on Eddie's hand. "I'm sorry, Mel, but I'm late for an important ballgame." Eddie then whispered into T.T.'s ear. T.T. nodded. Eddie grinned at me. "I just told T.T. what a great athlete you are and asked him if you could play with us. What d'ya say? We could use a pitcher."

Delighted by the invitation, I regretted again that I'd avoided these people for so long. I'd totally forgotten being an athlete. I had run marathons and road races and played tennis, baseball, and basketball. But I always took those things for granted. My athletic ability, once an important part of my identity, had been forgotten after "the poisoning." That terrible event and my mental illness had defined me. Nobody cares that you can swish a three-point shot when you're breaking furniture and writing curse words on the walls. I wondered what other parts of myself I lost sight of.

A month or so later, Eddie forwarded an email from a literary agent friend of his who wanted to meet with me. The agent told me I had a story worth telling, but I'd have to work with an editor to revise the entire manuscript.

Over the next few months, I worked on revising the manuscript. Whenever I grew discouraged, Eddie gave me a pep talk, encouraging me to keep working. "It's much too important a story not to share," he said. "You'll inspire other people who've lost so much as a consequence of mental illness."

As I persevered, I began to believe in the value of the book, along with my value as a person. I began to feel I was doing something worthwhile.

My self-assurance was further boosted when I heard a quote on National Public Radio by playwright Edward Albee. He said he liked working dead-end jobs because it allowed him to save his creative and emotional energy for what really mattered to him: his writing. I reminded myself of this quote whenever I felt frustrated that I was walking and training dogs to earn a living, or when I disparaged myself for not living up to my "potential." More than that, I discovered that what Albee said was true. Working with dogs gave me time to think, time I would have missed if I'd been in meetings all day or taking care of patients. I began to understand that my occupation was a necessary stepping-stone to the next phase of my life. Even though I didn't know what the next phase would be.

Feeling better about myself translated into taking the risk of telling people about my book. It never ceased to amaze me that people did not shy away from me when they heard my story. My self-disclosure seemed to draw people closer to me. People often confided their stories. Suddenly, I was again a person others came to for advice and comfort in times of despair and confusion. "If you could make it through such heartbreaking losses and come out on the other side, you must be able to help me." I wasn't ridiculed or shunned. Some people actually tried to minimize or make light of what I had done. Others tried to take the responsibility away from me. I disliked this type of response because I wanted to own my mistake, but I understood that each person's reaction had more to do with him than with me. This is true in general. People project their own experiences, biases, and values onto any given situation and act or react according to their individual perspectives and perceptions.

At the family reunion in August 2003, Eddie and I organized a baseball game with his three sons, my two nieces, and my nephew. When Eddie had to abruptly leave the game, the kids turned to me to continue playing. This tiny incident was marvelous confirmation that I'd been accepted back into the world of the living. I felt so tickled. Before Eddie left to go back to France, I promised to visit him and his family in France sometime before the next reunion.

Eddie surprised everyone a few months later by coming to New York to run the New York Marathon. In his euphoria over the accomplishment of completing his first marathon, he thanked me for all my running and training tips. Congratulating him, I asked if he planned to run it again. "Not really," he said. "Once is enough."

"That's too bad," I said, "I was thinking if we planned to run it together next year, I'd quit smoking and start running again." I had stopped running after I adopted my third dog, Scutch, a middle-aged abused pit bull. Three dogs were so time-consuming and enervating.

"If it will get you to quit smoking," Eddie replied, "then let's do it!"

"Great!" I said. I'll start training in January.

On Saturday January 3, 2004, Jay and I returned home from a twilight walk on the beach around the corner from where I had recently moved, with the dogs. I had taken up photography, and I was downloading pictures of a winter sunset I'd taken during our walk. The phone rang. It was my mother.

"How are you?" she asked cautiously.

"Fine," I said. "I'm just getting ready to go out to do my dinner jobs." It was the end of the holiday week, the busiest time of the year for my pet-sitting business.

She paused for a moment. "I have very bad news."

"Is it Dani? The kids? Are they all right?" It occurred to me that it was unlikely anything happened to Dani; she had recently converted to Orthodox Judaism and kept a very low profile on Shabbat.

"No, it's not Dani. Did you hear about the plane that crashed into the Red Sea this morning?" Her voice trembled.

"The one going from Egypt to France?" I asked. "Jay and I were just talking about it. Everybody onboard was killed."

"Eddie, Isabel, and the boys," she said.

"No!" My world went dark.

"They were on vacation. Isabel's parents, brother, sister-in-law, and their kids were on the plane, too."

"All of them?" I screamed.

"Yes," she said. "Eleven in all."

"Your sister?" I asked, referring to my Aunt Jill, Eddie's mother. "She's in shock," Mom replied tremulously.

For the next eight months I went through the days robotically, experiencing everything through a haze of loss. I increased my therapy with Tim to twice a week, suffered paranoid episodes and withdrew from the world. I managed to fulfill obligations, but I felt detached from everything and everyone. Things that used to matter to me, such as the start of the baseball season, world politics, and the beauty of nature, seemed irrelevant. All I could think about or talk about was that Eddie was dead. No matter who I met, I talked about the plane crash and then had nothing else to say. Whenever I could concentrate enough to listen to the news, I thought, *What's the difference? Eddie's dead.* When I saw people smile or children play, I wondered why they got to be alive when Eddie didn't. I wished it had been me who died instead of Eddie. It would have been a lot easier for my family to lose me than to lose Eddie, Isabel, and their kids--*two entire generations.*

For months, I had to pull over by the side of the road when I'd start crying so much that I couldn't see to drive. All the while, I thought, *I'll never see him again. I'll never hear his voice. I'll never see his fingers and toes. I'll never play baseball with his boys.* I composed myself and continued driving with images of Eddie and his family still flashing in my mind.

I lost my sense of humor. Making people laugh had been one of my best skills. I even disconnected from Dani and her kids. It was painful to be with them. Dani said the tragedy should make me appreciate them even more, but I backed away, fearing something might happen to them, too.

My mother worried about me. She said I "absorbed sadness like a sponge." But what frightened her most were my paranoid fantasies, which revolved around Tim. I was convinced he was secretly trying to humiliate and destroy me. The rational side of me knew this was ludicrous. He'd been honest, consistent, and supportive throughout the course of our six-year relationship. But I reasoned, if Eddie's entire family could be wiped out in the space of a second, then anything was possible.

Throughout that time, Tim was fabulous. He did not become alarmed by my crazy thoughts. He convinced me I had the right to grieve. I had initially doubted that because I had not been there for Eddie in his darkest times. Tim encouraged me to call him or come to see him in between sessions if needed. He was kind, compassionate, and analytic all at the same time. He offered to meet with or talk on the phone with my mother to explain that I was grieving and that everything I was experiencing was in the normal range. I was not in a tailspin in the sense of being out of control. I was not a danger to myself. With time, I would get through this.

During those eight months, I felt like someone had dumped a batch of chemicals into me and I watched the concoction froth and come to a head like some weird science experiment. But not once did I worry about the outcome of the experiment. I knew this was not depression in the true sense of the word. I was not hopeless. I did not feel worthless; my judgment was not impaired. I was just excruciatingly and appropriately sad, preoccupied with the loss and emotionally detached. It never occurred to me to increase my Prozac or take any other drugs to help ease the pain. I reached out to my aunt and cousins and helped my mother in any way I could. I was definitely not the person I used to be.

In August, the month of the annual reunions, I sat down at the computer for the first time since the crash and reread the emails I'd saved from Eddie. I came across one from November 2003, in which he encouraged me to forge ahead with my book. He wrote, "Isn't life mysterious? It hands us tragedies beyond comprehension and then gives us the strength to transform them into something of value to ourselves and others."

Some might bristle at calling my story tragic. They would say it was tragic for Luke, and I would agree. I don't think the poisoning itself was tragic for me. It was a tragic mistake, for which I take full responsibility. It's something I will regret for the rest of my life. Not because of what happened to me afterwards, but because I hurt and nearly killed a person I loved. To this day, even though I've had no contact with Luke in sixteen years, I have warm feelings toward him. No, my story is not tragic, although it is surely sad on many levels. Rather, my story is one of mental illness, rehabilitation, and redemption.

Nobody would argue with calling the plane crash and the senseless loss of lives (there were 144 people on board) tragic. With that tragedy in mind, I finish this book--as Eddie so eloquently put it--to transform tragedy into something of value to myself and others. Millions of lives are shattered by mental illness. They and all their loved ones need to know there is hope.

That night, as I started to write for the first time in eight months, Eddie came through the window over my desk. He was wearing faded jeans, sandals, and a white button-down shirt. His hair was shoulder-length, as it was when we were in junior high. He hovered over me, between the window and the computer. "Hi, Mel," he said, as casually as if we'd met for a scheduled appointment.

"Eddie!" I cried. "What are you doing here?"

"I came to tell you you're doing the right thing. Keep going."

"What do you mean?" I asked. "Writing the book?"

He didn't answer. Instead, he turned to leave.

"Wait!" I cried. "How is everyone? Isabel and the kids, I mean."

But he was gone.

"Well, my dear cousin, this one's for you."

<end>